American Gladius

A Study of the M9 Multipurpose Bayonet System

CPT (Ret) Mack A. Pattarozzi

Schiffer Military History
Atglen, PA

Book Design by Stephanie Daugherty.

Library of Congress Control Number: 2008944099

Printed in the United States of America.
ISBN: 0-7643-3239-5

We are interested in hearing from authors with book ideas on related topics.

Published by Schiffer Publishing Ltd.
4880 Lower Valley Road
Atglen, PA 19310
Phone: (610) 593-1777
FAX: (610) 593-2002
E-mail: Info@schifferbooks.com.
Visit our web site at: www.schifferbooks.com
Please write for a free catalog.
This book may be purchased from the publisher.
Please include $3.95 postage.
Try your bookstore first.

In Europe, Schiffer books are distributed by:
Bushwood Books
6 Marksbury Avenue
Kew Gardens
Surrey TW9 4JF, England
Phone: 44 (0) 20 8392-8585
FAX: 44 (0) 20 8392-9876
E-mail: Info@bushwoodbooks.co.uk.
Visit our website at: www.bushwoodbooks.co.uk

Contents

Special Contributors

One of the most rewarding aspects of any endeavor, especially writing and research, is the interaction with other collectors and exchanging information with them. In all instances, I have found them to be excited, supportive of my efforts, and eager to jump in and get things moving!

Regarding some of these people, special thanks are in order to Major Darin Weaver, who frequently and graciously took the time to search out items and/or articles he knew I would want to investigate. Of special note was his discovery of the cover photo, which is incredibly artistic!

Special thanks also are in order to the National Archives and Research Administration, College Park, Maryland, for their research assistance, and those of the United States Patent Office, as well as their counterparts at the Deutschen Patent- und Markenamtes (German Patent and Trademark Bureau).

As ever, I am grateful to my wife Kim, who endured so many nights of me staying up until the wee hours. Through it all she has been, as she always is with everything, supportive; if for no other reason than she knew it was important to me - Thank you Baby!

Frequently overlooked are the publishers, and I think especially Schiffer publishing deserves a great deal of recognition, if for no other reason than Mr. Schiffer truly encourages aspiring authors by providing a venue in these lives we call history. No longer is mankind's story the prevue of the elitist intelligencia. Mr. Schiffer, thanks for giving us a voice!

Contributors:
Darin Weaver, PA-C , Major, TXARNG
Frank Trzaska
Joseph Bielik, PA-C
Paul Crank, Soldiers Magazine, U.S. Army

Ms. Pennington, Donvon Technical Library, Ft. Benning, GA
G.G. Greene Inc, Warren, PA
Society of American Bayonet Collectors
United States Army, Aberdeen Proving Grounds, MD
United States Army, Engineer Board, Ft. Belvoir, VA
United States Army, Infantry Branch, Ft. Benning, GA
United States Army, Infantry Journal
United States Army, Natick Research, Development and Evaluation Center, Natick, MA
United States Army, Rock Island Arsenal, IL
United States Army, TECOM, Ft. Hood, TX
United States General Services Administration, Washington, D.C
United States Marine Corps, Equipment Board, Marine Barracks, Quantico, Virginia
marcorsyscom.usmc

Introduction to **American Gladius**

The title *American Gladius* may sound alien and strange to some, leaving them wondering what in the world the author is talking about, and yet for those familiar with history, the simple mention of a gladius harkens images of Roman Legionnaires marching to battle in formation with their trusty swords held at the ready. As well, the initiated know that the gladius is as much an icon of the Legionnaire as the Luger is of the Germans or as the K-BAR is of the Marine Corps. Likewise, the M9 is quickly becoming, if it has not already, an icon of the American Army.

The M9 has been our standard bayonet now for over two decades with no plans in sight to replace it, and soon it will be the longest serving American bayonet, joining the ***M16*** as an enduring symbol of the American soldier. As well, the Army has chosen it as the centerpiece of the ***Combat Action Badge***, thus permanently fixing its imagine throughout the Army, and the nation. It is within such context that this book is called ***American Gladius.***

The realm of military blade collectors is phenomenal, to say the least, as it is composed of numerous large and small niches encompassing the entire spectrum of blades belonging to every nation on the globe both past and present. The specimens literally number in the thousands, and as such the collector's focus is thus both desirable and essential, whether for study or collecting.

Similarly, this work of necessity progresses along a razor thin line of topic content, deviating only enough to provide adequate context when the author believes it will serve the reader's interest. The result is, hopefully, a body of knowledge that illuminates every relevant facet of the M9 story while ideally navigating unimpeded through the realm of militaria and its ever present minutia.

Another relatively unique facet of this study is its contemporary nature, as the author has the distinct privilege, and advantage, of studying the M9 in its natural habitat, rather than as a solely historic relic. This situation offers the greatest opportunity to accurately capture the knife and its story in the purest of perspectives—if such a thing in history exists. That is, to present the *big picture* in a way that lends realism and an authentic feel for events that no future historian would be able to do, hard as he may try. Such an opportunity as this is historically enormous!

As well, this work chiefly focuses on this knife, its manufacturers, evolution, variations, accessories, and collectability with the objective to spotlight only those M9s of military issue, and to treat special issue, commemorative, and import clones as appropriate to exclude. Beyond that, the intention is to provide fellow collectors with a reference and a tool that will enhance their collecting experience through objective data as well as personal knowledge and experience.

In collecting military weapons this author has, too often, encountered collectors who hold completely flawed beliefs simply because they accepted *facts* presented without the benefit of a military foundation. In such cases, they believe the information because there is no reason for them to disbelieve it. For example, if one told these same people that there was a truck atop a twenty-foot flagpole they would likely think the reporter daft! Likewise, any G.I. would also think it absurd for stating the obvious—that is, that a truck (ball) tops every flagpole. This is not to preferentially aggrandize the military, nor is it to deprecate the civilian, but simply to confront and dispel misconceptions by applying a range of military knowledge and experience to a military subject.

Where collecting is concerned, the M9 represents an historical phenomenon heretofore unencountered by the bayonet collector in that it is a modular system, and because of its commercial origin it gives the term *representative collection* an entirely new significance! Historically armories, or commercial firms under exclusive contract, produced bayonets and delivered them directly to the military, where upon obsolescence they found their way onto the civilian market and ultimately to the collector. In such a scenario, there was no question as to the originality of such pieces, and their configuration generally conformed to a known evolutionary progression. The M9 collector is in quite a different situation, and as such, a very new perspective is necessary.

Because of the above, it is extremely difficult to put together a pure *GI collection* of M9s, firstly because the M9 is produced by civilian companies and available equally to the civilian and military customer; therefore, one is hard pressed to know which M9 is actually military issue and which is not. Secondly, because there are so few actual veteran M9s available; for nearly two decades the Army had no reason to surplus these bayonets out, so few are available to the collector. This situation makes the *representative collection* a virtual necessity.

On the bright side, most of the military M9s which have been on inventory are generally in factory fresh condition, as they have been safely tucked away in unit arms rooms. Further, beginning around 2002 or 2003, the Marine Corps purged its stock of five thousand M9s as the OKC3s were phased in, and that has been an awesome boon to collectors.

Similarly, in 2005 units of the 3d Brigade, 1st Cavalry Division turned in an unknown number of M9s which—the author has first hand knowledge—contained many rare first issue pieces. These are now entering the surplus market, and will doubtlessly make someone a great deal of money, as well as enriching the hobby overall. Otherwise, the only issue M9s come in ones and twos from GIs who have retained theirs after leaving the service.

What this situation leaves for the *M9-ophile* is a collection comprised primarily of commercial pieces having the identical characteristics of their issue counterparts; but they are not *original issue* pieces, for again, there simply are not sufficient quantities of original military M9s to satisfy the collecting community. On the other hand, this is a temporary situation, as at some point in the next five or ten years the Army is certain to replace existing M9s, at which point collectors will be in their glory.

The other unique M9 collector's dilemma has its source in the modular character of the M9, as it is virtually impossible to know if any one M9 system is *virgin issue*, since any part of the system is quite easily interchanged, and because nearly all parts are manufactured to military specification the situation is additionally difficult. In this same vein, distinguishing between variations is a virtual nightmare, and just one more reason why this bayonet series must be highly organized into a comprehensive and cogent hierarchy based on a common nomenclature.

Furthermore, it is the hope that this work will add a measure of context to the knife, that is, to transform the image of the M9 from one of a sterile, impersonal object to that of a weapon with its own character, personality, and history. Perhaps more than anything else it is the object of this study to demonstrate just what a classic bayonet the M9 truly is, as with the possible exception of the Marine Corps' OKC3S, there is no other bayonet in all of American military history which possesses such a one of a kind individualism while at the same time displaying so obvious an American personality of design as the M9!

A great deal of content is taken familiarizing the reader with such topics as the institutional bayonet doctrine, materiel acquisition and the history of Army nomenclature. In fact, there is as much ancillary content as there is material directly related to the M9. The precise reason for this is that all of these topics make up the backdrop of the M9's story; they are the landscape of the portrait if you will.

Additionally, a seemingly divergent and unrelated chapter is included, though one which is actually both necessary and germane, that examines the Marine Corps' OKC3S and their quite lengthy quest to replace the M7. Consequently, one might well question straying so far afield after going to such great lengths delineating the content and constraints of this study, though the rationale is precisely because the two bayonets share a common and parallel development.

Both the M9 and the OK3S came to be because both services were looking to replace the M7, and at least initially considered the M9 both corporately and separately. As such, it is not a great leap to assert that the Army and the Marine Corps began the same search, at the same time, and with a like intent, and yet both ultimately adopted relatively dissimilar replacement bayonets. More ironically, perhaps, is that both services acquired weapons that are historically so classic, or so unique in design that each has or will become icons of their respective service.

Finally, it is this author's sincerest hope that readers will find this study an interesting and useful reference which enhances their collecting experience, and one that opens a few other avenues of interest as well!

Please Do Enjoy!

1

The Big Picture

Genesis

The musket and bayonet appeared on the field of battle at roughly the same time. With gunpowder came the musket, and with it came the demise of the bow, spear, and sword as principle weapons of combat. As well, the musket virtually ensured the invention of the bayonet.

These precursors to the rifle were clumsy, inaccurate, and generally unreliable. Should the fuse, match, or flint fail the soldier was essentially helpless; not to mention that if it rained, or the wind blew the powder from the primer pan, then he was in serious trouble. In fact, the number of calamities likely to befall a musketeer was many, making the need for a reliable backup weapon woefully apparent very early on. The bayonet satisfied that need then and in the centuries since.

In the early days of musketry the standard tactic of infantrymen was to lay a volley of musket fire, then charge the opponent with bayonets fixed. By attaching such a knife to their muskets, soldiers essentially had a pike and a very effective killing tool. But times change; or do they?

In combat, the bayonet is the infantrymen's tool of last resort, and in the role of crowd control, it has traditionally been the first option, and the most effective one. It is the universal symbol of close combat and courage, a spirit weapon that inspires its user to aggressively confront and eradicate the enemy.

Unlike any other weapon, the bayonet is an instrument of purpose, and while it has happened, it is very rare to hear of an accidental bayoneting! Cold steel meets flesh as the direct result of a conscious intentional decision to kill! Finally, the bayonet is a weapon of stealth, highly selective and intimately personal!

The Eternal Debate

When considered as an organization, the United States Army is in a constant state of flux. Policies, Congressional mandates, and a host of other stimuli cause the Army to shift

Figure 1: Bayonet training at Quantico. (Marine Corps Photo)

doctrine and focus almost unceasingly. As an institution, it is quite another matter. In fact, in the Army there is a saying that "The Army never changes; only the names."

Certainly from this author's experience such a statement, while perhaps overly general, seems a given. Once one strips away the organizational clutter, ignores the political correctness, and puts mandates aside, the Army is as it has always been—an Army. It is not a corporate entity, nor a social program, and certainly not a job program for America's worst and dullest!

Officers still delineate and define the mission; NCOs still execute that mission, lead, and take care of soldiers. Soldiers still *soldier*, and if something can be broken, you can count on a G.I. to break it! All of these things are now, always have been, and always will be characteristics of the Army. There are, of course, many, many other truisms.

Figure 2: Infantry trainee on bayonet range. (U.S. Army Photo)

One such is the debate over the role of the bayonet, an argument which has continued unceasingly and unchanging from generation to generation, probably since General Washington's command. Through the years the Army, and even the Infantry Branch, has split into two camps. There are those who think the bayonet is obsolete, and those who maintain that it is an economical and essential tool of the infantryman and field soldier. And, while the details of the matter could easily fill entire volumes, for this discussion, we will examine events around late WWII, touching only on the most central arguments.

Major James M. Gibson wrote in the Infantry School Quarterly in 1953 that:

"There is no more controversial weapon in the family of Infantry than the bayonet. You have heard it said that even within a few yards a .30 caliber slug is quicker and surer than a foot of steel. That no man with a round in his chamber will bother to stick an enemy with the blade. On the other hand, there are those who will say '...a man who knows how to use his bayonet won't stop to reload, but will make use of it.'"[1]

Certainly, the Major lends considerable insight into the debate; though it is possible to criticize him for oversimplifying the point, he accurately represents both sides of the argument from a central perspective. This is so, in that adversaries of the bayonet bemoan it as essentially a weapon, which is anachronistic and made unnecessary by the advent of modern firearms. Proponents of the bayonet counter that with competent instruction

Figure 3: The bayonet symbolizes the *Warrior Spirit*! (Marine Corps Photo)

soldiers will naturally use it in the time, place, and circumstance for which intended. Further, he points out that the bayonet is a natural extension of the rifle, and that it completes a harmonic infantry fighting system.

To elevate the discussion another level, the Major astutely points out that many criticisms have been, and will continue to be, leveled at the bayonet, with the majority maintaining that it is a weapon which has no place in modern warfare; it is merely kept on through a die-hard attitude, and an unwillingness to accept change.

Yet, the evidence is conclusive that the modern Infantryman continues to have a very real need for this weapon, and that the bayonet will be with us for some time fulfilling its traditional role. It is not a question of retaining or discarding the weapon, but rather a matter of proper training and indoctrinating our soldiers in its proper use.[2]

Again, the writer adroitly captures a critical element of the debate, in that the bayonet is a weapon that requires proper training if it is to be effectively employed. Further, it is entirely true that if soldiers are not going to receive appropriate training in its use there is no meaningful reason for having it. Even advocates of the bayonet would agree with this

Figure 4: Egyptian memorial commemorating war dead. Warrior spirit? (Marine Corps Photo)

Figure 5: Marksmanship training incorporating the bayonet. (U.S. Army Photo)

position, though they would also be quick to counter that the right answer is not to get rid of the bayonet, but to teach its proper use.

Such instruction necessarily means overcoming the one natural hindrance, which is that it requires time, a lot of time! And because the Army never changes, time is in short supply, as training requirements compete with *OPTEMPO*3 and now real-world deployments, frequently resulting in an unwillingness amongst many commanders to commit to such a seemingly low priority task, if not an antiquated one.

Another aspect of the training is that the proficient use of the bayonet is most relevant to only one group of soldiers: those assigned a rifle. The majority in leadership positions have not traditionally carried rifles, thus they are not issued bayonets, and without intending criticism, it is easy to overlook the importance of matters one is not directly affected by.

Figure 6: Soldiers assume the *Attack position*. (U.S. Army photo)

Figure 7: Spirit of the bayonet. (Marine Corps photo)

The Art and Spirit of the Bayonet

Regardless, the art of the bayonet is not unlike dancing; there are steps, moves, and there is technique. As such, to be proficient with the weapon a soldier must first learn these essentials, and then he must practice them until they are second nature to him. The elements of bayonet drill must be such a part of a soldier's subconscious mind that when confronted with the appropriate situation he will automatically execute the correct move at the precise time, both aggressively and nearly instantaneously. Recalling his first instruction in the use of this weapon, the author can still hear Drill Sergeant Sablan on the bayonet range repeatedly parroting, "Ladies, there are two kinds on the battlefield: the quick and the dead!" Add into this mix profound aggression and you have the Spirit of the Bayonet.

There are many curriculums for teaching the bayonet. The author's intent here is merely to demonstrate the time consuming nature of this training, and as such has arbitrarily chosen FM 23-25 dated 29 August 1955. There may be more time sensitive approaches and there may be those much abbreviated. Here we look at FM 23-25.

Regardless of one's choice of reference, in order to train a soldier in the basics of bayonet fighting the Army determined, at that time, that eight instruction periods of one hour each would be necessary. That is one entire day. For those who are not familiar with the Army, or its methods, understand that these periods are to be broken up and generally scheduled to be taught on various days, most likely one period per day. Furthermore, once all eight periods are completed, the units will continue to schedule recurring periods of instruction throughout the training year.

Figure 8: Bayonet instruction the *old-fashioned way* circa 1917. (DoD photo)

The FM states that in order to develop the will and determination of the soldier to use the bayonet, the instructor must introduce the subject by outlining the scope and course of instruction, and to cite examples of actual combat use of the bayonet. The instructor should also explain that the spirit of the bayonet is the will to meet and destroy the enemy in hand to hand combat. That it is a state of mind that springs from the fighter's confidence, courage, and grim determination, and achieved only through vigorous training.

The first period concludes with teaching the concepts of bayonet fighting by explaining the purposes, uses, and principles. This is the point at which the instructor must truly sell his students on the spirit of the bayonet! In later periods they will have the opportunity to experience it, but the instructor must establish their expectations up front. One could also think of it as the period of inspiration; a time when the learner actually experiences

Figure 9: Instructor and Assistant demonstrate blocking movement. (Marine Corps photo)

Figure 10: Instructor and Assistant Instructor demonstrate the *thrust*. (U.S. Army photo)

inspiration via a concept, and develops the motivation to achieve a given set of standards in order to become what he presently is not.

In the final fifty minutes of the first period the instructor must explain, demonstrate, and conduct practical work in the basic positions, fixing and unfixing the bayonet, forming for bayonet training, and the basic movements.

The manual dedicates Period two to teaching the long and short thrust, while period three addresses the vertical butt stroke series, and concludes with the horizontal butt stroke series. Parry right and parry left are included in period four.

Once the trainees learn the basic movements they can begin actually practicing them in a meaningful, yet relatively safe manner. Period five is the first truly practical application of bayonet training using the very effective training aide known as the training stick, or Pugil Stick. Obviously, it is at this point that the fun begins for the majority of young post-adolescent men, as they have an opportunity to bludgeon each other without getting into trouble!

Pugil stick training is employed toward the end of the training cycle for basic trainees, and it is also incorporated into the confidence course, or obstacle course, for the infantrymen as a part of their *Advanced Infantry Training* (*AIT*). Naturally, it is an integral part of the infantry training cycle in regular Army Infantry units.

During pugil training the soldier learns how to practically execute the basic bayonet moves and counter moves, but the real value of the exercise is to practically demonstrate, and therefore teach, to the soldier the effect of these moves in real time against a real thinking opponent.

Figure 11: Students practice the *butt stroke*. (U.S. Army photo)

Figure 12: Practical exercise utilizing *Pugil Sticks*. (U.S. Army photo)

Figure 13: Rifles fitted with padded tips: *Pugil sticks* circa 1917. (U.S. Army photo)

Figure 14: Vigorous bayonet training circa 1916. (U.S. Army photo)

The trainee will quickly come to appreciate the complexity involved beyond simply going through the movements. Most importantly, though, he will learn that to engage in this type of combat with anything less than pure, raw aggression ultimately—every time—will end with his defeat. Failure to internalize the spirit and then allow it to drive the fight is an exercise in futility, as the soldier who embodies and deploys the spirit will win every bayonet confrontation!

Pugil training is simply the single most effective tool for teaching the practical aspect of bayonet fighting and, as an added bonus, a great way for young men to purge some of the pent up frustrations inherent to every soldier during periods of closed training courses, such as Basic Training.

Period Six is a review of the primary movements and live bayonet assault on dummies as in figure 2 above, and Period Seven teaches soldiers knife and bayonet disarming techniques and group tactics, such as the bayonet charge.

Finally, in Period eight the soldiers test under simulated combat situations by running an assault course.

As mentioned previously, this phase of training lends itself particularly well to the use of pugil sticks. Training exercises such as the one shown above in figure 16 are fraught with

Figure 15: Methods of knife and bayonet disarming techniques. (Marine Corps photo)

Figure 16: Group tactics – the *bayonet charge*. (U.S. Army photo)

danger. While one should expect danger to be a given, it is preferred that soldiers not be expended during training. Pugil sticks are a great tool to avoid such injurious scenarios.

Mystique of the Bayonet

To continue discussion relative to the assertion that the bayonet is impotent without proper training, and that such training is time intensive, it is easy to appreciate this facet of the debate when one considers that basic bayonet training requires four hours of instruction just to get the trainee to a place where he can actually begin learning technique.

This leads us to another facet of the debate, which is that the bayonet actually imbues a *spirit*, an emotional state of aggression. Proponents for the bayonet insist, and in this author's opinion rightly so, that soldiers must approach combat with an attitude of unbridled aggression, and that the bayonet facilitates such a state. Some call it the *Mystique of the Bayonet*.

In an earlier article Major Schiller F. Shore wrote: "Our infantrymen are taught to close with and capture or destroy the enemy. This is the ultimate goal of all training…I think it is the bayonet and what goes with it - the spirit of the bayonet, offensive-mindedness and the will to kill…All these things are tied in, in some intangible way, with the bayonet on the end of a rifle…the sight of cold steel brings fear to the defender and confidence to the man who knows how to use it if he has to…by *deemphasizing* the bayonet…we strip ourselves of a spirit weapon that cannot be replaced…The bayonet is a tradition that we should not discard."[4]

Opponents actually deemphasize the above philosophy by slighting tradition as merely a die-hard attitude, an unwillingness to accept change. Like many misguided people in today's society, they place no significance on tradition, and sadly, they do not realize that

Figure 17: Obstacle course. (U.S. Army photo)

Figure 18: Teaching the proper use of the M9. (U.S. Army Photo)

Figure 19: WWI Marines Bayonet Charge. (Marine Corps photo)

the Army, at its core, is in fact the embodiment of tradition. Somehow, they can accept and see value in concepts such as institutional memory,[5] but are unable to recognize that tradition is essentially a manifestation of the same phenomena.

If the bayonet is not a spiritual weapon, it most certainly is a psychological motivator, either for aggression or passivity, depending upon which end of the blade one finds one's self.[6] Naturally, opponents also adamantly argue that the alleged psychological attributes associated with the bayonet are overstated and overvalued. In their opinion, a loaded rifle has an equally intimidating effect.

Patton said it best when he commented: "very few people have ever been killed with the bayonet or sabre, but the fear of having their guts explored with Cold Steel in the hands of battle maddened men has won many a fight."[7]

To temporarily abandon the conceptual in favor of the empirical, the author will take the liberty to relate personal experience as it pertains to the psychology relative to engagements with cold steel. As a young and zealous soldier, the author had the privilege of participating in numerous *riot control* operations during the early Seventies.

These skirmishes were generally limited to left-wing protestors yelling and throwing rocks, bottles, and an occasional Molotov cocktail. Recalling such encounters, with deep satisfaction, it is unequivocal fact that the protestors had absolutely no respect for, or fear of,

Figure 20.1: The preferred method of crowd control. (Marine Corps Photo)

CS gas. They simply threw it back, and when faced with batons they still pressed forward in an effort to push skirmish lines back, while frequently a few exceptionally aggressive ones would attempt, and sometimes succeed, in wrestling sticks from their owners.

Usually the Commander tolerated their antics until they started grabbing batons and striking shields. At that point, he would order the *reserve* formation forward to relieve *skirmishers* (those with batons). At the instant the reserves (with bayonets) appeared the protestors' yelling never failed to ebb, as if by magic, to a dead silence!

As word of the bayonets spread from the front to the rear of the mob, the volume would then pick back up, as protestors raced rearward, widening the gap to a *safe* distance from which to resume hurling their objects. As the reserves advanced they again retreated, attempting to maintain their imaginary safety margin.

And so it went until the protestors were pushed well away from the gates, where eventually they simply dissipated. However, at no time did even one protestor challenge the bayonets in any way, nor were there any attempts to grab the knives—so much for the *alleged* psychological effect of the naysayers!

By this point, the debate should be in relatively sharp focus; therefore, let us move from the major arguments to those of lesser prominence, though not of lesser importance. When one looks objectively at the bayonet as a weapon, its one undeniable function should be clear to both opponent and proponent alike. Regardless of any multifunctional role, the bayonet is now, as it was at its inception, intended to be a weapon of last resort. It is exactly because when a soldier has fired his last round, and thrown his last grenade, the final viable option available to him is his bayonet. A very sobering thought!

Captain Carlton G. Barber makes the case in a 1959 article: "Nobody claims that the bayonet is a major weapon. It is, however, a necessary one because - in addition to its more positive roles - it gives every rifleman last-resort protection...In confused, close-in action, the rifleman at times must destroy his enemy immediately, without time to reload or fire a rifle. In such a situation, the bayonet may be the difference between success and failure - between life and death. It is always loaded and a split second thrust operates it."[8]

The good Captain makes his point well, as it is one thing to banter the pros and cons of such a weapon and quite another to actually take away a weapon that just *might* save an American soldier's life. Further, when viewed from the macro level the cost of equipping an Army wherein every soldier, and certainly every infantryman, with a bayonet is minimal relative to most other weapons systems.

Someone called the Marines - Again!

If this author has learned anything in his nearly thirty years as a soldier, it is that when a problem is presented and discussion ends the Marines always come up with the most elementary and straightforward solution. This usually leaves everyone else involved slack-jawed, as they realize they have just witnessed the obvious clarity of simple logic! Now, once again, our Marine comrades have rescued us from ourselves and *snapped the proverbial cap* on the bayonet issue!

One of the better, albeit freshest, arguments for the bayonet comes from ***MCMAP*** (***Marine Corps Martial Arts Program***) subject matter expert in edged weapons, Homer Brett: "A bayonet has something a bullet doesn't have: less than lethal force. It can be used for

Figure 21: Soldiers in Haiti - Fixed bayonets add an element of seriousness! (U.S. Army Photo)

crowd control, psychological control, and you can use it for killing. You can stalk someone with a bayonet. You may not want a round to go off because everyone will know where you are. If you can't escape without killing that guy, then you can stalk him and bayonet him."

At this point it is interesting to note how the Army would react if the bayonet did go away, and one could justly argue that such has never happened would technically be correct. However, just such an event did *almost* happen in 1957, and may have inspired good Captain Barber to write his article in protest.8

Examining Army Infantry Board Report Number 2811, dated 17 June 1959, we see the following statement regarding the issue's background: "...The United States Army Infantry Board evaluated the standard bayonet-knife (M5E1) as a combination utility-fighting knife in early 1957 when the Army first envisioned that rifles of the future would not require bayonets. The Board found this bayonet-knife unsuitable and recommended submission of several other type knives for evaluation. The test bayonets arrived for evaluation in June of 1958, however, the plan to eliminate the bayonet from the rifle was revoked in early 1959 by *DA* (*Department of the Army*), and as a result the Service Test of the Fighting Knife was terminated."

Certainly, it appears from this reaction that, as an institution, the Army feels the need to have some sort of knife. Whether it is called a bayonet or a fighting knife there is an apparently strong, innate desire to equip soldiers with a blade to supplement the rifle.

As in the past, the issue has once again come full circle. Today the debate has swung back the other way, but this time it is known as the ***Marine Corps Martial Arts Program*** or ***MCMAP***. The creation of former Marine Corps Commandant General James Jones, who officially brought it into being via *Marine Corps Order* (*MCO*) 1550.54. General Jones hailed it as a revolutionary step in the development of martial arts skills for Marines, as it replaces all other close-combat related systems preceding its introduction.

According to the Marines MCMAP had its beginnings at the time of the Marine Corps' creation, when Marine boarding parties used their special martial abilities, bayonet, and sword techniques to carry the skirmish.

Figure 22: The South Korean Army has for many years incorporated the U.S. Army bayonet into their traditional art of self-defense, tae kwon do. (U.S. Army Photo)

Likewise, in World War I the Marines used their bayonets to augment unarmed combat techniques, which proved highly effective and useful in the pervasive trench warfare of the day. The interwar years saw Major Anthony J. Biddle adapt forms of boxing, wrestling, and fencing with close combat techniques, and at the same time Captains Samuel B. Griffith and William Green spread their knowledge of Chinese martial arts to other Marines throughout the Corps.

According to the Marine Corps, such skills and techniques were the precursors to a system of combat fighting dubbed the ***LINE*** system, or ***Linear Infighting Neural Override Engagement***. This system of close combat is derived from various styles of martial arts, and was used from 1989 to 1998.

Retired Marine Ron Donvito developed the LINES system after extensive study of human anatomy and various martial arts, even though it is not in itself a martial arts program. LINES is also known as the ***7 Deadly Moves of Combat*** philosophy, and was intended to be employed within specific combat conditions, such as limited visibility, extreme mental and physical fatigue, when facing a numerically superior force, and intended to produce nothing less than the enemy's demise. At the same time, the system's techniques are such that one can easily learn and retain them through repetition.

In 1998, Quantico convened another Course Content Review Board (CCRB), which began searching for a more effective system. The CCRB's efforts resulted in the adoption of the Marine Corps Close Combat Training Program, which the Marines fully implemented in 2000 as part of the Marine Corp Commandant's ***Summer 2000 Initiative***, wherein the General tasked LtCol. George Bristol and MGySgt Cardo Urso with establishing the MCMAP curriculum at the ***Martial Arts Center of Excellence*** or ***MACE***.

Figure 23: Ft. Benning military police practice hand-to-hand combat techniques. (U.S. Army Photo)

Figure 24: Marines' martial arts training. (Marine Corps Photo)

Recently, the Commandant announced his goal that all Marines would receive training in entry-level martial arts skills and earn the opportunity to achieve higher levels of expertise. The director of the Marines' martial arts program, Lt. Col. George H. Bristol, said that at some point, "...all Marines, regardless of age, sex, rank, or job will do this training."[9]

MCMAP is designed to further develop the complete warrior, and consists of a blend of proven disciplines including judo, karate, and jujitsu, coupled with bayonet and knife-fighting techniques. The program also combines the three warrior disciplines of mental discipline, character discipline, and physical discipline.

Like the Spirit of the bayonet, mental discipline is the development of a combat mindset, and is reinforced—inculcated if you will—through study of the art of war. Character discipline develops through the firm integration of ethics, values, integrity, and leadership, whereas physical discipline is fighting techniques employing the rifle and bayonet, edged weapons, weapons of opportunity (stick, club, gun), and unarmed combat; all of which are complimented through combative conditioning. Through such combat sports as boxing, wrestling, and wooden trainer bayonet fighting a warrior attains combative conditioning, which is no more than the physical stamina and ability to fight while fatigued in a battlefield environment.

Figure 25: Marine Corps' MCMAP structure and belt system. (Marine Corps Graphic)

Through MCMAP, Marines develop confidence in their own combat skills, as well as confidence in the abilities of their fellow Marines. In the end, the process fosters the art of teamwork, which is a fundamental and essential component of every battlefield operation.

With the advent of MCMAP all Marines are required to

Figure 26: All Ranger and SF candidates are given extensive hand-to-hand combat training. (U.S. Army Photo)

become proficient at the entry-training level, which is represented by the tan belt. For those more motivated warriors belts in gray, green, brown, and six degrees of black belts can also be earned denoting advanced proficiency.

As often happens, Marine Corps initiatives have influenced general military thinking, though few are likely to admit it. Even so, Army infantry recruits at Ft. Benning, Georgia, are now required to receive 15 hours of hand-to-hand combat training incorporated into their 14-week *Advanced Infantry Training* (*AIT*) course. As well, all Ranger School candidates must now complete an additional 18 hours of hand-to-hand combative training, which includes boxing.

At the top of the infantry hierarchy, and always state of the art, the Army's Special Forces adopted the Marine Corps' LINE System in 1998, teaching it to their candidates during the ***Special Forces Qualification Course*** (***SFQC***, or the ***Q Course***), ***Phase II***, and remediate it as part of phases III and V.

In October 2007, the Army replaced the LINE System with their own version of MCMAP, calling it the ***Modern Army Combatives Program***, or ***MACP***. After graduation from Special Forces training, these soldiers undergo further specialized hand-to-hand combat training which is tailored to the mission needs of each unit.

Surprisingly, the Navy and Air Force have also gotten on board with their own requirements for martial arts training, which is usually only offered to members of special operations and law enforcement units. However, the Air Force and Navy recruits do not receive bayonet or hand-to-hand combat training.

At least for the present, the military recognizes the importance of close combat and the use of the bayonet. And, unlike the past, this time the emphasis has been near universal and instituted on such a grand scale that one is tempted to believe the issue will finally be put to rest. However, if history is any reliable indicator it is highly likely that the next generation will lose their appreciation of cold steel and attitudes will once again swing back the other way. Nonetheless, one can only hope that the cycle has been broken for good this time! But, the Army never changes, and most likely neither will this debate!

Figure 27: Fixing an M7 bayonet. (Marine Corps Photo)

Goodbye Saigon - Force Modernization

To understand the development of the M9 it is helpful to know something of the Army's recent history that led to the knife's acquisition in the first place. Such knowledge lends context, and in turn allows the collector to form a picture in the mind's eye of his subject, rather than simply a list of dates and facts. In this case, what the Army needed in the early seventies was a program of modernization to support its post-Vietnam change of mission.

The 1970s found the Army fully engaged in the throws of tumult, as Vietnam was fast fading and all could see great change on the horizon. With the end of the war would come a massive exodus, motivated by individual soldier concerns or because of organizational restructuring. In either case, a tremendous downsizing was in the offing and uncertainty was pervasive.

The draft had left a legacy of ill discipline and an undeserved public perception that the Army was ineffective, comprised of hooligan dope-smoking draftees who were poorly led by an NCO Corps of near illiterate incompetents. Few in the public recognized, or perhaps even knew, that American Forces in Vietnam had lost not one battle, and that while the dregs of society certainly were in our midst, most maneuver, or combat, units contained a core of cadre who were loyal, disciplined professionals completely dedicated and occupied with leading highly effective units.

Further, in all fairness, many, if not most draftees were outstanding soldiers who contributed greatly to their unit's missions, having faithfully answered America's call; they served their country well, and comported themselves honorably! The trouble was that the newspapers, six o'clock anchors, and leftist journalists could not report any of that. No, they were superbly effective at smearing the American military, poisoning a large number of the younger generation's view of the Armed forces!

Nor was the Army leadership blind to the image that the media fabricated, and they knew that somehow the Army must emerge from the dark days of Vietnam, and the ill effects of the social revolution of the 1960s. So too, they understood that the Army must become a peacetime force of volunteers. Their answer was the ***Modern Volunteer Army***; the ***MVA*** would replace the conscripted force, and the MVA would restore the Army's image to America and the world!

Figure 28: U.S. Army Natick Laboratory's vision of the future soldier. (U.S. Army photo)

Meanwhile, the skeptics cackled in early 1974 that the volunteer Army was a lost cause, and that it was only a matter of time before the draft would have to be brought back. And, during the first four months of the year recruiting results tended to support this pessimism, as the Army fell some 12,200 men short of its recruiting goal.

Conditions within the U.S. Army Recruiting Command, or *USAREC*, were partially to blame, because recruiting duty was very unpopular and historically, with the exception of popular wars, quotas were difficult to attain; given the country's mood and the military's unpopular view recruiters frequently failed to ***meet mission***. If that was not enough, USAREC removed unqualified recruiters, causing a shortage of approximately 1,000 and raising stress levels even higher and general morale lower.

To remedy the situation USAREC offered incentives to volunteers, and manned the Recruiting Stations with competent personnel. An innovative program called *Hometown Recruiting* was implemented wherein after completing Basic and Advanced Training select enlistees were detailed to their hometown recruiters with the goal of attracting others from their communities.

Figure 29: New approaches - period recruiting posters. (Army/Marine Corps photos)

The result was that by the end of November 1973, USAREC had nearly reached full strength. At the same time, Recruiting Command reversed the trend in recruiting and was able to meet the Army's manpower requirements. As of 30 June 1974, Army strength stood at 782,897, or 1,297 above its authorized quota of 781,600.[10] The MVA was succeeding, but numbers were merely one facet of the of the whole.

Army leadership recognized that if the force were going to truly transform itself, it would need to develop a completely new Army culture; one of professional ethos, individual responsibility, and integrity, as well as an acute sense of soldier welfare. To this end, race relations received head on attention; military discipline became a top priority, and criminal prosecution was aggressively pursued by agencies of the Military Police and Judge Advocate General, as well as administratively under the auspices of the Adjutant General.

The very potent ***Expeditious Discharge Program*** (*EDP*) became the primary tool for local commanders to rid units *expeditiously* of criminals, drug users, malcontents, and even poor performers. The EDP became the Commander's magic scalpel to remove cancers from the body of his unit, as unlike traditional administrative means, under the EDP there was no requirement for upper echelon approval or reams of paperwork. It was fast, simple, and final. Once initiated, it was routine to complete the process within two weeks; no rehabilitative transfers, no retraining, just rapid and final *dud* removal! It worked better than Alka-Seltzer, and Commanders and First Sergeants loved it!

Figure 30: Bradley Fighting Vehicle: conceived and designed as part of the new *MVA*. (U.S. Army Photo)

Alcohol and drug programs, including the new innovative technology of mandatory drug testing, combined with the EDP served as tremendous deterrents, as well as super tools, to rid the ranks of the drug culture. In short, the Army turned inward in its effort to address every conceivable problem. The result was generally both effective and well received.

By 1976 the Army was well into its transformation, and the *Warrior Culture* was steadily taking hold. Then came the Carter Administration, and under its feckless policies and miserable leadership the U.S. military found itself on a starvation diet. Its budget suffered dramatic cuts, and all programs suffered from under-funding. However, the quality of soldiers, and their lifestyle, continued to improve, but the hum of change became nearly inaudible.

Nevertheless, just when things looked blackest 1980 arrived and everything changed. The excitement returned, and for the first time in the memory of most, we had a person in President Reagan that exuded leadership, optimism, and made people once again proud to be American! Moreover, his Administration constantly portrayed soldiers in a patriotic light, while expressing great favor and appreciation for the Armed forces.

In reality, the military was Reagan's club with which to beat the Evil Empire,[11] and he spared no cost where that objective was concerned. If soldiers needed something to execute the mission they got it, and it was the best money could buy. The days of operational stagnation, budgetary famine, and doing more with less were just a bad dream!

Perhaps Reagan's most brilliant and skillful ploy against the Soviets was the *Star Wars* program. The genius of it was the Administration's sly propaganda initiative of graphic scenarios depicting globally positioned, orbiting satellites zapping Russian ICBMs worldwide simultaneously with *death rays*; a system that if real was capable of rendering all Soviet missiles useless!

If true, and that was the central dilemma for the communists, what such a thing meant to the Kremlin was that in a *whiff* they had nothing with which to threaten the West. Worse, they were now at Reagan's mercy, and therefore virtually powerless! Such a prospect must have been as frightening as it was maddening to the Kremlin!

Figure 31: The seventies saw women integrated into the main force; no more WACS. (Marine Corps Photo)

Precisely because Star Wars required an elaborate positioning system for satellite guidance, maneuver, fire control, and target acquisition, the need for a method of precision navigation was central to the overall system. For the American military, Star Wars was a shot in the arm for numerous programs that had been in the works for years.

Precision global navigation had for decades been a military objective. The Navy and Air Force primarily relied on the ***LORAN*** (LOng RAnge Navigation) system to navigate globally, while the Army used traditional maps. LORAN allowed users to triangulate and calculate their position and speed based on radio transmissions, and though it worked well, it had many disadvantages, not the least of which was large bulky radio equipment. What the military needed was a precise, reliable, universal, and compact system capable of use by aircraft carriers or individual soldiers. That system was the ***Global Positioning System*** (*GPS*), and it fit into the grand Star Wars scheme perfectly. Best of all, from the military perspective, Star Wars was a virtual guarantee of full project funding.

Figure 32: The PLGR GPS gives the individual soldier exact navigational capability. (U.S. Army Photo)

First conceptualized by the military in the late 1960s, GPS became a program and received funding by the ***Joint Program Office*** within the Department of Defense. In December 1973, the *Defense System Acquisition and Review Council* (*DSARC*) approved a proposal for the GPS program, and by the mid-1970s the system underwent ground testing.

The first GPS satellite launched on 22 February 1978, and all indications were that the program would bolt ahead with early completion. Unfortunately, the Challenger disaster prompted a halt in the program in 1986, seriously delaying development. To everyone's relief the launch program restarted in 1989, and in that same year, the Magellan Corporation introduced the first hand-held GPS receivers.

These highly portable and accurate devices were alternately known as ***Slugger*** and ***Plugger***,[12] (PLGR, or *Precision Lightweight GPS Receiver*) capable of triangulating satellite transmissions and thereby giving the user his exact position. Moreover, while these devices did not replace maps, they did provide U.S. forces the capability of navigating anywhere on Earth to pinpoint locations!

In 1983, the Army decided to freeze active duty strength, thereby diverting their funds to the priorities of modernization over personnel expansion. This, combined with a slower than expected growth of the Defense Department's budget, reduced Army expectations in both areas.

Nineteen Eighty-Seven found the Army focusing on close operations and the weapons systems supporting them.[13] Pursuant to a warfighting capability study conducted by the Army Staff, Leadership zeroed in on critical systems essential to fighting and winning on any battlefield. The same report established priorities for acquisition of weapons systems. Programs and technologies necessary in basic operational requirements were used to determine essential weapons systems.

Army leadership decided that the essential operational capabilities for conducting combat operations were reconnaissance, surveillance, target acquisition, command, control, communications, battlefield lethality, battlefield sustainment, and equipment necessary to enhance soldier and unit performance. Using this report, the Army fashioned its policy for developing and fielding weapons into the year 2000, as doctrine led technology.

Figure 33 – Development of today's small arms, such as this *Squad Automatic Weapon* (SAW), was another product of the MVA. (U.S. Army Photo)

From these policies came the impetus for adoption of such weapons systems as the Squad Automatic Weapon (**SAW**), replacement of the venerable .45 caliber pistol (*M1911A1*), and adoption of the Kevlar helmet, along with a new equipment load bearing system. In fact, new equipment appeared across the board, and naturally included the ***M16A2*** and the M9 bayonet.

Therefore, it is because of all the aforementioned events that the M9 came to be the Army's newest, and most unique bayonet, and while the search for an improved bayonet greatly predates these events, the actual adoption of it was doubtlessly driven by events responsible for the force modernization by Uncle Sam, and of course - Uncle HO!

Figure 34: Development of today's small arms was another product of the MVA. (U.S. Army Photo)

2

Materiel Acquisition

The Army Infantry Board

Harkening back to days past, Testing and Evaluation began very simply, and for many years consisted of a handfull of facilities with a simple hierarchy. Many of us remember the old *Infantry Board* as the be all and end all of weapons evaluation. If anyone was *in the know* about new equipment, it was the fellows at Ft. Benning, though little did we know even then that a relatively gigantic infrastructure already existed, nor could anyone of the day have foreseen how large and complicated it would become.

The Army established the Infantry Board on 31 March 1903 at Fort Leavenworth, Kansas, under the command of the ***General Service and Staff College*** (today known as the ***Command and Staff College***). From about 1911 to 1919 the Infantry Board was inactive, and whether a result of its inactivity or routine realignment it was moved to Fort Benning, Georgia. In 1931, the Army chose to integrate the Infantry Board into the Tank Board at Fort Meade, Maryland, and in turn, tank testing moved from the Infantry Board in 1940 and consolidated with the *Armored Force Board* stationed at Fort Knox, Kentucky.

With the emergence of parachute units by countries such as Russia and especially Germany, the Army, in 1940, established the *Airborne Test Platoon* and placed it under the auspices of the Infantry Board. This special airborne activity was later redesignated the *Airborne Board* and transferred to Fort Bragg in 1945. In August 1940, Lieutenant William T. Ryder, commander of the Army's Airborne Test Platoon, made history as the first American Soldier to make a military parachute jump.

The Infantry Board was redesignated the *Army Ground Forces Board Number 3* in 1945 and remained at Fort Benning, Georgia, until January 1957, when it was essentially renamed the *U.S. Army Infantry Board* and became a virtual icon at Ft. Benning until 1988, when it was redesignated the *Test and Experimentation Command Infantry Board.*

In 1991, the Infantry Board at Fort Benning was closed and its mission assumed by the newly established *TEXCOM Infantry Test Directorate* at Fort Hood, Texas. In 2002, TEXCOM was redesignated the *Operational Test Command.*

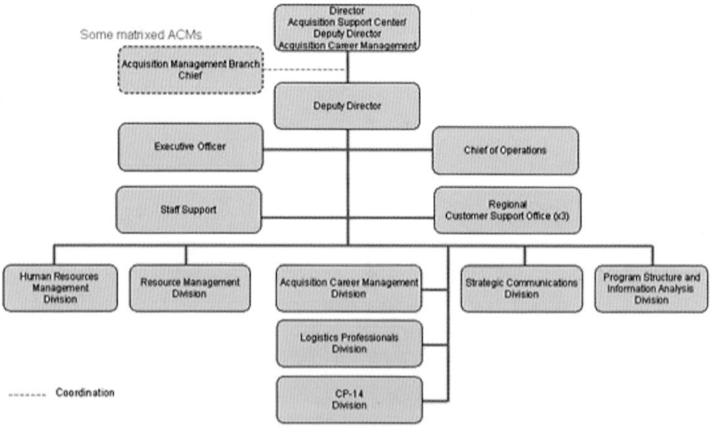

Figure 35: Organization chart depicting acquisition in the macro. (Library of Congress)

The *Tank Board*, created in 1920 at Fort Meade, Maryland, fell under the command of the Infantry Board in 1931, where it remained until 1939, when it transferred to Fort Knox, Kentucky. In 1940, it was redesignated the *Armored Force Board* and later redesignated again as the *Army Ground Forces Board Number 2*, remaining at Fort Knox.

In 1948, it was redesignated *Army Field Forces Board Number 2*, with no change in mission or structure until 1957, when it was redesignated the U.S. Army *Armor Board* , and in 1965 it was consolidated with the *Engineer Board* at Fort Knox. In 1988, like its counterpart the Infantry Board, the Armor Board was redesignated *TEXCOM Armor and Engineer Board*, deactivated at Fort Knox in 1990, and reactivated as the *TEXCOM Armor Test Directorate* at Fort Hood, Texas.

The Army's Test and Evaluation Command

Probably the single most interesting aspect of the acquisition process is that of testing and evaluation. From this process, collectors can obtain and study the physical attributes of their pieces and often pick up valuable clues for identifying rare variations of a given item.

Unfortunately, like most programs, *T&E* has evolved into a monstrous, complex bureaucracy that few can navigate even with an organizational flow chart as a map. Figure 36 demonstrates this intricacy quite well, keeping in mind that the chart is not a detailed representation, but a macro view of an enormous process!

Figure 36: Organization chart depicting acquisition in the macro. (Library of Congress)

Principle Activities of the Test & Evaluation Command

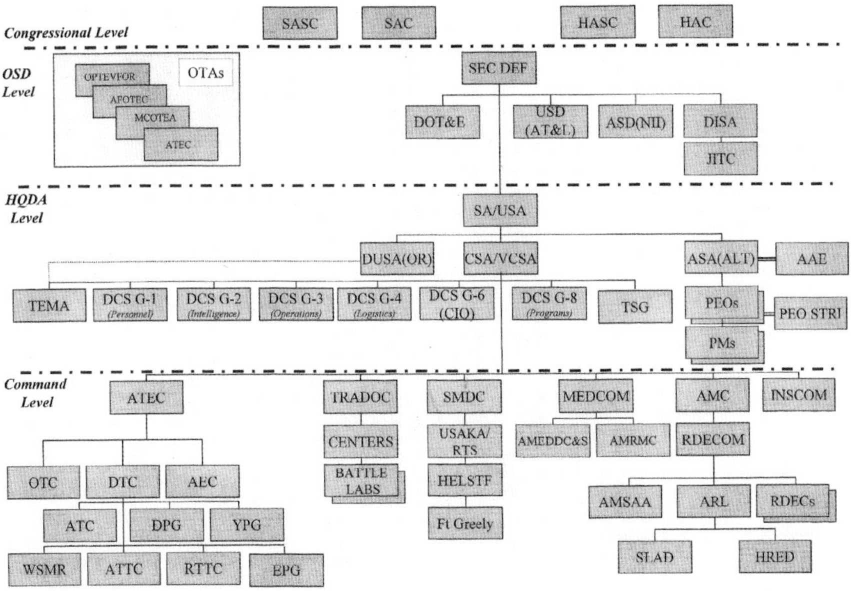

Figure 37: Test & Evaluation organizational structure. (U.S. Army graphic)

These organizations are a perfect testament to the Army's penchant for moving, consolidating, redesignating, deactivating, reflagging, and rotating! The Army is forever shuffling its house around which is frustrating, to everyone actually, but practically necessary in order to accommodate and support changes in mission and programs, though often it seems to be an unwritten rule that people and organizations are not allowed to become too entrenched in any one place.

For those who seriously study and collect bayonets there must come a time when it is necessary to confront the monster that is acquisition. It may be as simple as studying a contract, or for those brave souls, tracing the piece's progress through the complete acquisition process from proposal to actual issue. As such, it is incumbent upon the author to present the reader with at least a cursory overview of the acquisition process.[14]

Solicitations and Specifications

The basic process usually begins with the Army identifying a need for a particular item and passing their requirements up the *Chain of Command.* At some point, the acquisition process will become involved, and if such an item is not already in the system, they will search for the item by issuing a solicitation, which appears on numerous government websites, and in periodic publications with the intention of attracting appropriate business proposals.

All interested private manufacturers then submit their proposals for consideration and, if accepted, must provide a working prototype of the item to the appropriate agency for testing and evaluation.

In many instances more than one prototype will be required, and naturally, not at government expense.

From somewhere deep within the bowels of the bureaucracy the responsible agency assigns a project *Program Manager* (*PM*), who assumes overall responsibility to supervise and coordinate all aspects of evaluation, which usually begins with one of many Test and Evaluation activities putting the candidate item through a series of tests to insure that it meets military specifications.

In the case of Army and Marine bayonets, Rock Island Arsenal is the proponent agency to conduct specification testing *in accordance with* (*IAW*), the applicable *Military Specification*. For the bayonet, that publication is MIL-K-70606; however, any item may fall under one or more applicable specifications, and currently there exists in excess of 22,000 MILSPECS.

Fortunately, the majority of items will not be the subject of all 22,000, but may in fact be required to satisfy the requirements prescribed in a significant number of *MILSPECS*. And, while this process may seem convoluted, complex, bureaucratic, and unnecessarily *complicated*, it is critical that weapons contain the grade of steel that the *Society of American Engineers* has determined can withstand the forces likely to be encountered, or that the handle of the bayonet does not break down when subjected to certain chemicals and is capable of insulating the soldier's hand should he cut through an electrically charged wire.

Procedurally speaking then, and in the simplest of terms, a number of commands exist to develop and evaluate certain equipment, which may fall under the auspices of the *Army Material Command, or Medical Command*, or the *Tank and Automotive Command*, or others depending on the type and nature of that equipment. Each of these commands will utilize numerous and differing installations during the development of the equipment.

Army Arsenals and Depots

Natick Laboratories- Research, Development and Engineering Command

In-house acquisition is carried out at many sites as the graph above indicates, and to explore each one in depth would simply be impractical and beyond the scope of this writing; however, major players such as *Natick Laboratories*, which is part of the *Army's Research, Development and Engineering Command* (*RDECOM*), merit a brief mention.

In 1953, the Army established the *Natick Soldier Research Development and Engineering Center* twenty miles west of Boston, Massachusetts, on Lake Cochituate; it is seventy-eight acres and composed of fifty-six buildings. Natick's primary purpose is to research and test systems in feeding, protection, and mobility.

Since establishment its mission has remained the same, though the breadth and complexity has expanded exponentially, and today its scientists, engineers, and equipment designers provide soldiers a wide range of field feeding and life support systems, clothing, precision airdrop systems, and ballistic, chemical, and laser protection systems. The lab is also involved in other testing and evaluation functions, and was in fact involved to some extent in the Marine Corps' *OKC3s project*.

Figure 37.1: Natick Laboratory; twenty miles west of Boston, Massachusetts, on Lake Cochituate. (U.S. Army photo)

Figure 37.2: Above: a Quartermaster NCO demonstrates the latest Army rations circa 1930s. (U.S. Army photo)

Rock Island Army Arsenal

For those readers groaning that Anniston tested bayonets, that is correct; however, in the past numerous and sundry locations performed this same function. However, today this aspect of evaluation comes under the auspices of TACOM, which conducts its operations utilizing seven specialized facilities, but has its headquarters in Warren, Michigan, where it is responsible for managing the Army's fleet of ground combat

Figure 38: Rock Island Arsenal, nestled in the Mississippi River. (U.S. Army Photo)

and tactical vehicles. There the Army develops future ground vehicles and associated weapons systems, as well as sustaining the Army's vehicle fleet, and procures the bulk of our military materiel.

However, to a vast extent, procurement related activities take place at *Rock Island Arsenal* (*RIA*), in Illinois which is also engaged in the entire spectrum of armament acquisition, and functions to provide manufacturing, installation support, and logistics for all tenant interservice agencies. And, as it operates the only active Army foundry, it manufactures a multitude of armament and equipment, such as artillery and artillery mounts, recoil mechanisms, aircraft weapons sub-systems, small arms, and weapons simulators, as well as weapons parts and components, and chemical and petroleum systems. The arsenal accomplishes all of these critical tasks with a force of 250 active duty personnel and 6000 civilian employees, making it by far the largest and most comprehensive of TACOM's facilities.

Established as Fort Armstrong in 1816, Rock Island Arsenal sits atop Arsenal Island (a 946-acre island) in the Mississippi River, situated between the cities of Davenport, Iowa, and Rock Island, Illinois. Completed in 1817, Fort Armstrong served as one of a series of frontier defensive fortifications in the Upper Mississippi Valley following the War of 1812 and as a Headquarters for Army forces during the Black Hawk War in 1832, and afterwards remained as an ordnance depot when regular Army forces were withdrawn in 1836.

Rock Island Arsenal, officially established in 1862, subsequently functioned as a manufacturing site for Army field equipment (chiefly leather goods) and other accoutrements, as well as weapons for the military until the1880s.

Figure 39: Aerial view of Rock Island Arsenal; old arsenal in foreground. (U.S. Army Photo)

Figure 40: Colonel George Davenport. (Library of Congress)

The first Commander of Rock Island, George Davenport, originally came to Rock Island as the sutler for the Army at Fort Armstrong. By 1818, he resigned and established a more lucrative trading post on Rock Island and during the Black Hawk War.

Taking advantage of his background as a sutler,[15] he served as quartermaster for the local militia, and the Army, which earned him the honorary title of Colonel, as well as $20,000 in compensation. Following the Black Hawk War, Colonel Davenport became very prosperous and influential, and by all reports was uncommonly well liked by both the local Indians and settlers. So much so, that the city of Davenport, Iowa, was mapped out and named after him, and the first meeting to bring the railroad to the area was held in his home on the island.

Figure 41: The Davenport mansion, built in 1833, near the site of old Ft. Armstrong. By 1906, the house was abandoned and dilapidated. Fortunately, a local association rebuilt it. (Library of Congress)

Unfortunately, in 1845 members of a river ruffian group known locally as the *Banditti of the Prairie* murdered him in his home.[16]

During the Civil War, the Union Army operated 21 prisoner of war camps, including Rock Island from 1863 to July 1865. In the vernacular of the day, the *Rock Island Prison Barracks* held some 12,192 Confederate soldiers, of which 1,964 died. These dead are buried in the Confederate Cemetery, which are the only surviving remains of the prison barracks.[17]

After the war, in 1865 Brigadier General Thomas J. Rodman arrived on the Island, becoming the second Commander of Rock Island, and transformed it into a true arsenal on a grand scale. He devised a master construction plan calling for ten large manufacturing shops, five on each side of the island's major east-west thoroughfare.

Figure 42: Brigadier General Thomas J. Rodman. (Library of Congress)

Figure 43: Commanding Officer's Quarters. (Library of Congress)

Originally, the five shops on the North row were designated *Armory Row*, and were dedicated to the manufacture and overhaul of small arms, whereas South row was designated Arsenal Row and served to manufacture and overhaul general ordnance. These shops formed the manufacturing core of the arsenal and were supplemented by a variety of administrative, living quarters, maintenance, storage, and utility buildings.

Figure 44: Rock Island Arsenal Headquarters, Bldg 360. (U.S. Army Photo)

While it seems unimaginable that the Army would be as insensitive to the American taxpayer as to authorize the building of quarters so unnecessarily elaborate and wasteful, Colonel Rodman actually did in fact design and construct the Commanding Officer's Quarters. The building is an Italianate villa completed in 1871, having an unbelievable 50 rooms totaling—a nearly unprecedented, and obscene—20,000 square feet of living space! Not surprisingly, it is the second largest government single-family residence in the United States, with the exception of the White House!

With regard to the apparent opulent wastefulness, it is possible to take some consolation if one considers that the Arsenal was, aside from a mammoth production center, a centerpiece of American military technology and national might. Washington fully intended for other world powers to behold the Arsenal and be intimidated. From such a perspective, it is a bitter pill more easily swallowed!

Figure 45: Rock Island Arsenal Bldg 68, shop H. (U.S. Army Photo)

Completion of the residence occurred in the fall of 1871, a few months after the Colonel's death. In fact, Rodman saw few buildings actually finished during his lifetime, although his successors, such as Lieutenant Colonel Daniel W. Flagler—the third commander—closely followed his original plan, and continued construction of the arsenal buildings throughout the Nineteenth century.

Figure 46: Rock Island Arsenal Bldg 68, shop H, 1st floor (04 July 1904) showing Pratt & Whitney rifling machines for manufacture of the Model 1903 Springfield rifle. (U.S. Army Photo)

Figure 47: Rock Island Arsenal Bldg 68, shop H, 2nd Floor showing Browning machinegun parts being made. (U.S. Army Photo)

Figure 48: Watervliet Arsenal circa 1918. (Library of Congress)

Watervliet Arsenal, New York

Watervliet Arsenal, New York, is now, and has since the early 1800s, been the world's premier producer of cannon. Guns produced at the arsenal include the 120mm smoothbore for the Army's M1A1 main battle tank. Other guns produced there include howitzers and mortars, as well as recoilless rifles, employing the latest and most highly sophisticated technology in the world. Uniquely collocated with Benet Labs, Watervliet has the capability to design, carry out research, and develop and field test prototype pieces, as well as to put the products into final production. Few facilities are this comprehensive.

Figure 49: Self-propelled howitzer at Watervliet Arsenal. (Library of Congress)

Figure 50: Precision machine shop. (Library of Congress)

Picatinny Arsenal, New Jersey

Picatinny Arsenal, New Jersey, is located in the Northwestern part of the state, and was established in 1880 as an Army powder depot. In 1902 a shell loading line was added, and in 1907 the Army's first propellant powder factory was built on the installation, resulting in the post's name being changed to Picatinny Arsenal. With the conclusion of World War I, the Army augmented Picatinny with research and development laboratories, and following a horrific explosion at the Lake Denmark Powder Depot Congress appropriated 2.3 million dollars to rebuild the arsenal.

At the outbreak of World War II, Picatinny Arsenal was the only munitions plant with the capability of manufacturing large caliber ammunition, which included production and assembly of the complete shell, propellant, charge, and fuze. Following the war, the arsenal's mission focus changed to that of research and development of armament. It is officially known as the *Army Research and Development Center* (*ARDC*), and operated under the auspices of *DARCOM.*

Today, Picatinny provides research, development, engineering, and production support for advanced weapons systems, producing large numbers of new weapons and munitions. One well-known arsenal invention is the *Picatinny Rail System*, which increases the mission capabilities of such weapons systems as the M21, M16A2, and M4, as well as many other

Figure 51: The Picatinny Rail System mounted on an M21 sniper rifle. (U.S. Army Photo)

Figure 52 : The Picatinny Rail System mounted on an M4 carbine. (U.S. Army Photo)

assault type weapons. The rail system allows the attachment of numerous special devices to the weapons using a standard mounting apparatus.

The Arsenal has recently been involved in development of the XMB; a new infantry weapon system, a multi-configurable 5.56 mm modular system consisting of four weapon variants: the *Special Compact Carbine* (*SC*), *Designated Marksman* (*DM*), and the *Light Machine Gun /Auto Rifle*, with all variants featuring semi-automatic as well as automatic firing modes. The Carbine would be the standard individual soldier's weapon, and if adopted, would replace the M16 family of rifles.

Figure 53: M1 Abrams tanks on the reassembly line. (U.S. Army Photo)

Anniston Army Depot, Alabama

Anniston Army Depot, located in Northeast Alabama, is a state-of-the-art maintenance facility that has the distinction of being the *Tank Rebuild Center*. It is the only Army depot with the expertise and resources to perform maintenance on all families of heavy and light-tracked combat vehicles as well as their associated components. The depot is responsible for the maintenance and storage of conventional ammunition and the storage of chemical munitions waiting demilitarization.

Red River Army Depot, Texas

While the Arsenal is under command of the U.S. Army TACOM, other commands, such as the *Defense Logistics Agency, Defense Reutilization* and *Marketing Office*, *Department of Army Center of Military History*, *Health Services Command*, and *Soldier and Chemical Biological Command* share the facility.

Red River Army Depot West of Texarkana, Texas, provides depot level support for the Army's light vehicle fleet. This consists of the repair, rebuilding, and modification of Bradley Fighting Vehicle series vehicles, the *Multiple Launch Rocket System* (*MLRS*), and tactical wheeled vehicles. The depot also performs maintenance and testing on both the Hawk and Patriot missile systems, and is best know as an ammunition storage facility that covers an impressive 9,000 acres.

Figure 54: Gen. Richard A. Cody (Vice Chief of Staff) inspects the Bradley. (U.S. Army photo)

Sierra Army Depot, Herlong, California

The final facility presented is Sierra Army Depot, which is located near Herlong, California. Sierra has traditionally served primarily as a munitions disposal site that receives, stores, issues, maintains, and demilitarizes all forms of conventional munitions.

However, beyond its role as a disposer, Sierra's location in the high desert, to a significant extent, makes it a natural storage facility for all forms and types of equipment. Consequently, large-scale operations to provide worldwide logistical support in the form of maintenance, assembly, and containerization and rapid deployment of equipment, referred to locally as Operational Project Stock, comprise the bulk of the facility's mission.

This includes the Inland Petroleum Distribution System, Water Support System, and Force Provider, as well as Army Field Feeding Systems, Large Area Maintenance Shelters, Landing Mat Sets, Bridging, and Reserve Component Hospital Detachment Associated Support items to name but a few of the enormous variety of combat infrastructure.

The chances that a collector's search would lead to Sierra Army Depot are extremely remote, but in the interest of completeness, it is essential to include it no matter its brevity.

Figure 55: *Miles* of armored vehicles parked at Sierra Army depot. (U.S. Army Photo)

By this point is should be obvious that for research into recent weapons Rock Island Arsenal is the single most important facility, and as we have seen, an item may be sent there for specialized testing, or it may actually be manufactured at the arsenal.

Other Means of Acquisition

Assuming that an item meets specifications, it will pass from TACOM to TEXCOM, where it will undergo a second phase of testing. Field testing, or Operational testing, is a trial of the item under actual field conditions by the same type of (Infantry, Armor, Artillery…) soldiers who will eventually be issued the item. It is possible for any unit to be selected to put an item through field trials, but such a unit must consist of soldiers who are reasonably expected to actually use the item at some point in the future.

For the item that outperforms all others during field trials and also meets or exceeds military specifications, price, etc., a contract is a virtual certainty. Afterwards, at a specified date, the item will enter into the supply system and be available for issue to the end users. The military acquires most, but not all, items of equipment by this standard means.

Another means of acquiring supply items is through the *Open Request*, using a purchase order to buy items off the shelf. This method is very popular in today's military, and was instituted as a means of rapid acquisition of equipment that is not currently stocked in the DoD supply system.

For instance, let us say that the Commander of A Company, 1st Battalion, 26th Infantry, has a priority need for 100 M9 bayonets. Currently there are two companies contracted to provide these items (Ontario Knife Company and Lan-cay), and of course both meet military specifications.

The Company Commander, through the Battalion Supply Officer (S4) and with approval from the Battalion Commander, can order directly from these suppliers and pay for the items from unit funds. He can also purchase them through the General Services Administration (GSA) and use the unit credit card as payment and, naturally, the items can be UPS'd or FEDEX'd overnight.

Today many companies manufacture items of military significance, and they insure that military specifications are met precisely in anticipation that some agency will purchase their items. This is a profound and badly needed change in the way the military acquires supplies and other items. Again, for those of the bureaucratic bent, we will address the subject of materiel acquisition later in much more depth.

Local purchase is a common means of acquiring common purpose items such as office supplies, etc., and units can buy them directly from local merchants using the unit credit card, but the Army encourages Commanders to patronize small and/or minority businesses.

There is a unit budgetary allowance available for such purchases, but is limited by each individual command, and naturally managed using the Quarterly fiscal system.[18]

One of the oldest and least official means of acquisition is local authorization for wear of distinctive unit items. A good example of this is the leather belt and oval U.S. belt buckle worn by soldiers of the 3d Armored Cavalry Regiment. The Regimental Commander authorized these items for wear in the early 1970s as a means of boosting unit morale, and the practice has continued with each successive Regimental Commander. This practice encourages each soldier to purchase his own belt and buckle from local or mail order sources. As long as the soldier remains assigned to that unit, the items are authorized for wear.

Figure 56: Distinctive belt buckle worn by members of the 9th U.S. Infantry (Manchu's). (Author's buckle)

Other examples are the 9th U.S. Infantry (Manchu's), who have been authorized to wear a distinctive unit belt buckle since the early 1900s when they participated in the Boxer Rebellion in China. Likewise, Officers and NCOs of the 1st Cavalry Division are encouraged to purchase and wear the traditional black Stetson hat for unit social and ceremonial functions.

Such practices are the proverbial *down and dirty* explanation of how items end up in the hands of soldiers. It is useful to the collector to know the basic process of acquisition in order to appreciate the individual history of a given item, and in some cases such knowledge will be required in order to actually evaluate some pieces.

An in depth presentation of Defense Logistics, while perhaps interesting to some, would require volumes, and frankly, the expertise of someone many times more proficient than this author. Even so, it is the author's opinion that it is useful to take every opportunity to educate the collecting community on such issues, as they are germane to the hobby.

The Politics of Acquisition

One very interesting aspect of collecting is the inevitable uncovering, or discovery, of a multitude of dynamics associated with a given object. It is not unrealistic, in fact, to say that even the poorest of observers cannot avoid a confrontation with at least a few of these dynamics during his collecting career!

This is true precisely because no person and no relic ever has, nor ever will exist in a vacuum. We, and our artifacts, occupy space within our society, and thus share in the associated social and cultural dynamics. That is to say, that if one studies the artifact, one will eventually discover something, and usually it is interesting, about the people who created or used it!

Having said that, if one absolutely cannot abide politics, it is well that he not collect any form of militaria, for verily the politics of it will most certainly follow him home! It is inevitable. There is, though, no need for anxiety, because if one approaches the issue in the correct manner it can be very interesting and enlightening.

Admittedly, the preceding is exemplary of the longstanding controversy surrounding the procurement issue and, while this is not a political book, one must not dismiss the politics exactly because they have in one manner or another influenced the creation of the artifact. One does not have to like the politics, one does not have to agree with the politics, but one does have to be at least familiar with the politics in order to speak intelligently on the subject, or understand and appreciate the item's history.

It is important to understand a little of the procurement process, and be aware that this process is laden with political baggage and pork barreling. Fortunately, a very astute and adroit Marine Corps officer has gone before us and done a magnificent job of condensing this complex, nebulous, and tedious dynamic that we call political procurement or acquisition. The following is a further condensation of his treatise, but with the salient points preserved.[19]

Major Gary E. Slyman, in his article *Political Aerodynamics: Technical Decisions in a Political World, Why the Acquisition System Cannot be Reformed*, explains that:

"since the Civil War and until now there has existed a great dissatisfaction with the system of weapons procurement. The military, taxpayers, and Congressmen all have complaints with various aspects of the system. Charges that it is incapable of keeping pace with technology; laden with fraud, waste, and abuse, or accusing the military of *gold-plating* weapons; everyone involved has a complaint.

Yet such a system has somehow managed to produce the most technically advanced weapons the world has ever seen! In fact, our level of technical advancement is responsible for our position as the planet's only true superpower. Yet despite it all, there remains a great need for serious systemic change in the procurement system."

The Major points out that:

" no matter the many attempts at reform over the years, all meaningful change has failed to come about, and in is his opinion the truth is that reform in acquisition demands a transformation of the politics affecting the process. That because this country has traditionally ascribed civil control of the armed forces, and that Congress, is Constitutionally, mandated to raise and maintain the our nation's military it is therefore necessary, in order to achieve honest and meaningful change, to reform every area of the process. Such change must occur at the Congressional level, exactly because the flaw of acquisition reform has historically been a failure to change the political mechanism in any effective way."

The article stresses that the acquisition system is composed of technical, military, and political dimensions, wherein the technical dimension represents the transformation of technology into the weapons that the military employs to secure our nation, and that the political dimension is the use of tax dollars for the procurement of those weapons.

As such, the acquisition community must focus the majority of their efforts on the technical and military dimensions, specifically with regard to technical research as a means of satisfying military requirements, with the military dimension focusing on the end product, which is security of the nation and its allies.

Not surprisingly, Major Slyman saves the political dimension for last, emphasizing the critical element of reformation as being legislative. To this end, he relates how the acquisition system analyst Thomas McNaugher views the political dimension in terms of access and accountability, where access ensures a fair opportunity for the private industry to compete for acquisition dollars, and at the same time ensures each tax dollar is properly spent through honest accountability. Very adroitly, he explains that a unique defense sector economy has evolved because of access, which is based on monopolies, subsidies, lack of competition, and a market where the government is the customer and the regulator.

If his opinion seemed veiled to this point, he unsheathes his ire with the whole system when he charges that:

"the bureaucratic organization, which now regulates the system, is the ultimate handiwork of accountability and that acquisition dollars are supposed to be spent enhancing national security not creating jobs, or providing economic stability or growth to select localities around the country. Unfortunately, however, this is precisely what has happened and the realization of such a social has sadly influenced too many defense-spending decisions. In other words, the situation has exacerbated and enhanced pork-barrel politics!

While the afore mentioned dysfunctional state has evolved, the acquisition objectives have historically remained that of efficient procurement of effective, and easily supported weapons. Sadly, the whole weapons procurement system has evolved into the present overregulated, cumbersome, and unresponsive bureaucratic process that, fortunately during times of crisis has been temporarily suspended in favor of measures which encourage, and make possible efficient, and timely delivery of weapons and materiel in sufficient quantities for the military."

On the brighter side, the article contends:

"...reform and streamlining of the process is taking place, though not quickly, or substantially enough, through repeal of cumbersome rules and burdensome specifications, and Defense acquisition is increasingly employing commercial technology to optimize time and money while gaining more technological advantage.

While the situation is far from healthy, the system is generally trending towards a process, which employs a centrally controlled, and less restrictive system, in which the actual acquisition is decentralized. And, though all of the improvements, and reforms have improved, the overall system change has not come about to the extent necessary to provide a truly efficient, and effective acquisition system based on honest methods. To do this, to understand the real issues that trouble the system requires examination of reforms that historically have failed to be implemented.

One can categorize those recommendations requiring very simple implementation into either budgetary or issues of expanded competition wherein the deficiencies are results of an institutionalized biennial budget and modification of the Planning, Programming, and Budgeting System (PPBS). The sorely needed intervention lays in an expanded integration of the two practices while the challenge and hindrance to both is that they are politically sensitive in that, the power of acquisition emanates from the budget, and hence those able to, and responsible for, creating it.

While one simple remedy would be to create a biennial budget, such an act would have an effect tantamount to stripping military control from the Congress, as well as its ability to influence specific special interests. On the other hand, the expansion of competition would result in increased use of market-based systems through modifications to the defense industrial base, and that would destroy the current monopoly relationships."

The article's obvious conclusions are:

"1 - the problems with the acquisition system have been very well identified (many times over), 2 - the implementation of reforms have failed to significantly change acquisition, and 3 - it is a very difficult and slow process to implement reforms."

Another, not so obvious, conclusion is:

"...that the recommendations implemented are treating the symptoms of the procurement problem. Though treatment of the symptoms is essential, treatment of the disease will make the symptoms disappear. Weapons procurement is a political process that is accomplishing considerably more than acquiring weapons. It has become a social program that has jobs, economies, special interests, and votes all tied to it.

Reforms have not taken place exactly because of their impact on the Planning, Programming, and Budgeting System, and that because acquisition reform is not in the best interests of those that benefit from the current pork-barrel system, although the impression that reform is going forward does benefit them. That is to say, that the driving forces behind these military and technical decisions are political, and not national security concerns, and that true and meaningful reform is simply not possible until the focus is properly on national security, and not individual's political careers and interests.

Civilian control over the military emanates from the Constitution, and the power it vests in the Congress to raise and maintain the military while conversely, the President is charged with command authority of it, each being essential to provide a balance of power. In order for acquisition to proceed effectively, and efficiently, it requires clear political objectives so that the military can easily establish its objectives."

Clearly, the article charges that in particular the Congress has shirked its responsibility in the process, as its political objectives transcend those of national security. Major Slyman concedes:

"The many threats to the United States' vital interests has never been, nor is now easily quantifiable. In deterring a threat, we face the question of how a threat to our vital interests translates into a military capability. The money spent to develop that capability must then be justified. On the economic side, it is difficult to measure the return on the defense investment. There must be the justification of any money spent against the opportunity cost of domestic spending. In peacetime, this is a daunting task."

He suggests:

"by examining acquisition's three dimensions, technical, military, and political, it is apparent the technical and military dimensions are relatively manageable. Militarily, threats to national security require definition and the development of requirements to counter them. The priority, severity, and volatility of the threats are open to political interpretations, which complicate the threat evaluation. Since threat evaluation is a subjective process with monetary implications, anyone who perceives an interest in the outcome imbeds themselves in the debate. However, once defined and accepted, the military requirements of how high, how fast, and how big then becomes a technical problem. The technical solution is the conversion of a requirement into a weapons system within the given constraints. The political dimension is the determination of the funding level, the contracting to ensure fair access, and the accountability of the funding. This dimension is subject to continual tinkering to support competing interests.

For change to occur those able to effect it must consistently want it and in the current situation there is no incentive for them to do that precisely because big business has manipulated the politicians to the point that they essentially have monopolies while small business and minority businesses are afforded preferential treatment while lobbyists keep even the worst programs funded. By maintaining the current acquisition mess all interested parties benefit from institutional protection that is except the American taxpayer."

There are four recommendations from this brief study:

"• Continue with the reforms underway.

• Implement a review of the top down reforms from a bottom up perspective. This is to ensure the accomplishment of the desired goals to the lowest level.

• Reform the PPBS, the requirement generation process, and Life Cycle Management Process into a more integrated system. This must include Congressional Involvement at the initiation of a program.

• Increase competition where possible in the defense sector.

The desired end state for weapons acquisition is a market-based, competitive, defense industry that responds to the military's needs. The integration of the Life Cycle Management Process and a budget process must take place, with multiyear procurements for stable programs as the standard. Getting there from here is a difficult process, but the United States can ill afford to maintain the status quo. The military must take the lead, forcing Congress and the Executive Branch to mold the current systems into a workable integrated process."

Major Slyman did an outstanding job of delineating the problem, and placing the ultimate responsibility where it truly belongs: square on the politician's shoulders! The problem is fixable, but Congress is both the problem and the fixer. But then, figure the odds!

3

Quest for the Magic Blade (MPBS)

Multipurpose Functionality

In medicine, the drug capable of killing any organism while having no untoward side effects is known as a *magic bullet*. It is the ultimate omni-purpose drug, being at once all things to all users. Such a drug, of course, does not and cannot exist, and yet medicine continues searching for it. Likewise, the Army since its formation has been determined to find the magic blade, which is also a knife, a bayonet, a pry bar, a wire cutter, an entrenching tool, and yes, even a flamethrower!

While one could use any of a thousand objects as an example, we highlight the pocket can opener, not exclusively for levity, but as an example of just how ingrained multifunctionality is in the American military culture. Truly, it is as pervasive as *hundred mile an hour tape* (sort of like duct tape) or paint!

When one wonders why the Army would invest so much time, money, and effort into fielding a multifunctional bayonet, the reason is simple: breaking things, eradicating the enemy, and getting as many uses out of every object as possible *is what the Army does*! They do, because it is how they think, and all humor aside, it is in part because if the American soldier is anything, he is incredibly resourceful!

As well, for generations virtually every G.I. attached his favorite P38 to a key chain, or wore it with his dog tags, just to have it handy. We also know that most carried, or will carry, that same little can opener throughout life; partly from habit, and partly because it is a token representing many, many significant memories! Otherwise the P38 was chosen because there is a significant number of people who collect these tiny implements and very little is written about them.

To get back on message though, it would be a titanic task to exemplify soldierly resourcefulness better than to examine the tiny, seemingly inconsequential pocket can opener. A mammoth task, because the P38 is possibly the most famous, basic, and prolific of all multi-tools ever issued by the American military, even though, ironically, no one

Figure 57: Above: a patrol leader exploits the multifunctionality of the M4 combat knife. (U.S. Army photo)

intended it to be such. Even so, it may well exceed all others in the number of tasks it is capable of performing, though of course such would depend on whom one were to ask.

Its nomenclature allegedly originates from the ability to open the standard C-ration can by puncturing it 38 times, hence the P38.[20]

This amazingly simple, one and one-half inch, flat piece of stamped metal was invented by the Subsistence Research Laboratory of Chicago in just 30 days during the summer of 1942. What is most amazing to this author is that in its more than fifty-year history the P38 has never been known to break, rust, or need sharpening, nor has its design been changed in any significant way.

To avoid being labeled as antiquated, it is acknowledged that C-Rations have

Figure 58 : Front and rear view of the P38 pocket can opener.

long since succumbed to the more convenient MREs (Meals Ready To Eat), and yet, the phenomena that is the P-38 is alive and well. It survives even in this digital age exactly because it has scores of other uses stemming from its unique integration of ingenuity and creativity that all soldiers seem drawn to and unable to escape from. And, while it is no longer issued with rations, P38s may still be found in surplus stores and camping outfitters for a couple of bucks.

Of course, its best application is that for which the Army issued it—to access chow sequestered in cans! Naturally, in certain situations, that capability alone puts it high on *Joe's hierarchy of needs*. As well, soldiers have universally discovered the P38 to be an extremely simple, lightweight, multi-purpose tool. Finally, as any engineer will attest, the simpler a tool is, and the easier access is to it, the more it is ultimately used. Not surprisingly, the P-38 has all of those qualities.

As an aside, and for those interested, this author can enumerate the following uses he has found for his: can opener, screwdriver, fingernail cleaner, fishing hook, paint can opener, box cutter, bottle opener, prying tool, chisel, seam ripper, wire stripper, marking tool, letter opener, and measuring device.

While the P38 is ingenious in design and construction, it seems that regardless of how effective a device is someone always tries to improve on it. Naturally, that happened with the P38 in the form of the *P51*. As demonstrated in the following photo, the P51 is of very similar design, but is somewhat larger than the P38. Also a multipurpose instrument, the P51 is a bit more comfortable on the finger, given its broader dimensions, but is less rugged and durable, as it tends to bend. In addition, some P51s have electroplated surfaces, with what appears to be nickel, predisposing it to surface flaking and subsequent rusting, though plated models are generally of foreign manufacture.

While the P38 is not what most would consider a premium relic, many different companies have manufactured it over the past fifty years, and thus created a more than adequate number of varying markings with which to organize it into a tidy and interesting little collection. In view of its excellent collectability, and for the reader's edification, a data matrix is provided in Appendix G.

Figure 59: Comparison of P38 (left) and P51 (right).

There are examples of the military's penchant for multipurpose devices available ad infinatum, the P38 being just one minor specimen. But the American Army is not the only military enamored by multifunctionality. In fact, it is reasonable to assert that, given the very nature of armies, most such organizations seek the same qualities in their equipment for generally the same reasons.

One of the most popular, from an historical perspective, is the German Army, specifically the *Wehrmacht Heeres* of World War II fame. Popularly known simply as the *Wehrmacht*, this entity is all the more relevant, as many American military traditions have their origins in the German, British, and French Armies.

In that vein, it is interesting to note the degree to which the German military, like our own, places great value on its individual soldiers. And, similarly, the *Wehrmacht* invested a great deal of time and resources in soldier training and equipping, as well as genuine interest in soldier feedback.

Though the leadership's expectations of performance and sacrifice were high, so too was their commitment to leading the best trained and equipped fighting force on the continent if not in the world. The Leadership was completely obligated to providing all the essentials for their soldiers to fight, win, and survive, as the Chain-of-Command was well aware that dead soldiers did not win battles.

In fact, Field Marshall Rommel was fond of saying that "The best form of welfare for the troops is good training." Conversely, he absolutely believed that if a leader did not properly train his soldiers that that leader was derelict in his duties and placed his soldiers in mortal danger. Rommel firmly believed that soldiers fight exactly as they are trained (or untrained).

Moreover, like Rommel, the *Wehrmacht* as an institution, constantly strove to care for and properly outfit their soldiers. As an institutional culture, all leaders availed an acute ear to what soldiers said they needed to make their jobs more efficient or enhance their general morale and welfare. Many new weapons, uniform changes, and even tactics came about through soldier suggestion and Army experimentation.

Figure 60 – SG 42 showing stamped ordnance code cof or Carl Eickhorn of Solingen. (W.D. Weaver photo)

Prompted by complaints from the field, Army High Command and the General Staff of the Army began looking for a suitable close quarter knife. Their intent was to issue a close combat knife to Infantrymen fighting on the Eastern front, where savage hand-to-hand combat with the Russians had proven the bayonet impotent. What they wanted was a bayonet that could also function as a fighting knife. If that sounds familiar it is—how times do not change!

In this vein, it is interesting to read an 18 October 1943 entry, which appears in the *Kriegstagebuch*, Department II of the Army General Staff, that it was determined that:

"Soldiers have frequently expressed their desires that the bayonet 84/98 be abolished. For the first time they will be given the Bayonet 42, the Army dagger and the Flieger-Kappmesser for combat trials."

The participating units were to be the 17th Infantry Division, 78th Stu. Division, 28th *Jäger* Division, 2d *Gebirgsjäger* Division, Army Group A, Army Group Middle, Army Group North, Geb Aok 20, and one other. These units were each to be issued 100 Bayonet 42s, 100 Army daggers, and 100 *Flieger-Kappmessers*.

Figure 61: SG 42 extensive use of stampings and Bakelite form hanger, scales, and scabbard. (W.D. Weaver photo)

The telegram continues:

"The purpose is to test these side weapons compared with others in order to find a substitute for the previous bayonet as soon as possible. An official report on the evaluation is to be submitted to the general staff 4 weeks after arrival of the weapons to the evaluating units. The divisions will include in their reports what position they take on the side weapons evaluated..."

Until documents containing the responses to the OKW's telegram are located, one cannot know the opinions of the commanders, nor their evaluations, preferences, or reasoning. Nonetheless, for those of the historical ilk it is equally impossible not to yearn for the same; certainly, this author does.

First developed in 1942, the *Seitengewehr* 42 was intended to replace the SG 84/98 as the standard infantry bayonet. Significantly shorter than the 84/98, it measures in at just about 181mm, or 7 ½ inches. Recall that 7 inches is the cited maximum length that the ideal close combat knife would be.

The prime contractor for the knife was Carl Eickhorn, as evidenced by the ordnance code *cof* and *Waffenamt WaA 519*, and is obviously designed to accommodate economy of manufacture. Reminiscent of many later war weapons, it employs parts that have been stamped, and has few pieces that required more expensive and time-consuming milling procedures.

Other economical features include the extensive use of Bakelite[21] in the fabrication of its scales and scabbard. Very noteworthy is the ergonomic handle, which is extensively ribbed and arched. These features make it incredibly comfortable to hold while providing a very positive grip. The blade is very sharply pointed and quite sufficient for piercing, as well as being flat ground, which adds to the design's general strength.

Figure 62: SG 42 showing a very sharp point and flat ground blade well suited for stabbing. (W.D. Weaver photo)

Adding to its favorable points, the SG 42 includes a small muti-functional tool that is integral to the handle. This tool consists of a corkscrew, awl, can opener, screwdriver, and blade.

The addition of a multi-functional tool kit gives the SG 42 added desirability as both a close combat knife and a generally good field piece while offering a much-needed improvement over the SG 84/98. What actually became of the project is unknown.

Shortly afterwards new weapons intended to replace the K98 began appearing, and rifles such as the G43 and Stg44 were fielded, and in both cases, the bayonet lugs were omitted. Obviously, it was felt that the troops could do without bayonets. Nevertheless, as an example of parallel multipurpose thinking and design it is a wonderful example.

Many other designs have been proposed and/or tested that are very insightful, and others which are quite bizarre. For example, in the late 19th century the Army investigated a design capable of serving as both weapon and digging tool. The *Trowel Bayonet* was essentially a long, scooped, slender spade suitable for entrenching work, or when attached to a rifle, as a bayonet—quite a gruesome affair when one reflects upon its probable effect.

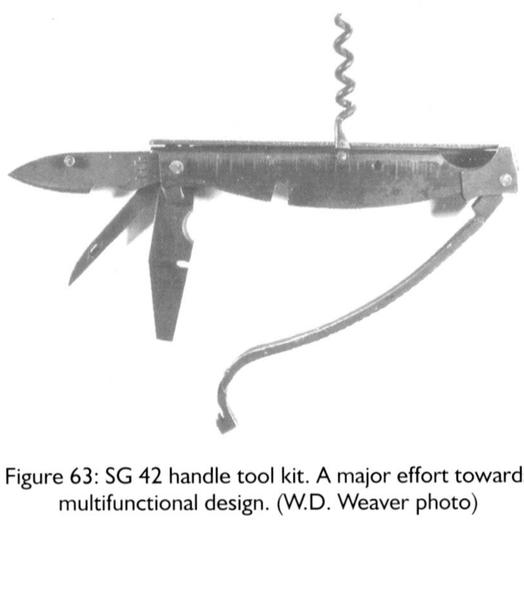

Figure 63: SG 42 handle tool kit. A major effort towards multifunctional design. (W.D. Weaver photo)

This unlikely marriage was the result of Lieutenant Rice's Patented Entrenching bayonet. First issued on a trial basis in 1869, the concept was simply to enable the infantryman to quickly excavate a shallow, hasty fighting position, affording him both cover and concealment. The trowel bayonets were issued with a detachable handle to improve the grip when detached from the rifle.

The concept was viable, and passed field trials as an entrenching tool; however, in its multifunction-role as a bayonet it was rather lackluster. Apparently, the large surface area created by its broad blade resulted in insufficient penetration. As a result, the Army cancelled production and the trial pieces were withdrawn from service.

While Lieutenant Rice's design was one of the earlier efforts to equip soldiers with a multifunctional bayonet, the design's greatest flaw was its failure to perform a bayonet's primary function, that of penetrating the enemy.

Interestingly though, the Army first tried incorporating the wire cutter into the entrenching tool and not the bayonet. In the early 20th century, there was a multitude of designs to this end, none of which amounted to much, though the time and effort were significant.

Just Silly!

Admittedly, it is only logical that the bayonet should be adapted to a multifunctional role, and certainly, the Army has endeavored to do so for quite some time, which is a good thing for the soldier. On the other hand, one has only to examine an M9 to see that the Army, and Phrobis, went to some length to incorporate every conceivable function into the weapon's design no matter how small. Frankly though, some of the features[22] are just plain silly, and most likely the result of the designer's overzealous attempt to present a product with as many bells and whistles as the imagination could conjure up in order to secure the contract.

That is not to say, given the nature of the acquisition system, that such efforts are necessarily bad things ***because*** any reasonable designer would do the same as they are merely trying to give the Army what it wants, or in most cases what the designer ***perceives*** it wants. Certainly there can be no doubt that Mr. Finn was primarily motivated by the desire to provide the best tool for our forces and that naturally necessitated winning. Even so, some of the features are just plain silly.

The early M9 sports a wire cutter as its premier *multifunctional* feature, and while such a configuration is generally standard for most armies, one has to question the realistic value of it. Certainly, in the First World War such a capability would have been necessary on any battlefield, laced as they were with every conceivable type of wire barrier. One could even make a case for its usefulness in the Second World War. However, the days of pitched battles have given way to low intensity guerilla actions, and it is doubtful that the battlefields of Pershing and Eisenhower will soon, if ever, return.

On today's fluid, unconventional battlescape it seems that the only ones using wire are us, and therefore, while the actual necessity of a wire cutter is dubious at best, it could only be justified as *a just in case* tool; a good to have feature, if you will.

The same cannot be said of the bottle opener, which is integral to the cross guard of the early patterns. This feature is truly unnecessary, as not only do soldiers rarely encounter bottles requiring opening, but if they did, such caps are easily removed by resting them on any solid surface and simply smacking the cap at an angle with the hand. This, and other techniques, are common knowledge to most G.I.s who historically experienced little difficulty

Figure 64: American wire barricades are a common sight in Iraq. (Marine Corps Photo)

opening bottles, especially those containing liquefied grain product! However, in defense of the designer, it is understood that these are actually lightening cuts necessary to reduce the weight of the piece in order to keep it within Army specs. Viewed from this angle it is just short of genius to machine out useless weight and then call the result a bottle opener!

As to the desirability and utility of actual openers though, further substantiation of the argument can be found in the form of a 1944 memo from Lt. Col. James G. Frazer of Headquarters, U.S.M.C. Commenting on the evaluation of such implements incorporated into Pocket Knives, the Colonel scoffed that "Each Marine carries with him a bottle-opener in the form of his belt buckle...." He expeditiously disapproved the project.[23]

There are other glaring examples, but critique of them is most appropriate elsewhere. Suffice it to say that the Army has long searched for a means of incorporating a wire cutter into the bayonet's design, and though it began long before World War II there has been a long succession of attempts since that time. Some have been very creative, while others approach simple silliness!

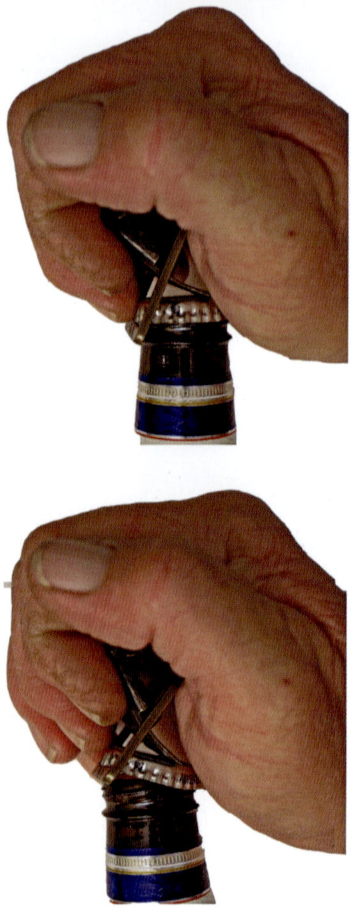

Figure 64.5: Defeating the bottle cap using a standard G.I. belt buckle.

4

Defining the Problem - Foundations of Design

As mentioned earlier, the military has, and has always had, a penchant for combination tools. In every period and every application, one can find requirements for items to have multiple capabilities. Interestingly, the bayonet was not the first implement that the Army sought to attach a wire cutter to.

Perhaps an equally appropriate tool to have a wire cutting capability is the entrenching tool—or shovel, as civilians know them. Digging and cutting wire go together well enough, and apparently the Army sought to couple these two activities as far back as the late 19th century.

In the case of the Multipurpose Bayonet System, it is no great feat to combine a blade that can serve as both bayonet and fighting knife. The problem comes when one tries to integrate a wire cutter into the mix.

Wire Cutter Bayonet Device

As far back as 1944, the Army was experimenting with the idea of a bayonet capable of cutting wire. In a confidential memorandum dated 04 May 1944, the Engineer Board requested that the Marine Corps Equipment Board at Quantico, Virginia, such a device. In part the memo states:

"The Engineer Board has been testing a type of wire cutter which attaches to the short bayonet. Its purpose is to give the foot soldier a wire-cutting device, which he can use quickly and without laying aside his rifle. Tests conducted so far with the original cutter shows that it works quite successfully on standard type entanglements, other than Dannert Concertina, both on land and in the water. On loose springy type wire such as Dannert Concertina, the cutter is not a success.

We are expressing to you under separate cover five (5) cutters and five (5) short bayonets. It is requested that you conduct service tests of this device to determine its suitability and desirability as an aid to combat troops in clearing lanes through wire entanglements.

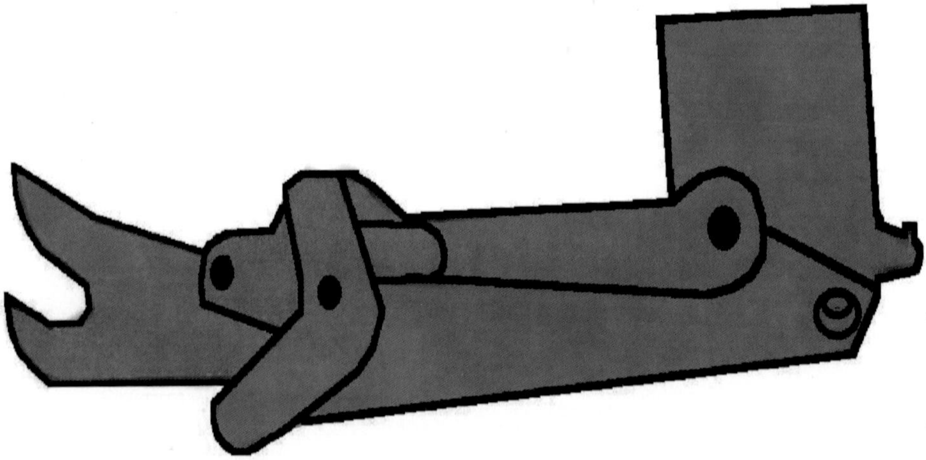

Figure 65 - Sketch of the bayonet wire cutter.

The bayonet wire cutter is a wire-cutting device constructed with a sleeve arrangement which slides over the blade of the M1 bayonet and locks to the bayonet guard by the same latch which locks the bayonet to the rifle.

The subject cutter is a system of compound levers, which operate the cutting jaws. The levers operate by a combined forward, upward thrust of the rifle when the user holds the weapon in a normal position. Alternatively, the device functioned while inverted as by a soldier cutting overhead wire from the prone position.

The normal position of the jaws is the open position, with operating levers folded closely against the bayonet blade and retained in such position by the action of a spring contained between the operating levers, which functions to re-open the jaws at the completion of each stroke. The open jaws permit the wire to enter the jaws before the cutting operation is begun. The upper jaw is shaped so that it projects ¼ inch above the lower edge of the bayonet blade in the normal position, which construction reduces the possibility of the wire failing to enter the jaws and becoming fouled between the lower edge of the blade and the operating levers.

The cutting jaws are 3/16 inch in thickness and are so opposed as to pass each other and cut by a shearing action. They are sharpened practically flat across the 3/16 inch thickness as in heavy metal shears and punches. The cutting edges of the jaws are curved at their forward tips to provide a wider opening with which to engage the wire and lead it to the rear of cutting section of the jaws. The jaw opening extends from the lower edge of the bayonet blade to a distance of ¾ inch below this edge, and will thus engage a strand, which lies within ¾ inch of the lower edge of the blade.

The ten inch bayonet blade projects 3 ½ inch in front of the forward end of the jaws and serves as a guide to lead the wire into the jaw opening when the forward end of the blade has its lower edge brought into contact with the wire and the rife is given a forward thrust.

The subject cutter when completely disassembled consists of thirty-two individual parts plus one assembly of three interconnected parts or a total of thirty-five parts. The device is simple to use and does not impair the use of the bayonet as a weapon."

However, as the old saying goes, good concept, poor execution! The Marines did put the device through field trials and had this to say about it:

"The foregoing tests indicate that the subject bayonet wire cutter, in the form submitted to the Marine Corps Equipment Board for test, is of limited adaptability for use against the various types of wire entanglements which may normally be encountered in Marine Corps combat operations.

The subject item is best adapted for use on high wire band, where there is little possibility of the bayonet fouling in uncut wires during the cutting stroke, and where the operator can readily make the thrust at right angles to each strand. It acts with fair results on standard double-apron barbed wire, although there is frequent fouling of the bayonet in uncut strands during the cutting stroke, particularly when the wire is slack. It is practically ineffective on concertina wire due to continued looseness of the strand, which makes it impossible to generate the required cutting force at the jaws. It is difficult to engage underwater wire in the cutter jaws when it cannot be seen."

It was felt that, at best, even with certain modifications discussed this cutter would but serve to supplement the standard cutter, and could not fully replace it.

Fighting Knife Project Number 2811

The next subject of evaluation regarded trials to select a fighting knife-utility knife.[24] This subject is germane for two reasons: first, simply because it is a multipurpose edged weapon, but more importantly because two of the three contenders were eventually adopted and produced later in some form as bayonets.

One might well wonder why the Army was investigating a multipurpose belt knife and not configuring it as a bayonet. The interesting answer is that at this particular point in history the Army had actually decided to phase out bayonets. In such an event, it was felt that the soldier still needed a long knife for fighting as well as other field applications. For those reasons, the search was on for the knife that could best fulfill those two basic functions.

What is bewildering about this entire situation is that if one is searching for a tool with a number of features, the act of adding one more is neither difficult nor unreasonable. That is, adding a ring and a simple locking mechanism is both simple and relatively inexpensive. Adding these two features enables the infantryman to attach it to his rifle if he deems it necessary. Unfortunately, there is no available explanation for why the highest echelons of

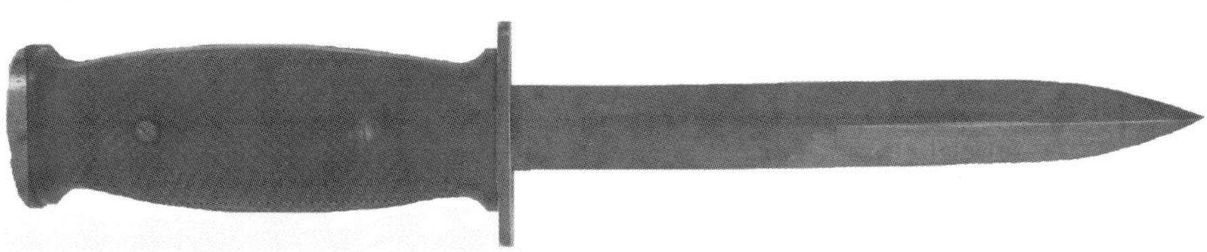

Figure 66: A - Test knife number 1 is a modified M4 bayonet knife.

leadership found it necessary to make the issue a *Federal Case* —though apparently they did. And so, execution of the case was begun at Fort Benning with the first contestant, Knife Number 1, which was a standard M4 bayonet-knife modified by elimination of the rifle attachment feature, sharpening the top of the blade for its entire length, and substituting the leather handle with one constructed of plastic.

Knife Number 2 was an M5 bayonet-knife also modified by eliminating the rifle attachment feature, and by sharpening the top of the blade for its entire length and substituting the plastic handle for an oversized rubberized handle.

Figure 67: B - Test knife number 2 is a modified M5 bayonet knife.

Finally, Knife Number 3 was a Marine Corps K-Bar hunting knife, constructed of blued steel with a blade measuring seven inches long and 1 3/16 inches wide. The blade's edge extended the entire length of the bottom and one third of the top, having a handle measuring five inches long and made of leather.

The test knives and scabbards underwent testing to determine which knife and scabbard was most suitable for Army use. All test knives were comparable in physical characteristics, in their suitability for airborne use, and the degree of organizational maintenance required.

None of the knives were found to be ideally suited for fighting, though Knife number 2 was rated superior to all others in the role of mine probe. Knife number 3 received superior ratings in durability, resistance to adverse conditions, and was particularly suitable as a utility knife.

The Army Infantry Board concluded that all of the test knives were suitable for Army use as combination utility-fighting knives, but that knife number 3 was the most suitable.

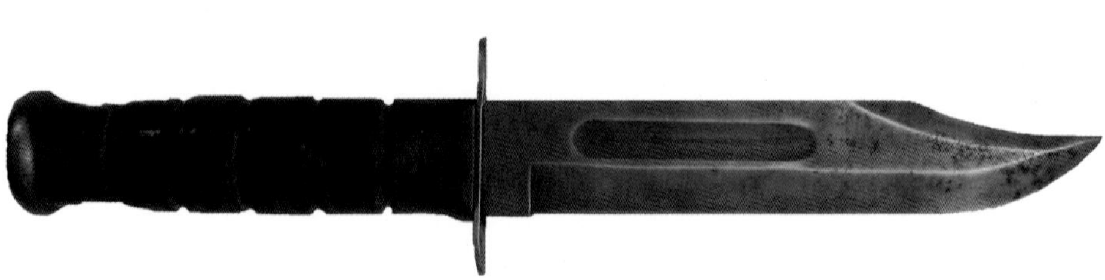

Figure 67.5: Test knife number 3 was a Marine Corps K-Bar hunting knife.

Advanced Development of a Knife Cutter Bayonet

Fast-forwarding nearly two decades since the Army evaluated fighting knife designs, and despite all of the rhetoric, we see that the bayonet survived. The KaBar blade configuration, for all of its popularity and practical advantages, was not approved, though soldiers did witness the adoption of the M6 bayonet for use with the M14 rifle. As well, by the early 1960s soldiers saw their trusty M14 replaced by the lighter, handier M16 and its companion bayonet, the M7.

Both weapon patterns, the M6 and M7, evolved from fighting knife designs of the 1940s and 1950s. However, serious consideration to eliminate the bayonet reached the highest echelons of Army leadership, and much heated debate followed with, as in times past, the bayonet proponents carrying the day. When the dust settled, the venerable weapon remained much as it traditionally had.

Still, the Army was without a multifunctional bayonet, though there was no lack of will. As usual, the folks in combat development continued to search for the elusive design, seemingly oblivious that the Soviets and Warsaw Pact fielded just such a piece shortly after WWII. One can only wonder why the Army turned such an apparent blind eye to the East! Nevertheless, such seemed the case, and reinvention of the proverbial wheel continued neither unarrested nor diminished.

The next push for a multipurpose bayonet came in 1974 via contract DAAD05-73-C-0564 under the auspices of the Land Warfare Laboratory of Aberdeen Proving Ground, Maryland.[25]

The particulars of this project were prepared for the Army by Benhof, Inc. of Long Island, New York, and involved five slightly differing designs based on the then contemporary M7 and the older M6.

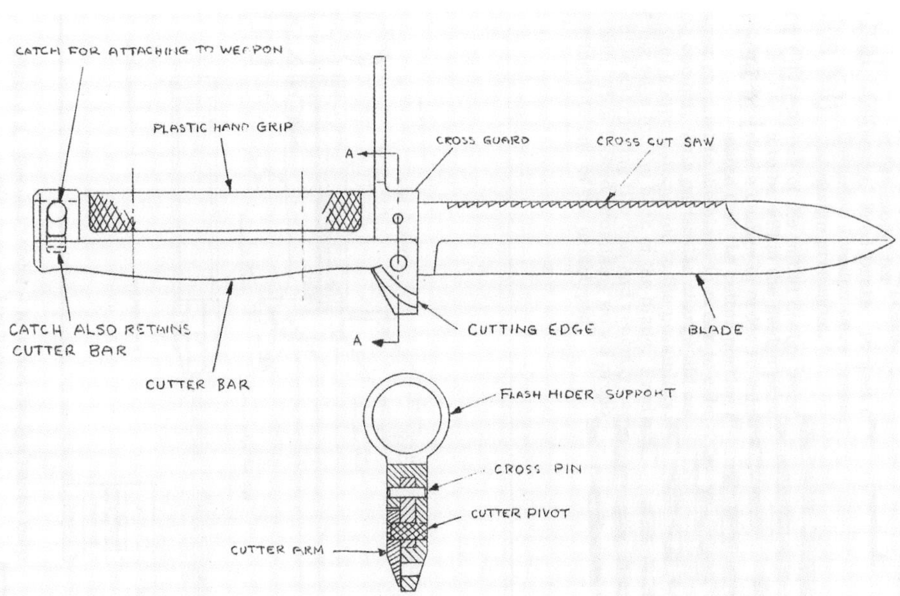

Figure 68: Drawing of initial pattern modified from an M5 bayonet knife.

The requirements set forth by the Army for this iteration specified a high quality, multipurpose Knife Cutter bayonet intended for use by the combat soldier in the defensive role, as well as to function as a multipurpose knife to aid in other tasks. The knife was intended for use by the soldier in instances of combat where he did not have access to cutting implements.

Barbed wire, both round and tape, present a tactical problem to the average infantryman. Explosives, artillery, and armored vehicles can destroy such wire entanglements, but these are not always available in such situations. The new design was to incorporate a compact tool capable of cutting tape and round wire. Whereas traditionally the Army focused on the infantry as the primary recipient of such tools, this time it decided to issue the knife as a component to be included in Army aircrew survival kits.

Following submission of the Preliminary Design and Visualization Plan (mock-up) and the Engineer Design Test Plan, project machinists fabricated five prototypes based on the following criteria:

1) It must have a positive attachment capability (to the M16 rifle) for use as a bayonet or as a probe for mines and booby traps.
2) It must be capable of cutting soft wire, barbed wire, and metal tape barbed wire.
3) Inclusion of a sharpening device component was necessary.
4) The design must incorporate an edge capable of cutting brush, Plexiglas, and light metals.
5) The weapon was required to possess a blade guard similar to the M7 with the balance and grip required for hand-to-hand combat.
6) The knife's weight must not exceed that of the M7 bayonet and scabbard, or one pound.
7) Its blade length must be no less than five and one-half inches, nor longer than seven inches, nor have an overall length of greater than thirteen inches.

The stated design priorities were first as a multipurpose knife; limited purpose saw; wire cutter; and lastly as a bayonet.The initial design was based on the M7 bayonet pattern and included an integral wire cutting device located beneath the cross guard. The cutter was a simple curved *tin snip* type wire cutter whose lever extended rearward and folded into the underside of the handle. The spine of the blade featured a crosscut saw.

This initial design was presented to the LWL Branch Chief, LTC Alexander Johnson, who made minor revisions. Subsequent discussion during that initial meeting resulted in

Figure 69: Prototype number 1.

some minor changes, which included the possibility of a carbide-coated cutting edge to replace the saw and a tungsten carbide sharpening stone.

The second design incorporated most of the above changes, including moving the flat tape cutter forward, and changed to a twin anvil configuration that the cutter bar sheared against, as well as a square notch machined into it for cutting round wire.

Figure 70: Prototype number 2.

When tested the device cut tape wire without problems, but required an inordinate amount of pressure to cut double strand, round barbed wire. As well, the cutter failed due to lack of hardening. Aberdeen pointed out that the knife, overall, was too heavy, and that the flat wire cutter needed redesign to prevent flat wire from sliding away from the cutter.

The second design was modified with the cutter redesigned to resemble a twin parrot beak, which was capable of cutting one strand of wire at a time and each having its own handle or lever.

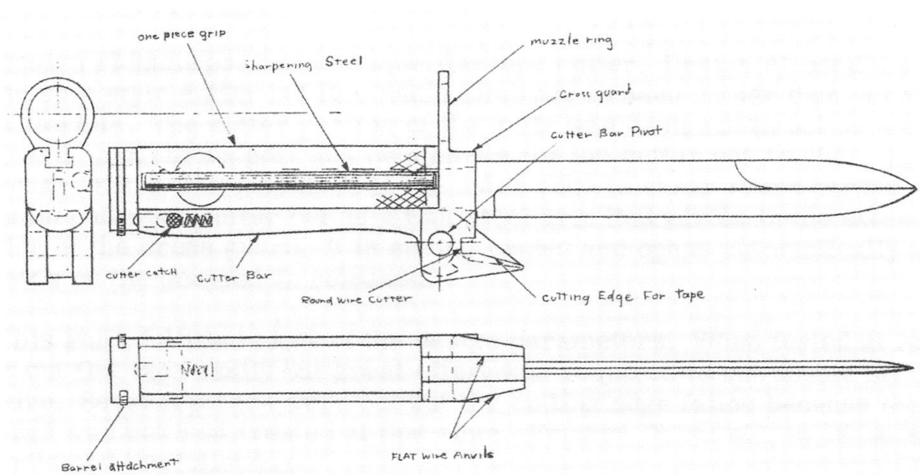

Figure 71: Drawing of second pattern also modified from an M5 bayonet knife.

As it turned out, they did not succeed in fulfilling all of the Knife Cutter Bayonet requirements before the Government terminated the contract for its convenience. In the report, the contractor laments that had the Land Warfare Lab remained in existence they could have, perhaps, brought the "good idea to a fruitful conclusion."

From this vantage point, it appears more than likely that prolongation of Lab activities would have served only in wasting more taxpayer money! During this experimentation, which is all that it really was, there is no evidence that the team investigated any parallel reasoning, nor considered any state of the art designs, nor explored historical designs or methodology! The investigators seemed singularly focused on using the M4 style bayonets with an incorporated lever operated wire cutter. Finally, in what can only be perceived as desperation, they actually proposed mounting a pair of wire cutters onto the butt of the bayonet—unbelievable!

Nonetheless, in the third design, the weight problem was generally overcome by reducing the thickness of the cross guard. Reducing the angle of the twin anvils relative to the cutter bar by ten percent addressed the issue of wire slippage, and the cutter bar was modified by a reshaping of the flat wire cutting edge from a straight to a long radius edge. These modifications corrected wire slippage and decreased actual cutting time.

Figure 72: Prototype number 3.

Night operations, with respect to the round wire cutter, had proven problematic, but they were remedied by adding a protrusion to the cutter blade. Upon opening the jaws, the protrusion extended at right angles and acted as a natural guide for the wire, directing it into the jaws. The round wire cutter received a modification and the cutter bar spring was lengthened, while the blade spine they left uncut, awaiting a tungsten particle cutter blade.

Figure 73: Prototype number 4.

Design number four maintained the basic twin anvil and cutter bar that was successful in cutting barbed tape, but the cutter they made as an integral part of the knife blade. In production, the knife blade blank included this projection as an integral feature of its stamping. The reversal was done first to provide additional leverage, and secondly, to move the round wire cutter up and under the blade. This location allowed the knife blade to guide the round wire into the cutting jaws.

The moveable cutter bar they formed from 1/8 inch flat tool steel and bent to form the twin anvils and hinge pin support. An additional 1/8 inch flat piece of tool steel they riveted to the moveable cutter bar. When employing the knife as a flat or round wire cutter, the extension handle opened in a manner similar to the opening of a jack knife. This, in turn, lifted the moveable cutter bar out of its seat in the grip. When folding the handle straight, a stop prevented it from traveling beyond 180 degrees.

Aberdeen tested this prototype and found it awkward to use, while it remained difficult to cut standard military round barbed wire. In place of the crosscut saw on the blade spine, prototype number four incorporated the tungsten carbide cutting edge.

The fifth and final design resembled a pair of wire cutters mounted atop the pommel, with the bayonet grip acting as one handle and the other handle doubling as a hand guard for the bayonet. It actually looks as ridiculous as it was desperate!

Figure 74: Prototype Number 5.

Metal Masters of South El Monte, California, and Gerber of Portland, Oregon, provided designs for the scabbard. Each incorporated sharpening devices, and initially they chose Metal Masters to provide a relatively new tungsten carbide coated sharpening steel. The device was 6 inches long by 5/16 inch wide, weighed 2 ounces, and resembled a round metal rod.

The investigators considered the Gerber scabbard design primarily because it was commercially available, and featured a chromium carbide coated, flat sharpening steel. However, due to excessive weight they rejected it.

With the Gerber scabbard no longer an option, the designers proceeded to epoxy a plastic pocket to the center front of an M1A1 scabbard to capitalize on the resiliency of the plastic, in an effort to provide a secure stowage for the sharpening steel. The final report states:

"Phase 1: Our Preliminary Design and Visualization Plan was presented to Land warfare Laboratories within the specified time. At this meeting we submitted a non-ferrous model for discussion and comment. Suggestions were entertained for improving the basic design. Benhof Inc. then proceeded to produce a tool steel model based on our original design and incorporating suggestions initiated at the meeting.

During Phase 1, a number of prototypes were produced. Since good design is evolutionary and not revolutionary, Benhof proceeded to develop a series of knife cutter bayonets. Each was an improvement over the previous design. If a proposed design or prototype reached an impasse because of some unforeseen difficulty, a different tact was initiated to alleviate the problem.

The prototypes were developed over a period of months of exhaustive testing. When simple leverage proved to be insufficient for the average individual, the next step was to provide additional leverage. This proved awkward and we proceeded to the more costly and complicated compound leverage. The results of this effort are detailed in the following Design Data portion of the report.

Phase 2: Phase 2 was to be the production of 100 knives based on a serviceable prototype. Since our efforts, research and experiments did not succeed in producing a Knife Cutter Bayonet that was 100% successful and because of the lack of additional time, production of the 100 pieces was not initiated.

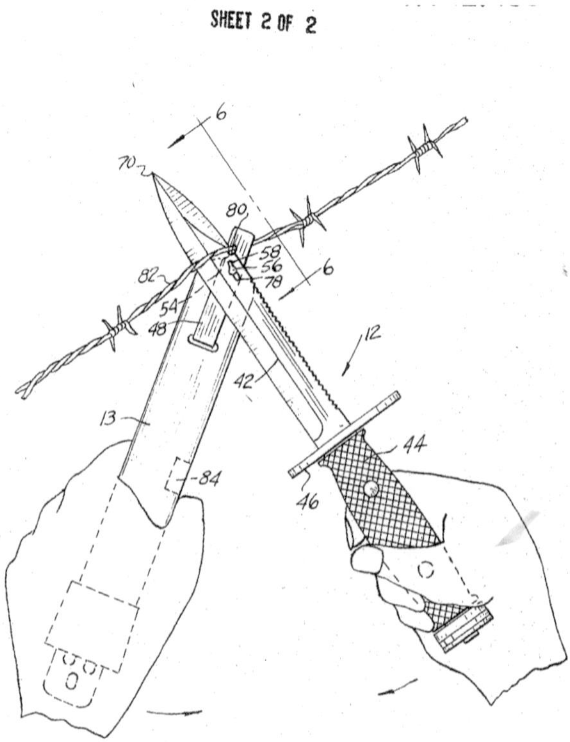

Figure 74.5: The Bauer wire cutter bayonet. And Benhof said it could not be done!

Conclusion: After extensive study and the production and testing of numerous prototypes and bench test fixtures, we have reached the following conclusions:

A. It is not feasible within the present state of the art to build a simple, inexpensive, compact combination Knife Cutter Bayonet.

B. In view of the fact that the U.S. Army has an inventory of M7 bayonets and effective compact wire cutters, the LWL and Benhof Inc. are in agreement that it would be to the government's advantage to retain the bayonet and wire cutter as two distinct items of issue."

What is most maddening about this project is that just the year prior Russell E. Bauer invented, and assigned to the Bauer Ordnance Company of Warren, Ohio, a patented bayonet based on a modified M7. It featured a saw-toothed spine and notched blade, which combined to form a wire cutter very similar to the Soviet AK and NWM/Eickhorn KCB70 bayonets. This design was completely capable of accomplishing exactly what Benhof's report claimed was not possible!

Product Improved Bayonet-Knife

In 1977 the Army launched another trial, this time consisting of a *Product Improved* (*PI*) feasibility test, though not directed toward incorporation of a wire-cutting feature. The objective was merely to change the M7 design so that the soldier had a knife and a reasonable replacement bayonet. In such undertakings, current issue equipment is simply modified in an attempt to produce an item that is better suited to the intended purpose than the original model. The Letter of Execution sums up the endeavor quite nicely:

"The need for a suitable knife to be used by the individual soldier in the field has a long been recognized, though the need for a knife is not adequately met by the M7 bayonet. The bayonet is still retained in the inventory as a standard item although its tactical value is questionable and a formal bayonet-training program no longer exists. The bayonet is retained because of tradition and its possible use in civil disturbance actions."[26]

At the request of USAIC, the U.S. Army Armament Command's *USAARMCOM*, fabrication of 40 prototype product improved (PI) knife-bayonets was authorized for this test. By letter on 7 December 1976, USAIC requested that TRADOC task USAIB to conduct Operational Feasibility FDTE to provide data to USAIC for use in support of a requirements document.

The Letter of Execution or LOE, received from TRADOC on 26 January 1977 substantiates the test was conducted at Fort Benning, Georgia, being initiated on 12 January 1977, and terminated 31 January 1977, due to the PI knife-bayonet's lack of durability.

The weapons tested were three. The current issue M7 was pitted against two M7 hybrids which were fitted with Navy Mark 2 blades, similar to the blades of the Ka-Bar, having serrated cutting edges mid-spine. One had its blade in the normal cutting edge down position, while the other bayonet's blade was oriented with the edge up.

Figure 75 : Prototype number 3.

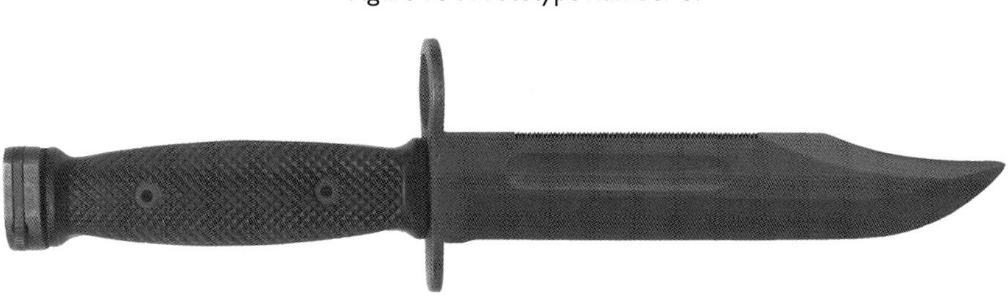

Figure 76 : Prototype number 3.

Figure 77 : Prototype Number 3.

Fifteen *PI knife-bayonets* of each design and 15 M7 bayonets were issued to 45 randomly selected Ranger trainees undergoing training at Ft. Benning. The items were used for 3 weeks on a *noninterference basis* and rotated among groups, so that by the end of the evaluation period each trainee had been given an opportunity to use each of the 3 weapons once. Each of the test soldiers were administered a questionnaire to obtain their opinions and observations concerning each test item.

The summary results were that the PI models suffered broken blades, cracked handles, and that the serration cut through Plexiglas, aircraft aluminum, and general vegetation only with great difficulty, not to mention that affixing the bayonets to the M16 rifle was cumbersome. Predictably, the majority of soldiers preferred the edge down model, and the same majority preferred the M7 bayonet over both of the PI bayonets.

5

Early Development

Rationale for Essential Characteristics

With regard to what the Army was looking for in a Multipurpose Bayonet System, the following is a very accurate representation, though exact wording from one Letter Requirement to the next varies somewhat. The essential features, however, have not changed significantly since World War II.

The following is an excerpt setting forth the rationale employed in the Letter Requirement as it relates to the M9. It is fundamental from an historic point of view to understand what the military was looking for, and this document is perhaps the single most comprehensive example of that concept:[27]

"Essential Characteristics: A non developmental acquisition (for an MPBS) is planned. Specific selection criteria will be established by a Source Selection Advisory Council (SSAC) and approved by the Source Selection Authority prior to release of a request for Proposal or conduct of any selection evaluations. This requirement provides guidance to the SSAC.

a. The bayonet has demonstrated its necessity as a secondary weapon in all past conflicts; however, the design and capability of the current bayonet does not provide the soldier with a practical field knife capable of being used as a multifunctional tool and combat weapon. A multipurpose bayonet system capable of performing as a combat/field knife, wire cutter, bayonet, and which has a limited capability to saw, would give the combat soldier a true multipurpose tool without increasing the soldier's load. In addition, the soldier would always have the necessary item in his fighting load when needed.

b. The M16 series rifle and the XM4 carbine are the individual weapons the soldier will be carrying in the near timeframeJ5

. The Multipurpose Bayonet System must be designed to complement the individual soldier's ability to close with and destroy the enemy in the event of weapon failure /misfire or when close combat (hand-to-hand) is necessitated.

c. The soldier needs the capability to cut barbed wire during cross-country movement and to cut through wire obstacles to attack enemy positions. During MOUT operations, electric wire may be encountered, as well as during stealth operations by specialists. Most common electrical wire other than field telephone wire (WD1) will be 240 volts or less which will require insulation to this level to prevent shock. The individual soldier will be required to cut/break banding material on ammunition/food containers. Standard band for small arms ammunition are constructed of the dimensions indicated per MIL-B-2427. Soldiers may also be required to cut ribbon barbed tape, both during the construction of friendly obstacles or during the breaching of enemy obstacles. Fifty wire cuts is the criteria that has been developed through surveys and interviews with infantrymen and other Subject Matter Experts. It is estimated that the service life of the system under intense combat usage will be one year. Fifty cuts will approximate one year of usage and ensure system durability.

d. A combat/field craft knife will require sharpening from time to time. Previous bayonets were not designed to be sharpened and used as a field knife or combat knife for hand-to-hand fighting. Many types of cutting, i.e., brush, small trees, etc., will dull any blade capable of being sharpened. A sharpening device will be desired as a part of the system so that the soldier can maintain the cutting capability of the Multipurpose Bayonet.

e. The Multipurpose Bayonet System must be constructed as a durable multipurpose tool in order to satisfy the need for the soldiers to perform a myriad of field tasks. The soldier will be required to break/cut banding material constructed of steel of dimensions indicated to open ammunition containers. Soldiers will also use the bayonet as a prying tool for various field crafts. This requirement will insure the system will possess sufficient ruggedness to withstand the battlefield environment.

f. A weight of not more than 1.8 pounds compares favorably with the current bayonet. When coupled with the multipurpose tool aspects, the system would be lighter than carrying additional tools such as wire cutters, saw, and other small tools. The Multipurpose Bayonet System must not add weight to the soldier's load yet provide him with a fighting knife that can be used for self defense, clearing field of fire, cutting camouflage and field craft. The total weight of 1.8 pounds and a blade length of not more than 8 inches with not less than 4 inches extending past the muzzle. The Surgeon General has determined that a minimum blade length of 4 inches extending past the muzzle of the rifle is required to achieve adequate penetration for inflicting incapacitating wounds.

g. A *V* ground blade is most easily maintained by the individual soldier and is best suited to the multipurpose aspects of the bayonet. A point shaped in what is commonly called a *Bowie Knife* design will provide more flexibility as utility as a field/combat knife and will allow the bayonet and scabbard to be used as a wire cutting device. A hand or blade guard will protect he soldier's hand and may be used to mount or affix the bayonet to the rifle. The rear of the blade should not be a saw but have the serrated portion to penetrate and rip/cut light metal (aircraft skin). Same as d, e, and f above.

h. The soldier must be capable of using the bayonet in any mode without diverting his attention from the situation at hand. The form and fit of the handle is critical to the individual soldier if he is to grasp the bayonet as a reflex or automatic action.

i. A serrated edge will give the soldier a weapon with true multipurpose capability. Light metals are the primary materials which are required to be cut to free downed helicopter pilots and will ensure the needed durability for more frequent usage against other weaker materials. Hemp rope is the primary material used for tie down material.

j. The soldier's load and how it is carried is an on-going effort; all items of individual equipment must be viewed as a system. The scabbard must be capable of being affixed to the soldier's load bearing equipment so that it will not move around, make noise, and must hold the bayonet securely. The scabbard must have a quick release to facilitate removal form the load bearing equipment so that the scabbard can be used with the bayonet as a wire cutting tool. In a combat situation the soldier must be able to react and use the wire cutter quickly; 10 seconds is more than adequate to prepare the device for use. It is not necessary, but desired, that the Multipurpose Bayonet System have the capability for limited sawing. Saws on the back of knife bladesare not efficient and may be prohibited under the Geneva Accords. The scabbard may have a saw blade attached to meet the limited saw capability.

k. Be constructed of materials that are non-corrosive such that the system, when used as a multipurpose device, will come in contact with POL products, insect repellents and other corrosive elements. The system must be resistant to these as well as rust and fungus. Reflective materials must be avoided as they are not conducive to the overall camouflage necessary for the soldier.

l. The rapid removal of the bayonet from the scabbard is critical should the soldier be forced to rely on it as a secondary weapon in a hand-to-hand situation. When affixing the bayonet to the rifle or preparing the scabbard and bayonet to be used as a wire cutter, the soldier must be able to accomplish these tasks without diverting his attention from the other combat tasks at hand. Ten seconds is adequate for the ***average*** soldier to accomplish any of these tasks. It is recognized that the soldier may be required to carry out his mission during NBC conditions or while dressed in bulky clothing. The Multipurpose Bayonet System should be designed so that he soldier can use the device under these conditions without an unreasonable increase in time required to remove the bayonet from its scabbard, affix the bayonet to the rifle, or use the scabbard and bayonet as a wire cutter. Climatic design types hot, basic, and cold will ensure that the system can be employed in all geographic areas of the world. Cold climate conditions are expected to occur in Alaska and in northern Europe to include Greenland, Iceland and Scandinavian countries. The current bayonet meets this requirement and the technical risk is considered low that the Multipurpose Bayonet System will be able to function in these environments.

m. The individual equipment used by parachutists is often different from non-parachutist's equipment and causes special concerns in affixing items of equipment or weapons to the jumper. The Multipurpose Bayonet System must not interfere with current rigging, parachute harness and equipment bag.

n. Neither the bayonet affixed to the rifle nor the manner of affixing the bayonet to the rifle can interfere with the standard day or night sights. It is unreasonable to adapt sights to accommodate a bayonet when this area can be addressed in the design of the bayonet.

o. The Multipurpose Bayonet System is viewed as a component of the individual rifle and may become the soldier's primary weapon in some situations. The system must be capable of withstanding NBC effects as well as the soldier when both device and operator are exposed to the same conditions. If contaminated, the system must be capable of being decontaminated to permit reuse.

p. The human factors of safety/health hazards need to be addressed during design/evaluation of the bayonet. The multipurpose aspects of this system require built-in checks against self injury to hands, fingers, eyes while using the Multipurpose Bayonet System for its intended purposes.

q. RAM Requirements. Quantitative RAM was determined to be inappropriate to the Multipurpose Bayonet. This passive system may contain, at most, two moving parts: a detent for attaching the bayonet to the Rifle, and possibly a hinged mechanism for a folding saw blade. A discussion among the points of contact) paragraph 3 below) concluded with the view that RAM characteristics were not applicable or essential to a Multipurpose Bayonet. Durability is a concern and will be key evaluation criteria of non development candidates.

r. The design of the bayonet must not drive the design or capability of the proposed individual weapon or day and night sights.

s. Marine Corps Organizational and Operational Concept: The Multipurpose Bayonet System will be used by the FMF (Fleet Marine Force). The bayonet will replace the M7 and K-bar knife throughout the FMF. It will be employed in all geographic areas and subjected to various climatic conditions. The bayonet will be used as a secondary weapon for close combat when mounted on the M16 series rifle, tactical shotguns and carbines, or as a combat knife. It will also be used to perform various field crafts such as cutting wire, limited sawing, or constructing and camouflaging fortifications."

Design Contenders

Qual-A-Tec began as a Research and Development Company originally located in Chino Valley, AZ, specializing in custom suppression and muzzle control devices until its closure in 1988 and subsequent move to Oceanside, California, where Charles Mickey Finn first conceived of and designed the M9 in its original form.

One version of Charles Finn's story is that he started up his Research and Development Company Qual-A-Tec in 1981 at the behest of tax attorney Fred Schumacher, whose prime motivation, auspiciously, was to take advantage of research and development tax loopholes. Other sources contend the company's conception was entirely that of Finn, a retired DOD weapons developer who designed devices for Special Forces and other covert government agencies, and specialized in custom silencers and muzzle compensators at his Qual-A-Tec facility in Chino Valley, AZ.

Known in his circles as *Q*—after the James Bond inventor character—because of his special weapons penchant, Finn also provided classified weapons systems to the U.S. government. Allegedly, when author Tom Clancy publicly used Finn's identity in the novel *Cardinal and the Kremlin*, Finn felt compelled to close Qual-A-Tec.

Certainly, it is no myth that Finn opened his company in an industrial complex on Production Ave. in Oceanside, California, and staffed it with family members, friends, and business acquaintances such as John Holm, Bob MacDonald, Rick MacDonald, Doug Olson, and Harry Camphuysen. To say that it was a very small operation would be an understatement, though to its credit, it employed some remarkably capable, motivated, and creative individuals, not the least of which was Mickey Finn's wife, and soul mate, Wendy Finn. She occupied arguably the most essential and influential position within the company. For, as any astute businessman will testify, the heartbeat of any organization is its Secretary and Treasurer, and Mrs. Finn was both.

Another associate, Harry Camphuysen, a weapons enthusiast, local pawnshop owner, and purveyor of Buck knives, ultimately facilitated Finn's meeting with Chuck Buck, Jr., whereupon he presented his ideas for what was to become the *Buckmaster* of the *Rambo* genre knife.

With the alliance of Buck knives came the formation of the company of Phrobis III, Ltd, of Carlsbad, California. However, all early M9s are marked *Phrobis III*, as the firm was the official business entity, though Buck Knives actually accomplished the production of the Buckmaster, and later the M9.

The actual birth of the M9 came when Mickey Finn and Doug Olson learned of the Army's *Request for Proposal* for a new bayonet and Qual-A-Tec put together a prototype, which they entered into the competition conducted by the Infantry Board at Ft. Benning, Georgia. And, while it is known that Finn and the Qual-A-Tec staff used the Buckmaster as a starting point for that early M9 design, it is uncertain exactly what inspired most of those design concepts.

What is glaringly obvious and supremely undeniable is that the wire cutter mechanism is a spitting image of that found on the Soviet AK bayonet (and Eickhorn's KCB series and others)! Obviously, given Finn's background he would have been very familiar with the Soviet system's design, as well as most others, and frankly among the best qualified to design the M9.

From the above Letter Requirement one gets the impression that the Army already had at least a fuzzy vision of what the bayonet should look like, as the LOR specifically mentions a quick release for the scabbard in order to facilitate its use in the wire cutter role, and that a bowie knife point was preferable.

If, however, they genuinely did not, one has to be amazed since, as we have seen, the Army had struggled for decades in search of a practical integral wire cutter. The only thing more amazing is that they could simply have *borrowed* it from the Soviets any time they wished! In the end they did, and what sweet irony that is!

Without straying too far afield, most will recall that during the Cold War military and industrial espionage was the order of the day. East and West spied on one another unceasingly as a means of maintaining their level of strategic, tactical, and technical advantage. The United States knew every piece of equipment in the Soviet inventory, and certainly, the Army was aware that the Soviets had fielded a bayonet that essentially

Figure 78: Note the profound similarity of the U.S. M9 bayonet (top) and the Soviet bayonet (bottom).

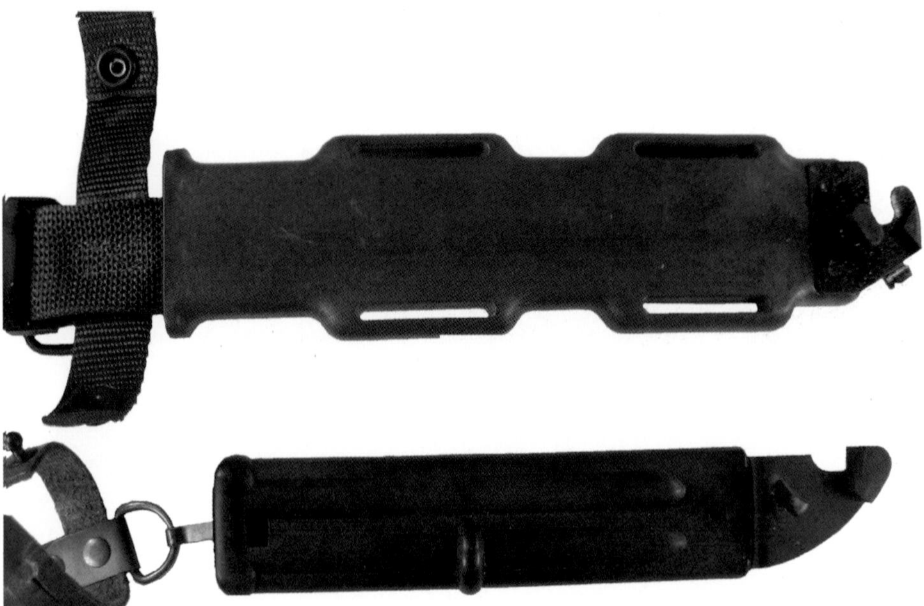

Figure 79: The upper photo is the M9 scabbard; the lower a Soviet AK bayonet scabbard.

satisfied its requirements for the MPBS some thirty years previously. Yet, by the mid-1980s, the M7 was still the issue bayonet, and the prospect of a successful domestic design appeared bleak at best.

It is mind boggling that so much time and money was spent on numerous failed design attempts when the Soviet model could have simply been adapted to U.S. specifications; as this author contends, it was in any event. This is even more baffling when one recalls the way in which the Soviets pilfered and stole American equipment designs seemingly on a regular basis!

Nor were the Soviets bashful about it, as they usually announced such as the "most recent Soviet advance or discovery," and each time their *recent advance* looked amazingly like one of our own *recent advances*! All musing aside, the AK bayonet is a very good design, masterfully crude, elementally simple, and one that is now widely used by many militaries the world over—most prodigiously in areas where eating utensils are uncommon.

Alas, in the end the Soviet design held sway, which is actually even more ironic when one considers that the bayonet wire cutter is one of the few honest and original Soviet designs. Moreover, while it took three decades before it actually happened, in the end, we took it from them. And, to add insult to injury, Charles Finn went a step further when he patented the design!

Perhaps Finn drew heavily upon the Soviet design, perhaps he did not—only he knows that. Yet, in all fairness to Mr. Finn, what is known is that he took considerable time in his patent write up to acknowledge the inventor R.E. Bauer who, in 1987, patented a similar wire cutter scabbard design.[28] We should not, therefore, be surprised that Mr. Finn was well versed in both knife design and requirements; that was, after all, what he did!

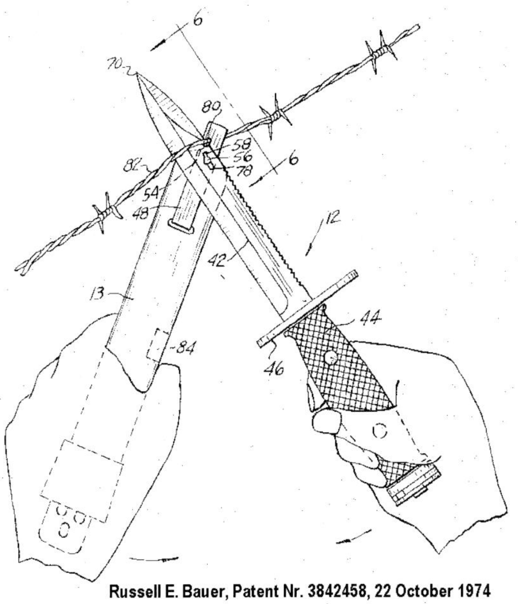

Russell E. Bauer, Patent Nr. 3842458, 22 October 1974

Figure 80: Illustration from Russel Bauer's patent submission depicting a modified M7 and his scabbard design in role of wire cutter. (The Infantry Board Trials of 1986)

In the collecting arena, one hears a great deal about Phrobis and its early role in the M9 saga, yet very little discussion relative to the other design contenders, most likely because Americans are success oriented. As such, they quickly forget history's losers and consequently many of the events that make history and the M9's development so interesting.

For example, forty-nine companies responded to the Army's M9 solicitation, and of those fourteen had the tenacity to produce and submit working prototypes. As for the other thirty-five, surely there were as many reasons for not following-up as there were dropouts, and some have suggested the principle reason was that the Army required fifty-five working prototypes, at the competitor's expense. Such argument contends that the requirement was too burdensome, causing many smaller companies to become discouraged, while others were simply unable to raise the necessary initial investment capital.

Whether or not the initial investment presented a formidable capital burden on small businesses, one cannot deny that for a company to spin up production in support of such a project is quite significant. Significant in terms of capital outlay and diversion of resources, however, the payoff would be a large and lucrative one to the tune of $15,641,000! Moreover, if done right, a company could potentially win subsequent contracts just as profitable, not to mention a whole lot easier, since there would be no R&D outlay, and no grueling evaluation. Yes, there certainly was plenty of profit potential to make a company forget the sting of fronting the trial samples! At any rate, by the time the Army completed its initial assessment of all design submissions, only six survived to compete in the trials.

Figure 81: The standard KCB-70 made by Eickhorn.

Specifics of the entire story surrounding the early trials have been elusive, generally yielding only snippets of one evaluation aspect or another. Yet, none avail a detailed account of the trials, and while perhaps frustrating, these snippets are nonetheless sufficiently significant to provide the collector some interesting information. Moreover, the potential for insight gained from them gives one a better appreciation of both the designer and the M9.

For instance, from an old issue of *Infantry Magazine*[29] we find that Twenty-Eight soldiers of the 197th Infantry Brigade conducted Operational Testing Phase II at Ft. Benning, Georgia, under the auspices of ARDEC and the Infantry Board from the period of 16 June through 16 July 1986. During the exercise, each soldier alternately employed each candidate system in a series of tasks designed to evaluate performance as a bayonet, field knife, and wire cutter. The Ranger Department provided six Ranger Instructors to evaluate candidate system's performance as a fighting knife.

At this point, it is important to note that the number associated with candidate companies is that assigned to their designs at the time of submission and indicate the *prototype's identity*, not its testing order or ranking. In addition, many companies routinely submit multiple designs when vying for contracts.

With the identity issue clarified, it seems that Ontario Knife Company got off to a bad start, albeit with a good design. Apparently, they patterned their prototype after the Navy MK III, and yet were unable to deliver it to Fort Benning within the time specifications, thus resulting in disqualification.

Number three in the evaluation sequence was Royal Ordnance, submitting a modified SA-80 bayonet and scabbard. Lending credence to the earlier assertion that the Soviet-style wire cutter design was in wide use, it is interesting to note that their candidate in fact sported a wire cutter plate similar to the Soviet AK scabbard. This design also included a fold out saw as well as a sharpening stone.

Eickhorn was a contender with number six, which was a modified version of their ubiquitous *Knife Cutter Bayonet* model. Not surprisingly, they subsequently offered versions of it to the Marine Corps as an alternative to the OKC-3S. And, not to let the argument

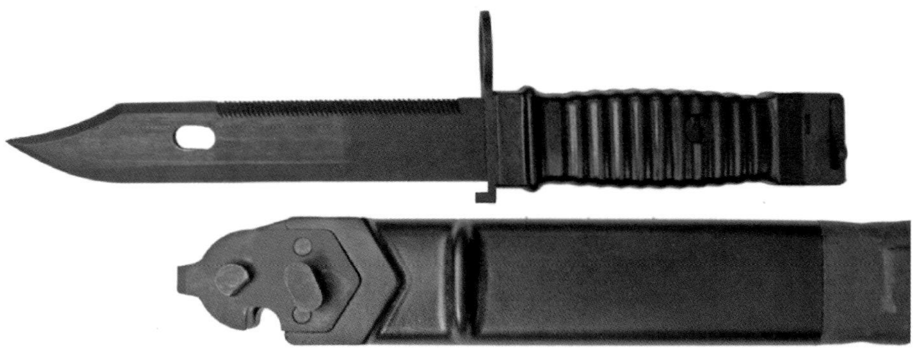

Figure 82: Shown is an Eickhorn KCB-70 made for the Stoner Weapons System trials in 1970, but it is altogether representative of the KCB series.

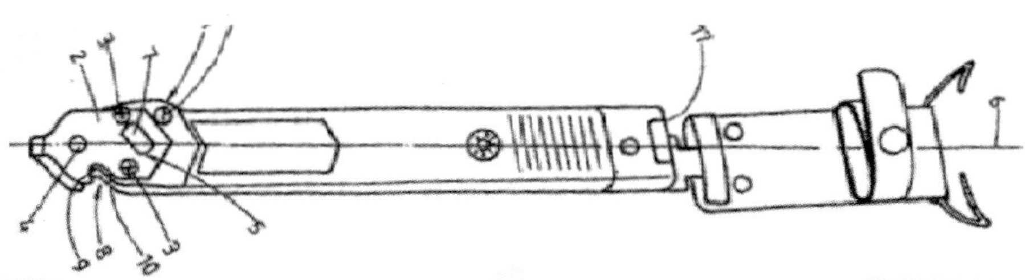

Figure 83: Above is a 1989 patent illustration of KCB series scabbard with quick release sheath amazingly similar to the one Eickhorn submitted for the M9 trials.

rest, Eickhorn's *KCB* design, like many others, bore a strikingly similar appearance to the Soviet AK bayonet.

Reflecting Eickhorn's record of accomplishment in winning Army contracts, their *XM9* lost yet again. Not daunted in the least, Eickhorn maintained with certainty that their entry was superior to the Phrobis M9. In fact, Eickhorn was so convinced of their product's superiority that they actually had printed on the boxes of their commercial M9 bayonets *the genuine and better M9*!

Imperial Knife Company (number twelve) featured a design employing a metal device that bolted on to the back of an M7 scabbard and functioned as the wire cutter. In many ways, it resembled the Bauer bayonet from the 1970s.

Marto of Spain submitted prototype number fourteen, which interestingly looked nearly identical to the Phrobis M9's blade, but with an oversized handle and featuring the only knuckle guard in the trials.

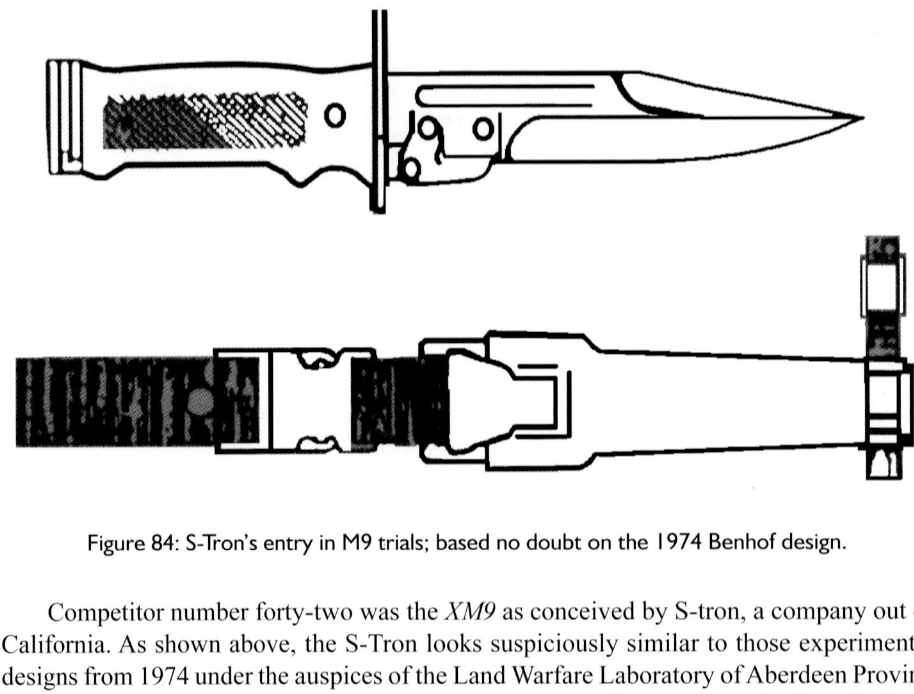

Figure 84: S-Tron's entry in M9 trials; based no doubt on the 1974 Benhof design.

Competitor number forty-two was the *XM9* as conceived by S-tron, a company out of California. As shown above, the S-Tron looks suspiciously similar to those experimental designs from 1974 under the auspices of the Land Warfare Laboratory of Aberdeen Proving Ground, Maryland, and conducted by Benhof, Inc. Obviously, S-Tron worked out the lever mechanism that had so greatly baffled the Benhof design team!

Lastly, only because it was the winner, is Phrobis' M9. Very interesting, and very unusual, is that of the 55 test samples provided by Phrobis for evaluation none suffered test failures. In fact, the M9 bested all other entries, specifically because of its performance and popularity among the soldier-evaluators. Beyond its objective qualities, soldiers were enamored with the knife's heft and comfortable handle, as well as its balance, certain purchase when wet or muddy, and generally just liked the way it handled. The Army, in what may be an unprecedented decision, chose the knife because of its zero failure rate and popularity amongst the evaluating soldiers, even though, at a cost of $49.56 per copy, it was the second highest bid price.

When later asked about the price of his knife Mickey Finn is reputed to have said that:

"Everything I design is the best, regardless of cost. In the weapons industry, if what you make has defects it costs lives. I couldn't live with that type of guilt."[30]

To get a better idea of the final bayonet trials results, the following graphic representing the cost comparison and failure rates amongst the above contenders as released in an Armed forces Journal article:

Entrant	Cost	Cutter	Blade	Handle	Scabbard	Total	Rate
Phrobis	$49.65	0	0	0	0	0	0%
Imperial	$19.75	0	1	0	2	3	6%
Eickhorn	$19.29	7	0	2	0	9	18%
Marto	$39.85	12	0	0	9	12	24%
S-Tron	$52.58	0	14	1	0	15	30%
Royal Ordnance	$45.00	1	5	9	31	37	37%

From the preceding summary, it is possible for one to get the impression that Phrobis candidates were perfect, that is not exactly the case. While true, in as much as no *mission failures* occurred, that is not to say there were not problems. Certainly there were, but they simply were not widely publicized, as to do so would have been counterproductive for both Phrobis and the Army.

Recall that once an item has passed *First Article Testing*, or *FAT*, and the *Operational Test*, the results are sent to, and reviewed by, TECOM for an *Independent Evaluation.*31 IF the evaluator is satisfied that the item met specifications as demonstrated by the testing data, then the item is determined acceptable for *Full Material Release*. In this case, Aberdeen Proving Grounds provided evaluation support as summarized below.

Survivability performance in a tactical environment, adverse environments, and NBC environments of the Phrobis was adequate, though it was noted that under salt spray conditions corrosion could cause earlier than normal replacement, unless the blade were well maintained and protected, but this was not of major concern.

During visual and mechanical testing, one sample of fifty sustained a broken bayonet retaining plate. However, because that same event had not occurred during the FAT, evaluators assumed that a quality control glitch probably accounted for the failure.

While evaluation notes show that, during Operational Testing, user soldiers overwhelmingly preferred the Phrobis in the bayonet and fighting knife role, ninety percent of those same test participants failed to put the bayonet into operation within the ten-second standard. As well, evaluators reported that a minor safety hazard existed in the wire-cutting mode.

Further, evaluators recommended anodizing the blade to prevent corrosion, conducting testing relative to storage limitations, and performing a time study analysis to determine if the time standards for deploying the bayonet were excessive—that is, too short. Offering a partial solution to the time standard evaluators asked that the item's location on load bearing equipment be considered.

Interestingly, approval of the Phrobis excluded issue to female soldiers, and the evaluator recommended limited additional testing to determine its suitability for use by them.

Of greatest significance was the recommendation to amend specifications requiring a stop on the cutter plate to prevent user injuries. This recommendation apparently registered with higher ups, as subsequent variations include two different stop designs.

The preceding represents the salient events of the *birth of the M9*, but the landscape—those transparent occurrences that created the stage upon which the story played out—must at least receive a passing mention for those readers who like the *rest of the story*.

In 1985, the Army Chief of Staff instituted a number of measures intended to improve the means of managing the research, development, and acquisition process. His goal was that of achieving better planning, improved management information systems, greater use of multiyear contracting, improved risk analysis, and better quality assurance management. To accomplish these goals the CoS appointed a *Competition Advocate General*,[32] whose function was to reduce obstacles to the competitive acquisition of high quality goods and services.

As part of the same stratagem, the Army Materiel Command overhauled the methods by which the Army developed and bought weapons, ostensibly improving quality, and accelerating the equipment development and fielding cycles. This was naturally in line with the CoS's intent of limiting development to four years, with two years for product improvement and actual field-testing. As well, the CoS declared that the Army must increase its use of state-of-the-art commercial items produced in existing commercial facilities.

What all of this meant, in essence, was that the CoS had committed the Army to slashing the traditional ten-year developmental cycle in order to provide soldiers with today's technology today, and not in ten years. This concept was widely known as *off the shelf* procurement, and was a publicly stated goal of Army acquisition.

The problem, with regard to bayonets, was that only one company was regarded to have the manufacturing capacity to provide an off the shelf bayonet, and that was Eickhorn of West Germany. Who determined this and why is not clear. As we shall see in Chapter Nine, this determination led to more than a little difficulty in the acquisition world.

At any rate, all of the other designs, including Finn's, were actually custom products. A fact that, in part, explains why Finn secured Buck's subcontracting services. The same situation occurred with future contract winner Lan-Cay, as in both instances the winning company had little or no production capability at the time of contract, relying instead on subcontractors.

As such, the Army's official plan was to select the best bayonet in an off the shelf purchase, as it was specifically not interested in a developmental design, nor necessarily the lowest price. The goal was the best, at the best price, and if that was $49.65 then that is what the Army would pay. Naturally, this was not the traditional mindset, and one that obviously some of the older contestants were unable to fathom or accept!

On the other hand, the concept of off the shelf procurement was to present problems for the M9, in as much as the Army rejected numerous product improvement modifications suggested by Phrobis.33 The real trouble was not the concept, but rather the politics of the procurement culture. Unfortunately, Phrobis was to become just one more victim of the same acquisition system that Major Slyman so adeptly illustrated in his article!

Further exemplifying the corruption of the system, we see that, during this period, the Army was conducting trials for a new service pistol to replace the M1911A1. And, while the Beretta 92 had won the trials, influential Northeastern competitors cried foul, demanding a reshoot. Because of their political sway, they intimidated the Army into conducting a full reevaluation, at great expense to the American taxpayer, though the results were the same and Beretta once again came out on top.

Probably emboldened by the pistol trials, a number of the bullish bayonet competitors, at least two of which were from the Northeast, also protested the M9 trials, with some actually filing lawsuits against the Army. Apparently, Eickhorn considered suing as well, but the cost caused common sense to prevail.

Nevertheless, it is doubtless that the Army was very reluctant to make any changes to any off the shelf article in view of the brow beating given it by these Northeastern political power brokers. Changes of such importance to Phrobis that it offered to make them at no cost to the government!

To make a bad story worse, Phrobis was awarded the M9 contract in October 1986, and the first of its M9s were issued to the 3d Battalion, 75th Ranger Regiment at Fort Benning in February 1987, a mere fifteen months following the official establishment of the letter requirement for the bayonet! As well, Phrobis completed its full contractual requirement in September 1989, which was so obviously impressive that the government awarded Phrobis the Exemplary Performance Award!

Start up operations for ventures such as this far exceed those of an existing company fronting prototype costs. They are rather staggering in their demand for capital outlay and other financial backing. No doubt, Phrobis was realizing a very modest profit from the M9 contract after paying overhead, not to mention expansion costs. Therefore, from Finn's perspective, it was the second contract, ostensibly promised to Phrobis early on, that would be the real *make or break* event.

Sadly, thanks to politicking, when the Army did announce the second contract (Spring 1992) there was no Phrobis to compete for it as in April of 1991 the company terminated operations - selling its patents and production machinery to Buck Knives. Obviously the events of the late Eighties and early Nineties (Operations Just Cause and Desert Storm) significantly diverted the Army's attention from bayonets, and much needed contracts for Phrobis, many (who will not be named here) still contend the real reason resulted from Imperial and Ontario's politically powerful affiliations in Congress, who no doubt cut out the promised 100% add-on contract from Phrobis, money that Finn undoubtedly depended on to continue operations.

One can only speculate how the M9 would have evolved had Phrobis survived and Mr. Finn remained a design influence. In fact, Phrobis did continue refining the M9 making improvements to the sheath, handle and metal components. This Phrobis dubbed the M9-A1, and while both the Army and Marines evaluated it neither actually purchased it. Plainly, the M9 is proof that Finn is one of those rare individuals capable of glimpsing the future as well as grasping the implications. For with the M9, Finn truly brought the bayonet from the shadow of the Dark Ages and fully into the 21st century. If only the political forces in our country could do the same!

6

Nomenclature

A Common Language

This chapter could have been placed almost anywhere within the text; for that matter it could have been an appendix. The reason that it immediately precedes chapters directly covering the M9 is to facilitate the reader's frequent reference to it. Or, at a minimum, so that it will be fresh in the reader's mind.

There is one primary objective in this chapter, and that is to establish a clear argument for, and system of, naming and organizing M9 variations into a logical hierarchy. Doing so will allow collectors to better study, appreciate, and organize their own collections—nomenclature is the chosen vehicle for accomplishing that. Additionally, there are some

Figure 84.1: Clips are bundles of ammunition that are loaded through the top of a weapon.

secondary objectives, which are to illustrate the need and purpose for nomenclature, as well as to present the Army, or military, nomenclature system, as many collectors struggle with it. Seldom has this author attended a collector function without encountering a score of questions related to nomenclature.

Aside from examining methods and systems, primarily we shall be discussing words, as when one really thinks about it, nearly every facet of modern life depends directly or indirectly upon them. Further, because collectors spend a majority of their time using words to relate to, and describe their particular pieces to other collectors, and as such, conversation usually takes place away from the physical items, words are the most precise means by which one collector can communicate with another, and therefore, words are obviously very important.

As an aside, and a pretty important one at that, is the fact that words are one of the first attributes of a person used by others to evaluate him, and it is only reasonable that one would want to have as keen a command of his language as possible. Further, though this certainly is not an English lesson, it is the intent to encourage collectors, at a minimum, to know their hobby's syntax. One cannot stress enough the fact that others almost always judge an individual by the words he uses, how he pronounces them, and how succinctly he employs them. This is to say, that people tend to assume much about us, whether true or not, simply based on our use of words.

Many of us come in contact with the public during our collecting activities at such places as gun shows, auctions, and the like. And, without trying to sound paranoid, we are in the public eye—they are watching and listening to us. It is therefore critical that collectors know and use the proper words to describe their pieces, not just as a means of clear communication, but also as a means of positively influencing that lay public.

A positive impression, therefore, is invaluable to those of us associated with weapons. For the sake of our hobby, not to mention our sacred freedoms, we must strive to present ourselves as the reasonable and educated people that we are. As well, our example must be such that it draws in new hobbyists while at the same time leaving a positive impression on the general public. It may be seen broadly as an investment in public opinion to insure their support should we ever have need of it.

To that extent, and in that vein, there are a couple of issues that if only corrected within this readership would be tantamount to a communication success. First is the use of the term *clip*. We hear this term bandied about on the television frequently by reporters when they describe a perpetrator as "having emptied the clip of his handgun…" in any of many crime stories. Examples such as this are illustrative of the misuse of a simple term in order to sensationalize a tragic event in order to further their own socio-political agenda!

Chances are that most collectors know the difference between a clip and a magazine, but with deference to those who may not, as a practical means of illustrating the importance of the proper use of words the following is offered for the reader's edification.

Clips are bundles of ammunition, which are loaded through the top of weapons as a means of inserting the ammunition into the weapon's *internal*, fixed or semi-fixed magazine. The clip may be an en bloc clip, as shown above, wherein the clip will remain in the magazine until all ammunition is expended.

Alternatively, the clip may be a stripper clip, in which case the firer will insert it into a special notch on the top of the rifle's receiver, and push the ammunition out of it and into the magazine. In other words, the firer *will strip the rounds from the clip.*

Figure 84.2: Above is a collection of both en bloc clips (1) and stripper clips (2).

Figure 84.3: A box magazine fitted into the magazine well of an M4 carbine.

Magazines are bundles of ammunition contained within a housing, usually in the form of a rectangular box shaped structure, which is inserted into a rifle, or pistol, and usually from beneath via the magazine well. There are a number of exceptions wherein the ammunition reservoir is a rotary or helical magazine, such as those used with the Ruger 10-22 rifles, the Calico 960, or the Russian Bizon, respectively.

Obviously, the topic of magazines and clips could fill many books, and the preceding abbreviated discourse is not all-inclusive, nor intended to be. However, if one simply knows the differences presented here, and uses them correctly, only the ignorant can criticize him.

It should be obvious by this point that the author considers words to be not just important but critical in the way that they are used, as well as essential that the right word is used within the correct context.

In the event that the topic seems trite and unimportant, consider that the Army views words to be of such import that it actually has a word for these particular kinds of words: nomenclature.

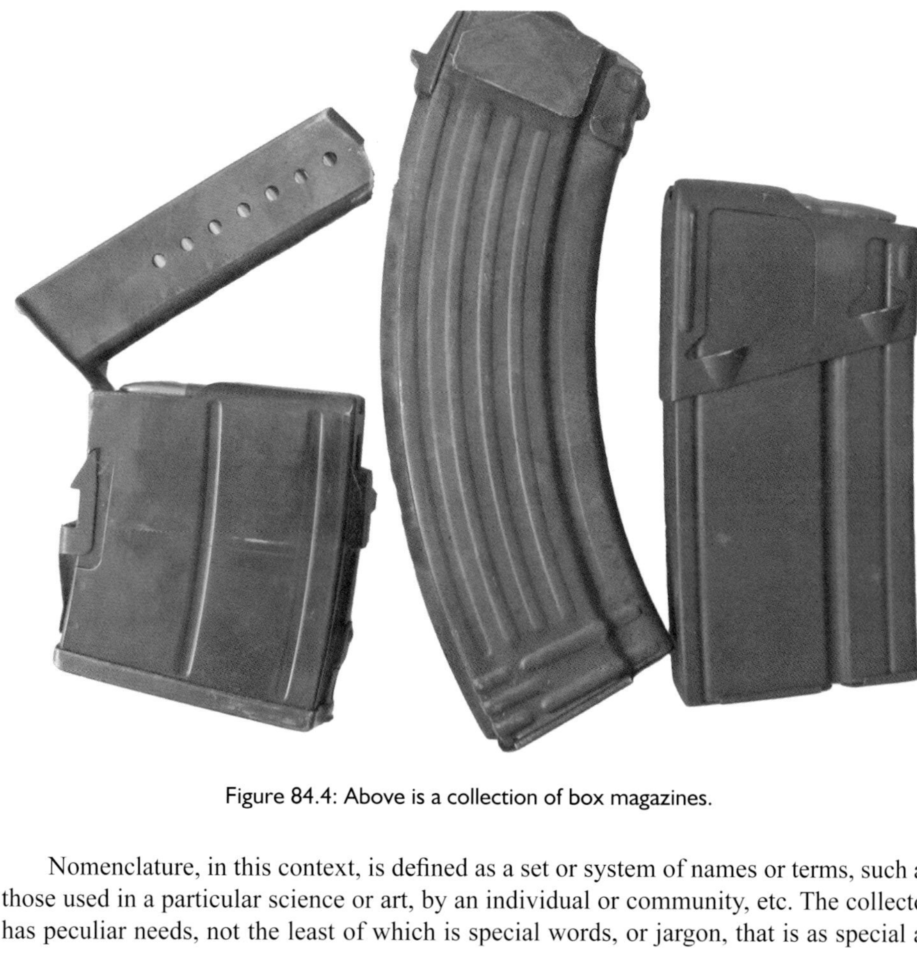

Figure 84.4: Above is a collection of box magazines.

Nomenclature, in this context, is defined as a set or system of names or terms, such as those used in a particular science or art, by an individual or community, etc. The collector has peculiar needs, not the least of which is special words, or jargon, that is as special as his collection is unique. Therefore, it is the specific intent of this chapter to offer a viable nomenclature as a tool for the collector, which will enhance his collecting experience.

Collectors of the M9 bayonet are at a particular disadvantage, as there is no system of nomenclature available to distinguish one variation of M9 from another. Moreover, considering there are at least nineteen distinct variants exist, for a collector to be at a loss for words is tantamount to being isolated from other collectors. This is unfortunate, especially when one considers that the average collector probably spends more time talking about his collection than any other related activity. Needless to say, anything that limits this facet of the hobby, in effect, also diminishes any resulting satisfaction.

It is this author's experience that a great many M9 collectors use a hodge-podge of terms, picked up along the way, to describe their pieces. And, though better than nothing, too often when one attempts to engage in a discrete discussion one is burdened with frequent clarifications, often resorting to drawing the piece one is trying to describe! The result is usually a very frustrated and tired collector!

The solution is a common, specific nomenclature that will enable any collector to easily discuss any given M9 with confidence that the other person, if also familiar with this system, understands exactly what the speaker is discussing, and that the subject M9 has been precisely distinguished from all others.

A simple example is set forth in Appendix B using photograph sets to demonstrate the basic nomenclature of various M9 parts, most of which are not necessarily unique to military edged weapons, but which can make describing the piece relatively easy. However, when it comes to describing one variation as opposed to another there is no official nomenclature, as all variations are known collectively as the M9 bayonet.

To remedy this situation, Appendix B also contains a matrix of M9 variations arranged by assigning pseudo model designations based on common physical attributes. Obviously, the matrix infers a linear progression of variant models. However, the cautious reader will not automatically assume, for instance, that because the M9/L1C appears after the M9/L1B that variation C occurred later than variation B. Such is germane for numerous reasons.

Foremost for the collector to understand is that in any manufacturing facility, numerous operations commonly occur simultaneously. Factories, especially those engaged in military contracts, are in a constant state of flux, and the government frequently interjects new specifications into the project; manufacturers are naturally obliged to comply.

Secondly, a large amount of information used in this work is of secondary source, or arrived at through comparative analysis, and though both sources are reasonably dependable, they are not beyond reproach, just as this text and the author are not. Moreover, while the material presented here is believed to be highly accurate, the reader is encouraged to keep in mind that this is a *study*, and not a sacred epistle.

Where collecting is concerned the M9 represents an historical phenomena heretofore not encountered by bayonet collectors, in that the M9 is a *modular system* and moreover, because of its commercial origin gives the term *representative collection* an entirely new significance!

Historically armories, or commercial firms under exclusive contract, produced bayonets and subsequently delivered them directly to the military. They remained in military possession until they remained, until they reached obsolescence and were disposed of into the civilian market and ultimately to the collector. In such a scenario, there was no question as to the originality of such pieces, and their configuration generally conformed to a known evolutionary progression. The M9 collector is in quite a different situation, and as such, a very new perspective is necessary.

Due to the unique method of M9 acquisition, it is extremely difficult to assemble a pure *GI collection* of M9s. This is primarily so because there are very few actual veteran M9s available, as for nearly two decades now, the Army has had no reason to surplus them out. But, perhaps more vexing is the fact that it is very difficult to discern an M9 sold on the civilian market from a military contract piece.

Compared side by side both are exactly alike, and because those that were on military inventory generally remained in factory fresh condition safely tucked away in unit arms rooms, being seldom if ever issued. Fortunately, this latter situation has improved since deployment of U.S. forces to Southwest Asia, in that all authorized equipment is currently in actual use.

Also, beginning around 2002 or 2003 the Marine Corps purged its stock of five thousand Buck M9s as the OKC3s began arriving, and that has been an awesome boon to collectors. Similarly, units of the 3d Brigade, 1st Cavalry Division recently turned-in an unknown number of M9s which the author has first hand knowledge contains many rare first issue pieces. These are, or should be, entering the surplus market anytime now, and will doubtlessly make someone a great deal of money, as well as enrich the hobby overall.

Otherwise, the only issue M9s comes in ones and twos from GIs who have retained theirs after leaving the service. And, even with recent situational improvements brought on by the war, the prevailing environment continues to force M9 collectors to assemble collections primarily comprised of M9s from commercial sources.

The other unique M9 collector's dilemma has its source in the modular nature of the M9 system. It is virtually impossible, for instance, to know whether any one M9 system is original, primarily because one can interchange any part from one system to any other with

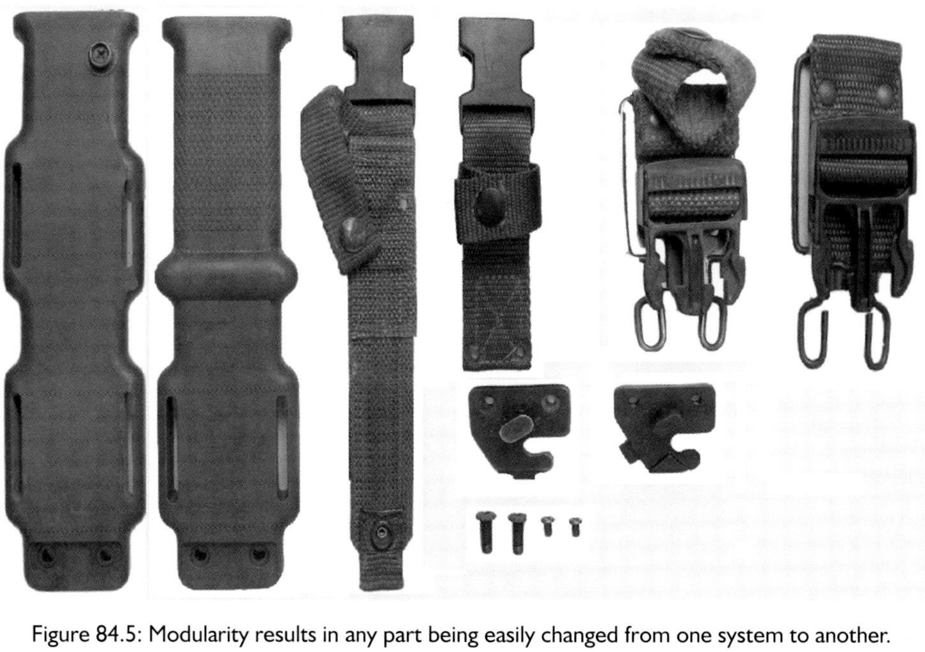

Figure 84.5: Modularity results in any part being easily changed from one system to another.

minimal effort, thus creating an M9 system to match any existing variation conceivable. Moreover, not only are parts interchangeable, but also because producers manufacture to military specification there is no way to identify *non-original components*. All of these factors coalesce to create an extremely challenging environment within which to collect the M9 bayonet.

Here, and in succeeding chapters, the reader will find a number of tools to make identifying and organizing his collection more manageable. Obviously, the use and availability of nomenclature is one of those basic tools, just as matrices are tools to enhance the use of nomenclature, which is offered here as an additional aid for the collector.

Having qualified the above points, it is well to emphasize that the purpose of the matrix is to group knives into common cohorts, which facilitates naming them as appropriate to their variation. Though no small task, the ultimate purpose is identification of cohorts so that the collector can speak of any variation and be confident he and his listener are referring to the same M9 system.

This matrix organizes all variations into *pseudo types* patterned after Army model designations. These pseudo models were arrived at using a format and method similar to Army model designations, but with information that most collectors are familiar with.

For example, all of the models are M9s, but after their organization into groups they are further identified by the maker, because most collectors already know that Phrobis III, Buck, General Cutlery, LAN-CAY, and Ontario Knife Co. manufactured the M9 or major components of it. Next, each model is segregated into its own unique subcategory according to physical attributes, such as its unique marking, marking style, or any unique recurring physical characteristic. The system is logical, easy to understand, and provides a means with which to identify any given variation.

For those accustomed to the military method of naming objects, the matrix will make perfect sense. For the remaining readers an abbreviated history of the military system will serve to enhance their understanding of it, and how it can be of benefit to the collector, whether in the search for new specimens or a more in depth research of an existing collection.

Standardization of Army Nomenclature

"The intent of the Army Nomenclature System is to provide an identification tool when there is a need to establish the identification of an item relative to other items. Such identification design is to facilitate the repeated reference to other items by using fixed top/summary identification, intended for use as the subject, in the process of verbal communication, all forms of correspondence and documentation such as drawings, standards, specifications, equipment lists, production schedules, contracts, and the like. Such a system provides a convenient means of differentiating between items having the same basic name but differing in design or functional interchangeability. This system is the basis for recording the status of an item relative to its overall history as a guide to authorization for development or modification, procurement, logistical support and readiness reporting."[34]

Naturally, Army nomenclature has not always been standardized, nor has it been in its present form. In 1924, the Army recognized the need for a standardized system especially pertaining to technical literature and cataloging. To study the problem the Army Ordnance Board, on 24 December 1924, commissioned a subcommittee consisting of a Major J.K.

Crain of the Ordnance Department Manufacturing Service, and Major C.G. Mettler of the Ordnance Department's Technical Staff.[35]

It is interesting to note in the text of the subcommittee's *Letter of Instruction* from the Ordnance Board that the Board already had the essentials of the system in mind, as evidenced by their instructions. The Board directed the two men to:

"...consider, make recommendations, and submit reports to the Ordnance Committee on matters pertaining to the proper designation for Models and Types while under development and proper designations for approved standard types."

The Board also forwarded this LOI36 to the men's sections, instructing their Chain of Command to report:

"... all matter of type or model designations and nomenclature, which arise in any of the named divisions that should be referred to this special committee."

The subcommittee's suspense date was 31 December 1924.

The first briefing of the full Ordnance Committee occurred on 11 June 1925, in which the sub-committee recommended all new designations begin with the letter *T* representing *type,* followed by an Arabic number delineating the design number of the ordnance item. To designate modifications and design changes the subcommittee recommended placing the letter *M* after the design sequence. To designate the sequence of modification, they directed that the letter *M* be followed by an Arabic numeral. Therefore, a first modification of the 16th succession of a rifle design would appear as *T16M1.* If an item was in development, but had not been approved for fielding the letter *E*, or experimental, would follow the modification sequence. In addition it would have a modifier just as the modification did, i.e. Arabic numeral. This example would appear as *T16M1E1*, representing the 16th modification of the model that remained in the experiment phase of development.

During the briefing critique one civilian contractor, a Mr. Whittett, pointed out that the adoption of this system would at once cause a large number of technical and training manuals to become obsolete. He recommended substituting the letter *T* with the letter *M* for model, to avoid publications obsolescence. He further suggested phasing in the *T* designation at a later date, to avoid confusion during the war, and that the transition be done incrementally over time.

When asked his opinion by General Joyes, Major Hardigg did not like the *T* designator, but agreed on the designation, at least in principle, but requested that the designation *Mark* continued to be used, as it was not only popular, but that many ordnance items were already designated with such. The critique was concluded by General Joyes, who stated:

"I feel that this discussion has brought to light some of the points that might well be considered further by the sub-committee and I realize the difficulty under which the sub-committee was working... I feel the subcommittee has done good work here, but it is of such an important change that I suggest Major Crain take the report back to see if the sub-committee can work out the question of designations of models in the light of some of the discussion that has taken place."

The follow-on, and second, briefing to the Ordnance Committee came to order on 30 July 1925. While the first briefing contained seven pages, meeting 28 was nine pages long, consisting of numerous changes in the system, but was not otherwise greatly different from those of meeting 27. The items of debate included catalog arrangement, distinguishing terms to differentiate ordnance items, and unique adjectives for caliber, weight, size, and/or use. Also discussed was the question of what was the most useful and distinctive term for indicating classes of ordnance, technical discriminators for items of the same general character, and finally, designation of experimental versus standard types of ordnance.

Catalog arrangement, it was decided, would continue to be dictated by the conventions of Field Service, which held that the principal noun, or item name, be designated by an alphabetic index word positioned before any item's title. The Committee extended the convention to include all drawings, markings, index lists, nameplates, and training regulations to avoid confusion. This practice remains today, thusly: Pole, Fishing, 1ea.

Catalog arrangement had been relatively easy, particularly because the committee had convention to rely upon. The task of identifying uniquely distinguishing terms for ordnance represented difficulty of the next order! After much struggling, the Committee decided that there should be published a standardized list of terms wherein similar items received a standard designation

Today the Army uses the term *extended modifier* to describe the information that follows the basic name of an item. The Committee addressed this standard, wisely choosing to continue the practice of placing the caliber, size, weight, and/or general application of an item after the basic name in order to clarify the item's identity, and to categorize similar classes of ordnance. The basic name would always precede the extended modifier in order to identify the category. An example of this is *Pistol, Caliber .45, Automatic: M1911A1* to describe the weapon; items of a similar category appear as *Cartridge, Pistol, Ball, Caliber .45, M1911*. And, regarding weight, one writes: *Truck, Cargo, 2 ½ Ton, 6x6*.

In the case of new words and/or acronyms, the committee decided to add words/acronyms provided they were inherently descriptive, and generally recognized by the term. The example used was that of the term tank, which was a relatively new term, but nearly everyone understood its meaning.

Finally, the Committee looked at designation of experimental versus standard types of ordnance.What they finally settled on was a method of annotating developmental progression of design, while at the same time providing for variance between similar design types, and simultaneously demonstrating minor design changes in two separate and distinct developmental classes. These classes pertained to items that were currently under development and those already fielded. For items currently fielded for testing but yet unadopted, the subcommittee chose to designate them with the letter *T*, meaning *trial*.

Using the system, an item being developed would be designated *T1* for the first model through T_x for the final iteration of a given design series. The *T* was sufficiently unique to preclude confusing the trial model from standard issue items currently fielded. Beyond this, the system provided for trial model modification by assigning alphanumeric sequence designators to show experimentation. The *T1* model would thus become *T1E2*, to represent the first trial model having had two experimental modifications; the *E* represented experimental.

The Committee determined that a *T* and/or *E* designator would represent all design development, and that a comprehensive file of the project was to be kept on a lessons

Figure 85: WWII vintage box of .45 caliber cartridges demonstrating nomenclature use in labeling.

learned basis, or for future study, should the state of the art progress sufficiently to make a failed design viable.

The Subcommittee further recommended that once an item passed all testing and evaluation, and was approved for general issue, that its nomenclature be changed by dropping the *T* and redesignating it with an *M* to denote its *Model*. They further recommended for Naval materiel that was not otherwise designated the descriptor could be known as *Mark*, to be followed by an Arabic numeral expressing its iteration, and to cease using Roman Numerals as identifiers. The Committee advised caution so as not to duplicate nomenclature within any given class, and that currently fielded materiel would not have their nomenclature changed.

For consistency, the Committee directed that new items enter into service uniformly, and thereafter be designated sequentially according to their design evolution. As such, when a given model was modified or altered, it would be classified using the letter *A* and numeral *1* to denote the first alteration; *A2* for the second alteration, and so forth.

A good example is the M16 rifle. It entered service with a three-pronged flash suppressor and chromium bolt. During fielding it was found that the flash suppressor became easily entangled in brush and that the bolt mechanism fouled after a very few rounds, causing it to jam, or preventing the bolt from completely locking in the forward position. After study and testing, the Army changed the flash suppressor to a closed tubular design or *birdcage*. Parkerized bolts replaced the old chromium units, and an added *forward assist* device made it possible to force the bolt into battery in the event of a malfunction. This modified M16 became the M16A1. Later added were new sights, round hand guards, a heavy barrel, and a three round burst sear, resulting in a designation change to M16A2.

The Committee found it necessary, and prudent, to specify that all new designations be annotated anywhere that the original model nomenclature might be found. This pertained to blueprints, drawings, the actual item, books, pamphlets, shipping labels, and so on, and that all classification books be stored in the same office as those with the nomenclature books for reference.

The Ordnance Committee approved this proposal on 30 July 1925, publishing it for review and approval of the Chief of Ordnance at the War Department. Subsequently, on 18 August 1925 the Ordnance Chief approved and disseminated it to all major commands in the form of *Order Number 614, dated 18 August 1925*. This was the genesis of today's Military Standard Nomenclature which, as with all systems, has since been modified a few times—the latest being 15 May 1987.

Implications of the Nomenclature System

At this point, many readers may want to skip ahead, as most people consider logistics a dry and most tedious subject. Before doing so, though, it is this author's contention that the well-advised collector who understands nomenclature does not exist without its corresponding stock number! They never travel alone! Moreover, a sound grasp of this relationship frequently makes research considerably easier, not to mention faster!

For those collectors driven to know everything possible about their subjects the following represents just how fascinating it is to observe the history of systems and methods; how they dovetail, are interrelated, and ultimately evolve. This is true of the nomenclature system and its relationship to logistics.

Equally fascinating is the Ordnance Department as an organization. Every weapon, their spare parts, and all related equipment has a drawing somewhere within the bowels of Ordnance—a concept capable of stretching the mind like a rubber band! There must literally be millions, and at least Ordnance claims to have drawings on every item since the inception of the Department! Finally, consider that every one of these drawings is numbered and cataloged! Staggering!

Well, staggering is exactly how Ordnance was feeling by the time World War II rolled around, as not only does Ordnance have to design, test, repair, and modify weapons, by necessity they also get deeply involved in the Logistics process. Recall that essentially Ordnance controls the Nomenclature System; it catalogs and archives item nomenclature, making it the *Proponent Agency37* for these official words. Therefore, if someone wants to name a screw, they must submit their request to Headquarters, Department of Ordnance, for approval.

Before the current stock numbers, Ordnance used a numerical system dating back to 1915, which listed drawings and parts by numbers, with each part represented on a given drawing, and both the number and the drawing assigned their own unique number. This practice most knew as the *Class and Division* system. Complimenting it was a cross-reference list by which the user was able to match any number with its corresponding drawing and vice versa.[38]

An improvement of the system came in 1915, when the Ordnance Department adopted *Drawing Lists* and *Parts Lists*. Using this method, when a drawing (for instance *drawing 1*) was assigned to the list of drawings for, say, Class and Division 3-16, it then became designated as 3-16-1. To a corresponding list of parts they assigned a similar number. The parts list carried a drawing number, except that a letter suffix was added sequentially, as in 3-16-1A, 3-16-1B, and so on. Parts were listed alphabetically, including the material and quantities required to procure or manufacture a given item.

Throughout World War I the Ordnance Department used the Class and Division System, during which time its inherent inadequacies quickly became apparent. In 1922, Ordnance created a new drawing system utilizing five distinct drawing sizes, each identified alphanumerically and sequentially. There were five standard drawing sizes: *A, B, C, D,* and *E*. Drawing number one of size *A* was *A1* and so on. Under this system, the only discriminator between the five different sizes is the letter. Without it one would have to pull each like numbered drawing to identify a part or assembly.

Standard parts, formerly shown on drawings in classification 30-2, came to be shown on B size drawings in the same general form using letter suffixes. In 1927, the first Ordnance Standard drawings came into use and consisted of separate series of drawing numbers and *piecemarks*[39] shown on letter size sheets. The drawing number consisted of three letters with an *X* plus a number. Letter suffixes were added to indicate the piecemarks. The first standard of this type was *TAAX1*. Because *TAAX1* strongly resembles the word TAXI, it was not long before widespread use of the term *TAXI drawings* unofficially replaced Ordnance Standard system in casual conversation.

The problem, on the macro level, was that each Department controlled its own piece of the logistics pie. In other words, Ordnance procured and cataloged weapons and related items. The Medical Department procured and cataloged all medical supplies and related items. Signal managed communications equipment and so on. Herein lay the problem; while what something was called had been standardized, individual stock or part numbers and their cataloging had not.

By 1941, just within the Ordnance Department three distinct numbering systems existed and were in general use: the *Class and Division System*, *Letter Size System*, and the *Ordnance Standard System*. Yet, the problem remained manageable enough, in the interwar period, provided a supply clerk could spend all day hunting down a set of .45 handgrips. Still, one's imagination can run wild conjuring up the logistical nightmares this must have caused on a daily basis!

Yet, overall, parts got ordered, and orders were filled soon enough. It is easy to imagine, during this period of military famine, that priorities were not quite urgent, a situation surely made worse by the nation's isolationist mood. Moreover, during this time the country had suffered through the Great Depression, as well as two of history's most devastating Influenza epidemics! Given these circumstances, it is not likely that Congress placed much impetus on the military's logistical readiness. The more practical reality lay in Joe and Joan civilian, busy either trying to stay alive or burying their families! Nevertheless, bad as it was, change did eventually rear its head in the form of Word War II.

Recall that in Chapter Two, Major Gary E. Slyman said in his article that "the evolution of the weapons procurement system has produced the large, slow, overregulated bureaucratic process now in place. However, the unresponsiveness of the system, in times of crises, has always been temporarily repaired." Well, whether the Army temporarily repaired the logistics system, or there were simply scores of highly motivated Supply Sergeants in perpetual motion, the War Department was able to supply our troops magnificently during the war, in spite of the clumsy supply system.

Amazingly, in 1943—exactly mid-war—Ordnance moved to regain logistical control, and sanity, by giving the Engineering Section of the Office of the Chief of Ordnance charge over all drafting room procedures. Of immediate concern was the coordinating of stock and parts numbers used by the Industrial Service, as well as that of the Field Service. The solution culminated in the most extensive change to the Ordnance Department's numbering system in the history of the organization.

The result was assignment of a new part number to every existing piece of then current ordnance material. The basic concept, while not profound, was a sensible procedure of assigning one unique, yet common number to each drawing, part number, and stock number. While the system was very utilitarian, and loaded with common sense, it was still inadequate!

Figure 86: Lid from wooden case of a surgical kit with the number heat stenciled into it.

Nonetheless, without getting any deeper, or further afield, it worked like this: the part number consisted of a seven-digit identifier, call it 1234567, allowing one the ability to look up that part to insure the correct item was being ordered the requisitioner could then reference drawing number A1234567. The alpha prefix identified the size of drawing (A, B, C, D, E). The stock number assigned to this part was determined by adding a standard nomenclature identifier before the part number, such as C040-1234567. This system applied to all current and previous items as of the fall of 1943.

All NEW items were to be organized using number series. The series 7000000 through 9999999 designated all new ordnance material except standard parts, *major end items*,[40] and tools. The series ran in sequence irrespective of the drawing size, and the alpha identifier for sizes was discontinued.

Existing drawings organized under the old system and still in use were converted to number series 5000000 and 6000000. As such, size A drawings became 5000000, B sizes became 6000000, C size became 5500000, D sizes became 6500000, and E size drawings would be in the 6900000 series range.

Tools, tool equipment, and accessories, as well as bulk material had assigned *Federal Stock Catalog* numbers (this is not the same as the *Federal Stock Number*) in the same manner as the part numbers. Ordnance Standard numbers use the series 100001 to 999999. Standard parts specific to the Ordnance Department are assigned numbers in the series 500000 through 999999. Packages containing spare parts, gear sets, etc., are in the series 5700000 to 5949999. Variations of the other systems they retained and or combined for specific items.

New Systems for a New Era

Post World War II couldn't have been more different from that of the World War I and interwar period, though it is true that mass demobilization did take place, and probably on a larger scale than was prudent. But this time the United States had won one war only to be face to face with a new enemy, and the very real prospect of another even larger conflict. Moreover, this time the boogieman was not the machinegun, nerve gas, nor even the tank, but the atomic bomb. America could not afford to slip into a snooze mode as she had done after every other war, and this time many great changes in rapid succession were to take place.

One of the first, and unprecedented, changes was the post-war reorganization that created the Department of Defense. Soon afterwards, in July of 1947, the *Army-Navy Munitions Board* established the *Cataloging Agency* to manage a single Department of Defense resource called the *Joint Army-Navy Catalog System*. Established soon after, in 1949, the *Federal Stock Number* (*FSN*) system entered use with an eleven-digit number, and the first FSN assigned.

On 1 July 1952, the *Defense Cataloging and Standardization Act* mandated a single catalog system for the entire Department of Defense, followed in 1958, with the establishment of the *Armed Forces Supply Support Center (AFSSC)* based in Washington, DC. Its mission: to maintain the Federal Catalog System and standardize item names used by the military services.

When the *Defense Supply Agency* was created on 1 January 1962, the Armed Forces Supply Support Center was renamed the *Defense Logistics Service Center*, becoming the central control point for the Federal Catalog System. The Defense Logistics Service Center was later renamed the *Defense Logistics Information Service (DLIS)*.

Unlike all past numbering systems, the FSN actually worked *remarkably* well, and provided actual useable information to field level users. More importantly, it provided, for the first time, interservice interoperability, which greatly enhanced Mission Readiness. What it did not provide for was Allied interoperability. If there were to be a war with the Warsaw Pact, it would be critical that U.S. Forces work effectively along side NATO allies, and that certainly entailed logistical support, both to and from NATO forces. To this end, the *Nation Stock Number* superseded the Federal Stock Number system to include NATO members.

Organization of the National Stock Number is such that the first two digits, the *Federal Supply Group (FSG)*, identify the property group to which an item belongs. The first two digits (FSG), combined with the next two digits *comprise* the *Federal Supply Class (FSC)* which identify the supply class (ammunition, food, etc...) to which an item belongs. The next two digits, the *National Codification Bureau Code*, identify the item country of origin. The final seven digits, the *National Item Identification Number (NIIN)*, is the number used by the military to control individual items in inventory.

Example: 1234-00-123-4567: FSG (12), FSC (12 + 34), Country Code (00), NIIN (123-4567)

Whereas Headquarters, Ordnance Department is the proponent Agency for nomenclature, the *Defense Logistics Information Service* located at the *Battle Creek Federal Center* in Battle Creek, Michigan, performs National Stock Number (NSN) assignments. Initiated whenever a new item enters the system repeatedly, or when a new weapons system enters into service, each NSN assigned to an item is the result of a careful review process called cataloging.

All U.S. military services, as well as NATO and allied countries, submit cataloging requests to DLIS for processing. The information is held in the Federal Logistics Information System (FLIS) managed by DLIS in Battle Creek. DLIS operates within the Defense Logistics Agency (DLA) and is the only organization authorized to assign NSNs.

National Stock Numbers are assigned based on the end use of the item, and include everything from large, complex items like a weapon or truck, to tiny individual components. As of 2005 there were about 14 million active and inactive NSNs in the Federal Logistics Information System (FLIS).

Obviously, this is not the complete story of the stock number system, its proponents, or intermediate and support organizations, and while such may be very interesting to some, it is far and away from our focus here. What is relevant in all of this is the concept that identification of an item is critical, and the means by which one accomplishes it must be discrete (precise) and accurate, and is the reason this author places such importance on an organized system of nomenclature for the collector.

M9 Nomenclature for the Collector

When initially considering how to approach the differentiation of the various M9s, a number of obstacles at once became evident. First among them is the reality that so many random terms for any given variation exist that one must resist the temptation to be intimidated. While old habits may be difficult to break, break they can, but only if sufficient effort is applied. After some reflection, the fact that, not unlike the Army's struggle during the interwar period, a common system is truly needed was supremely convincing to this author, and as of this date, no one else has taken the initiative to put forth any sensible alternative system. Having said all of that, in the final analysis perhaps a more troubling aspect is the question of what form any new classification system should take.

It seemed obvious that name recognition should be a large consideration, as any radically new or different term would require an even greater measure of appeal, and educating interested collectors would be even more difficult. It therefore just seemed rational, and practical, to include something as recognizable as the manufacturer's name in the designation.

What ultimately emerged is the following, which is an amalgamation of a number of the most common names and discriminators. All collectors will recognize the nomenclature's *M9* identifier, whereas the discriminator is primarily composed of the manufacturer and a quasi-Army model suffix assigned uniquely to each knife according to its differences from the others, where the difference may be manufacturer, markings, materials, or design. Every M9 fits into one of the following subtypes.

Overall, objectively, the following system will serve the collector well in his routine discussion of any given item. Using this system will also make reading this book much easier, as the author has put this new system to good use. Finally, because the classification system logically incorporates already familiar terms it is easy to learn and use.

The following matrix is an example of the Author's M9 classification system, which can also be found in greater detail in Appendix B, and will be referred to frequently in the following chapters.

	RICOSSO MARKINGS	FONT/REMARKS
M9P1	M9, Phrobis III, U.S.A. >	Flat "M" CRAZY 9
M9P2	M9, Phrobis III, U.S.A.	Flat "M" CRAZY 9
M9P3	M9, Phrobis III, U.S.A.,	
M9P4	M9, Phrobis III, U.S.A., PAT. PEND.	NARROW
M9P5	M9, Phrobis III, U.S.A., PAT. PEND.	WIDE
M9B1	M9-USMC, BUCK +, USA	SHARP TOP "M"
M9B2	M9-USMC, BUCK /, USA	
M9B3	M9-USMC, BUCK /, USA	
M9B4	M9-USMC, BUCK /, USA	
M9G1	M9, LANCAY, USA	GENERAL CUTLERY
M9L1	M9, LANCAY, USA	
M9L1-1	M9, LANCAY,USA	
M9L1-2	M9, LANCAY,USA	
M9L1-3	M9, LANCAY,USA	2d Contract blade
M9L2	M9, LAN-CAY,U S A	
M9L2-1	M9, LAN-CAY,USA	Early 2d Contract
M9L2-2	M9, LANCAY,USA	1st Contract blade
M9L3	M9, LAN-CAY,USA	
M9O1	M-9, ONTARIO KNIFE CO., USA	

Figure 87: Summary chart of M9 variations

7

The Phrobis Generation

Production

Up to this point, the majority of material presented has addressed peripheral, or ancillary, issues. However, in this chapter the focus will be to identify, categorize, and quantify significant changes throughout the history of the M9, thus establishing a confluent lineage or evolutionary pattern. Such methodology makes it possible to place any M9 into a category, which corresponds to its place on a timeline according to its production, and inherent variations as they pertain to the Phrobis generation of M9s. It is well to note that with few exceptions this is both possible and desirable.

Having said that, it is again stressed that the material presented in this chapter addresses only DoD contract M9 bayonets, and as stated elsewhere, other makers have produced, or continue to produce, other variations for foreign governments and the general civilian market. In as much as they are germane to the particular topic, commercial and other than U.S. M9s may be mentioned, but they are not a topic of study here.

While historically armories or commercial firms under exclusive contract produced bayonets, subsequently delivering them directly to the military, upon obsolescence they found their way into the civilian market and ultimately to the collector, leaving little question as to their originality or configuration. The M9 collector is in quite a different situation, and as such, a very new perspective is necessary.

Figure 88: The Phrobis III, Inc dolphin logo.

Because of this unique situation, it is extremely difficult to put together a pure GI M9 collection, as there are so few actual veteran M9s available. This is simply because, up until 2003, the Army has had no reason to surplus out such bayonets, and those on inventory are generally in factory fresh condition, safely tucked away in unit arms rooms. That generally leaves the *M9-ophile* with a precious few military issued pieces, and a myriad of commercial variations with which to build his collection around.

Readily identifiable genuine issue surplus bayonets are such based not on their condition, as a great number arrived from depot and never left the arms rooms. Consequently, they are generally found in a highly preserved state and are either in near or pristine condition. The presence of rack numbers painted, stamped, electro penned, or even scratched into them by unit Armorers is a good, though not a guaranteed indication that they are genuine military contract pieces.

Because there is no prescribed location, font, or other requirement for applying this identity system the collector will encounter a great variation of locations, fonts, and methods of marking. To this author's knowledge, there is no formal requirement that the markings be permanent, though the general practice is to use a reasonably permanent method in order to preserve the bayonet and scabbard's identity, which is matched to the rack number of its corresponding rifle. Simply put, a unit will issue M9 number *x* along with rifle number *x*.

For those unfamiliar with this system, it is a very old, simple, and expedient method whereby the Armorer records all serial numbered weapons on an inventory sheet, then beginning at the top, numbers them sequentially so that a given line number (thereafter known as the *rack number*) is keyed to a specific serial number. This provides a quick, simple, and easily recognized identity for that weapon.

While rack numbers make identification easy for serialed sensitive items like rifles, bayonets, gas masks, compasses, etc., do not have serial numbers. As such, these items have no intrinsic identity, so for them the rack number provides one. Usually a bayonet will have the same rack number as its rifle, and when being signed-out a note is made on the log if issue included a bayonet.

Because M9 bayonets are not serial numbered, and are off the shelf items, it is an easy matter for a soldier to purchase a new one and turn it in instead of the issued piece. While the legality of this is questionable, otherwise there is actually little wrong with the practice, as the unit gets a new bayonet, and the soldier gets his object of nostalgia.

WEAPONS/AMMUNITION CONTROL SHEET
For use of this form see DA Pam 710-2-1

UNIT: Bco, 1st Bn, 26th Infantry (M) — DATES: FROM — TO

ISSUE							TURN-IN		
RACK NUMBER	WEAPON SERIAL NUMBER	NOMENCLATURE	DATE/TIME OUT	AMMO & RDS	ISSUED TO: PRINTED NAME	ISSUED TO: SIGNATURE	DATE & TIME RETURNED	AMMO & RDS TURNED IN	SIGNATURE OF ARMORER
1	gxxx-x	Rifle, M16A2							
2	gxxx-x								
3	gxxx-x								
4									
5									
6									
7									

Figure 88.1: Note above that the first column on the left contains a rack number, which corresponds to a serial number in the second column. This dramatically decreases the time needed to issue weapons, and makes for easy and rapid identification of them.

Such situations are responsible for a great number of veteran M9s ending up in the hands of collectors, which is a good thing. Unfortunately, it also accounts for many collectors having variations that are not military issue and possess non-military features. Such situations greatly add confusion to the already complex issue, and this is a bad thing!

The following photos are a small collection of the many variations of rack number styles, as an example of what one can expect to see on *original* issue pieces. Note that the scabbard and the bayonet are both marked and keyed to one another, just as both are keyed to their respective *rack rifle*.

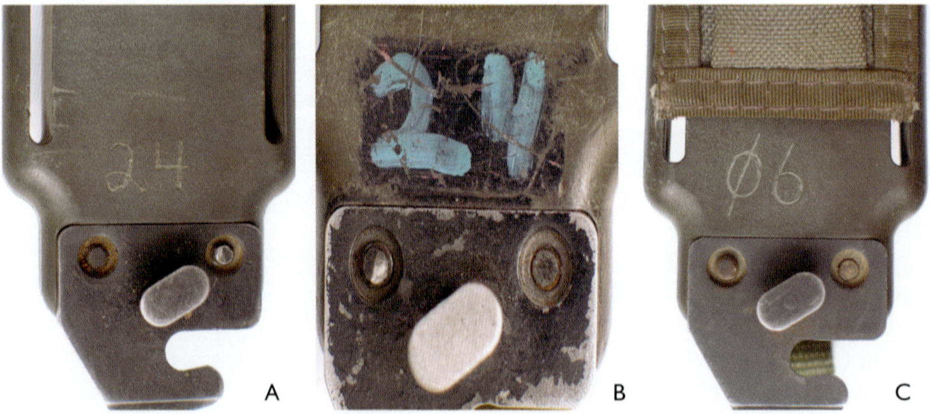

Figure 88.2 (A, B, and C): Above is shown just three of an infinite variety of rack numbers as they may appear on M9 scabbards.

Figure 88.3 (A and B): Above: corresponding rack numbers on the bayonet itself, which is keyed to the scabbard to facilitate pairing.

By way of description, the M9 MPBS, or Multipurpose Bayonet System, is comprised of a bayonet, a scabbard with integral sharpening stone, and a quick-release suspension assembly. By design, the M9 System should function as a bayonet, a general-purpose combat/utility knife, a saw capable of cutting through aircraft metal, a prying tool, and as a wire-cutting tool when used in concert with the scabbard. As well, the M9 is resistant to electrical voltage, as its handle is composed of DuPont's Zytel® material. Also provisional in the design is a flat tipped screwdriver, two machined slots on the hilt front capable of functioning as bottle openers, and the addition of an eyelet for attaching a lanyard. And, of course, the M9 is specifically designed and intended for use with the M16 family of rifles and carbines.

Unlike its M7 predecessor, the M9 bayonet is very robust, having a blade which is one and three quarters of an inch broad, by one quarter of an inch in breadth, and a full seven and one quarter inches long. By contemporary standards it is truly a rugged brute, and a classic one, which has become an American icon. Only the Marine Corp's OKC-3S, examined in Chapter 9, exceeds the M9 in strength, size, and aggressive appearance.

The M9's scabbard, as initially designed, accommodated a small sharpening stone glued into a preformed slot on the reverse surface, covered by a protective strap of heavy webbing, and secured to the scabbard via a button snap. However, even with this provision, historically it is not uncommon for the stone to become cracked or even completely dislodged from the scabbard. Such frailties as the sharpening stone are one among a number of reasons that the Army modified the design and eliminated numerous unnecessary features.

The U.S. Army purchased the first M9 bayonets via contract number DAAA21-87-C-0001 dated 06 October 1986, which for budgetary considerations is Fiscal Year (FY) 1987, at a cost of $49.56 per copy. The use of the Fiscal Year accounts for so many sources quoting 1987 as the year the bayonet was officially adopted, though 1986 is, in fact, the correct calendar date. Nonetheless, the contract was to run for three years, specifying delivery of 315,600[41] units with additional order options at the discretion of the Department of the Army.

For a variety of reasons, Phrobis sub-contracted the Buck Knife Company to produce the M9 and, in the end, Phrobis and Buck delivered 325,000 units, thus fulfilling their contractual obligation to the Government in 1989. Therefore, with the completion of the contract, the two companies were effectively free of any obligation except to one another. And, while it is not uncommon for companies to participate in serial ventures, for Buck and Phrobis such possibilities were, apparently, not only ill advised, but also mutually unacceptable, and a parting was in the offing.

While the exact details of the difficulties between Buck and Phrobis are not well known, at least to this author, the idea of an amicable, pleasant parting of ways seemed unlikely given that the relationship had been frictional from the start. Whatever the actual details, Buck and Phrobis terminated their contract citing mutual convenience as the reason. The resulting settlement awarded Buck production rights within the United States, while Phrobis' founder, Mickey Finn, retained control of Phrobis III, Ltd., and associated trademarks. His M9 production rights, whatever their specifics actually were, reverted to the Army upon completion of the contract.

It is interesting to note that Mr. Finn went on to actually patent the M9 bayonet system. His patent, dated 18 April 1989, includes the entire MPBS system, leading one to assume that in view of such he would have been free to do as he pleased with his design. Chances are, though, that there is more to the story than meets the eye.

Figure 89: The MPBS (M9) system—designed for use with the M16 family of rifles and carbines. (U.S. Army photo)

Nevertheless, in the end each company went on to produce M9 style knives for the commercial markets as autonomous entities. However, with Buck's machine shops gone Phrobis was forced to look elsewhere for someone to actually produce its M9s, eventually contracting with Marto of Spain.[42]

Buck continued M9 production aimed primarily at U.S. civilian markets, but also struck some contracts with foreign governments, such as Australia, Abu Dhabi, and Japan. Certainly not one to retreat into obscurity, Buck went on to compete for U.S. contracts, such as a small open bid project for the Marine Corps requiring production of 5000 M9 systems. Buck had actually bid against Phrobis for this contract and won, making these 5000 knives the only M9s ever produced exclusively by Buck.

The Phrobis M9P1

The first of these weapons began arriving in units around the middle of 1987, and with them came some unique and interesting challenges for unit leadership and soldiers. If one understands the concept of training, and what it means to *be trained*, it is a short stretch to understanding comfort zones. Until this time soldiers trained with the M7, and no one worried much about sustaining cuts, as the typical M7 bayonet was about as sharp as the leading edge of a Hershey bar! The M9 was an altogether different animal!

In keeping with Buck's tradition of superior blade production, and excellence in fit and finish, M9s being delivered in 1987 possessed a truly razor sharp edge. Many

Figure 90: The M9; issued as a complete kit like the one above.

careless soldiers, accustomed to the blunt M7, immediately fell victim to the M9, creating a seeming epidemic of sliced fingers and variously skewered appendages. Leadership reacted by instituting M9 safety training and modifying various SOPs, and where parades once included fixed bayonets they now featured fixed, *sheathed* M9s. Likewise, other bayonet exercises required sheathing as a safety precaution. Without doubt, this new weapon was more knife than bayonet, as early users are ample proof!

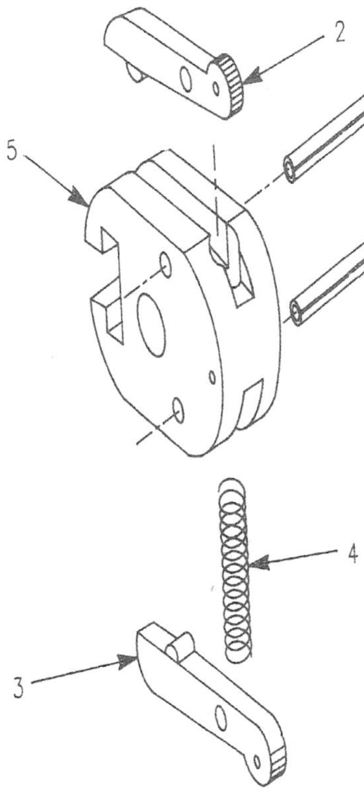

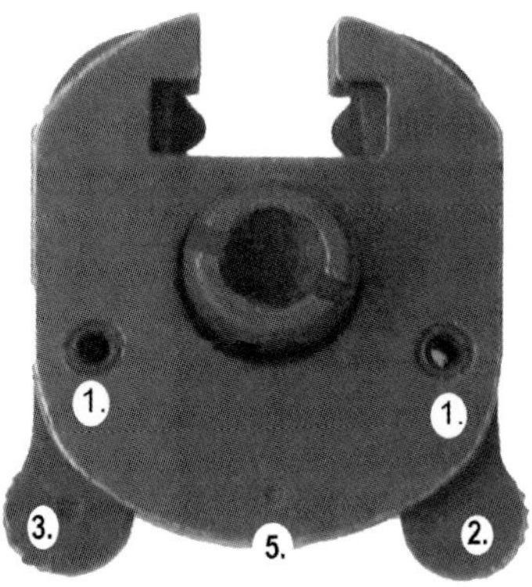

1. PIN, SPRING
2. **LEVER, LOCK RELEASE (RH)**
3. **LEVER, LOCK RELEASE (LH)**
4. **SPRING, HELICAL, COMPRESSION**
5. **LATCH, PLATE**

Figure 91: Latch Assemblies on all M9P series are identical in design.

The M9P1 is the first iteration issued, and easily recognizable by its ricasso markings: *M9, Phrobis III, U.S.A.* >; it is frequently referred to as the *3 line chevron* M9, as the *greater than symbol* symbol is the premier feature distinguishing the M9P1 from the rest in this series. This variation is addressed later in detail, as the focus of this section is to examine each component of the MPBS system individually, beginning with the *Latch Assembly.*

With the exception of the P1, the latch assembly of the M9 is for all practical purposes identical to that found on the M7. In the case of the P1, whose sides have a very noticeable, rounded appearance, standard assemblies are flat sided as in the photo below, because as with other entities involved in designing machines, the Army strives to use common components when and wherever possible, whether for fiscal considerations or logistical interoperability. Aside from those considerations, this particular latch assembly is very ergonomic, and thus quite easy to operate with one hand. It is also extremely reliable and simple, as one can discern from the diagram below.

One can easily disassemble the M9 by removing the *cap screw*, using either a hex wrench or large flat-tip screwdriver. This screw, located by looking at the face of the *latch assembly* (as in the above diagram), is directly in the center of the assembly.

After removal of the cap screw, one may separate the latch assembly easily from the rear of the handle and the *tang extension*. The handle can then be slid rearward and removed from the tang extension, leaving only the *blade, hand guard, and tang extension.* Compared to the M6 and M7 bayonets, disassembly of the M9 is a snap, and just another reason for its popularity with the Army.

Not only did soldiers naturally warm to the brutish M9, but found it to be surprisingly ergonomic. While the gently curved scales of the M7 are comfortable, they do allow for maximum purchase, whether wet or dry. The M9's scalloped *Zytel®* handle offers excellent hand traction, and unlike the M7's comparatively fragile scales, the M9's handle is just less than indestructible, exactly because of its resin composition.

Figure 91.1: Above and left is the M9P1 latch plate, whose sides are slightly curved compared to the one on the right, which is the design found on all other variations and has very straight sides.

Interestingly, DuPont's versatile Zytel® nylon resin is not new, as DuPont chemists developed it in the 1930s. During World War II the U.S. government encouraged plastics substitution in an effort to conserve strategic metal reserves, which encouraged DuPont to apply its new nylon resin to the production of engine gears, cams, valves, and ball bearings.

Following World War II, DuPont chose the name Zytel® for its new resin plastic, promoting it as a lightweight, heavy-duty industrial and engineering material. And, while DuPont talked up Zytel's® ability to resist heat and corrosive chemicals, the material tended to crack when notched by faulty molds, or its surface became scratched.

Figure 92: The M9 handle is a one-piece molded structure made of Zytel®, which is resistant to heat, corrosive chemicals, and has the ability to insulate the user from high electrical voltage.

Zytel's® propensity to crack was overcome in 1973 when DuPont researcher Bennet N. Epstein created *Super Tough Zytel® ST* by mixing small amounts of other resins into the original formula. Epstein's application proved fortuitous during the oil shortage of 1973, as Zytel® ST was ideal for automotive fuel tanks and certain interior components, as well as strong enough for molding into engine parts; all measures that saved gas by reducing vehicle weight.

Soon afterwards, other manufacturers began using Zytel® to make parts for appliances and many other home and sporting good products. Since then *Zytel® HTN* or high temperature nylon, has been formulated for use where poisonous chemicals and environments characterized by extreme temperature and/or humidity exist.

Returning to disassembly, the next step is removal of the tang extension, which secures the hand guard against the rear of the blade. Accomplishment of its removal may be effected using any one of a variety of wrenches. Turning the tang counterclockwise until it separates from the blade assembly allows the hand guard to slide off, completing the disassembly process.

The removable tang extension is quite a useful innovation, in that it allows the soldier to maintain an overall tight condition of all the components. In the case of the M6 and M7, the entire assemblies are held together by peening the end of the tang into a rivet configuration. Should the riveting become loosened, a vice and hammer are required in order to repeen it—obviously not a field operation. With the M9 no such situation will occur.

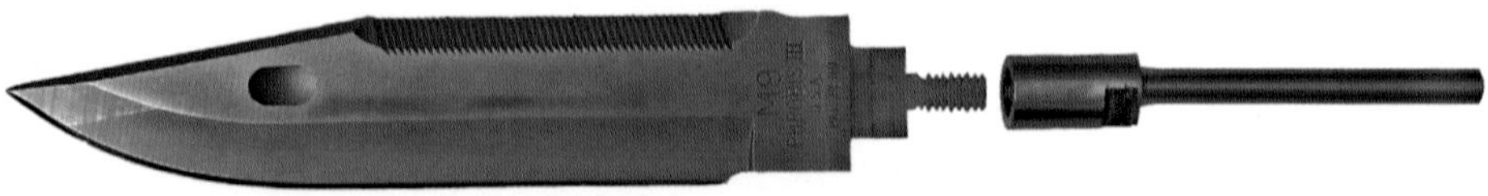

Figure 93: Removing the tang by turning it counterclockwise until separation from the blade assembly.

The hand guard, pictured in Figure 94, is probably the most multi-purpose component of the entire MPBS system. This flat, stamped piece of steel serves to attach the bayonet to the rifle, protect the hand from sliding forward onto the blade, has two bottle openers, maintains tension on the blade as part of the overall assembly, and has an eyelet to which a lanyard may be attached. That is five functions in one; not bad for a piece of flat steel!

The M9P series absolutely exudes Buck quality, the halmark upon which the Buck Knife Company's reputation is built! Especially impressive are its fit and finish, as well as being wonderfully complimented by the Buck process of bead blasting. This finishing process gives the metal a marvelously uniform satin finish and, in spite of its silver appearance, it actually does not reflect light as much as one might imagine.

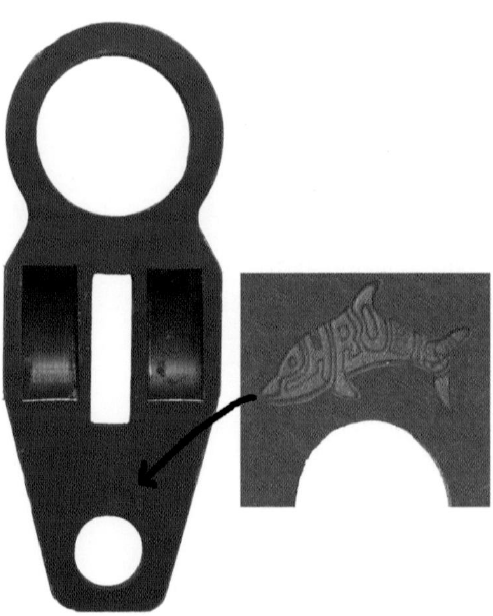

Figure 94: Phrobis logo shown here is stamped on all M9P series bayonets.

In fact, everything about the early M9s was simply dazzling in quality! That is not to imply that other Army equipment is generally inferior, as any such suggestion would be nonsense; however, even superior equipment can appear perfectly utilitarian. And, while the M7 is a fine bayonet of excellent quality, next to the M9 it appears anachronistic, even crude. The M9's flashy, brutish refinement was not what soldiers were accustomed to, and was, in part, responsible for its immediate popularity.

The original M9 quality was in part due to the superb materials used, such as the 425 stainless steel[43] and heat-treating to provide the cutting surfaces with 58 to 59 Rockwell C hardness, the blade being 54 to 55 Rockwell. Even today, it is standard at Buck Knives to put each blade through a precisely controlled and duplicated heat treatment.

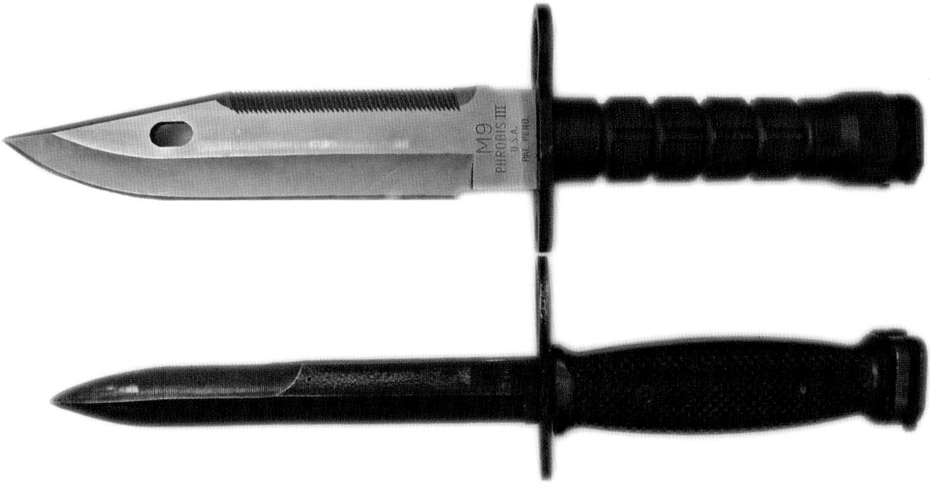

Figure 95: While both bayonets are quality pieces, the M9 exudes refinement.

At Buck, heat-treating consists of raising the steel to a *high temperature* (company secret), then cooling by allowing it to return to room temperature. The blade is then placed in a cryogenic freezer where the temperature is below zero, after which the blade is again allowed to return to room temperature. Finally, the steel once again undergoes heating, wherein it is very slowly raised to between 350 and 950 degrees depending on the steel type and knife function. For instance, high carbon steel, of 420 grade, undergoing this process would come out at 58 on the Rockwell Scale of Hardness.[44]

Of particular interest to collectors are the numerous *faux pas* that have occurred during production, resulting in unusual variations which are now highly sought after. Ironically, the initial M9 contract actually kicked off with technically flawed knives, which the reader will discover is not unique to this variation, but is just one of many changes and associated anomalies that have plagued the weapon throughout its entire production span, and consequently is responsible for nearly twenty different M9 variations.

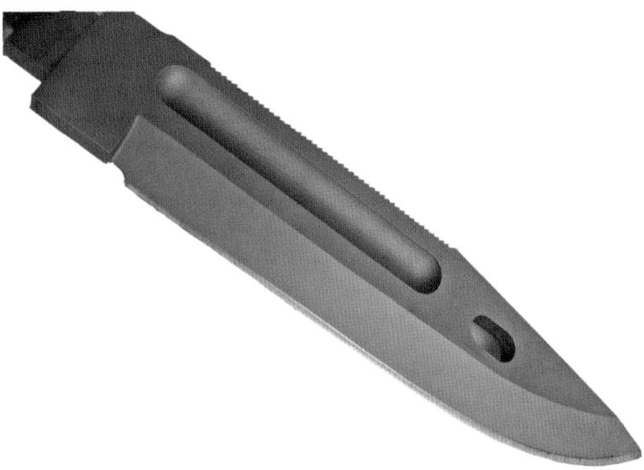

Figure 96: Early M9s came from the factory with a razor sharp edge and the marvelous bead-blasted finish that is characteristic of Buck quality.

The P1, or *first generation* M9 as produced by Buck, is immediately recognizable by the greater than symbol stamped into the obverse ricasso as shown above. As it happened, the initial run of M9s came at a time when Buck was phasing in a new date coding system for its knives using simple keyboard symbols to represent dates of manufacture, which were routinely stamped into the ricasso of all Buck knives.

It is not unreasonable, then, to see how Buck knife makers probably just complied with the new company policy without giving it much thought when they stamped the *chevron* into the M9's blades. In fact, in the rush to get the first M9s to user units Army inspectors did not stop production, even though the marking was not in compliance with the *Technical Data Package,* which specifically detailed how each blade was to be marked. Perhaps they actually overlooked the flaw, or perhaps they did not consider it worthy of note, as it did not effect performance or function of the knife; their reasoning is not known.[45]

Figure 97: The P1, or first Generation M9, is often referred to as the 3 line chevron M9.

What we do know is that *someone* noticed, because Material Review Report Number 002, dated 16 January 1987, put Buck on notice that the *chevron* was an unauthorized marking, and that such activity must stop. Buck subsequently acknowledged the order in an interoffice memorandum dated 20 January 1987,[46] but this was after 1200 of the bayonets left the production line, and 1034 had entered the logistics pipeline. The remaining 166 Phrobis held back for use in constructing commemorative presentation plaques. This one, small, innocent mistake has resulted in the most sought after and rarest of all the M9 variations.

Caution is advised, however, as other knives from that year also bear the date symbol, though fortunately, just as obvious is the marking *Buck 188* on the flipside (reverse ricasso). No military contract bayonet should bear any markings on the reverse ricasso.

YEAR	SYMBOL	YEAR	SYMBOL
1986	<	1996	⊃
1987	>	1997	∩
1988	∧	1998	∪
1989	∨	1999	⊏
1990	×	2000	⊐
1991	+	2001	⊓
1992	–	2002	[illegible]
1993	/	2003	⊤
1994	\	2004	⊥
1995	⊂	2005	[illegible]
		2006	⊣

Figure 98: Buck date symbols. Generally, a corresponding symbol is stamped on the ricasso of all Buck knives denoting the date it was made.

Also noted by Buck Quality Assurance, these early M9s possessed discrepancies, such as uneven hollow grinds, dips in the grind near the point, flat spots and rolls on the edges, broaching tears, and improper application of the oxide coating to the *cutter plate, quillon, and latch plate*. Some further observations included improper cleaning of parts prior to application of the coating, as well as instances of raw material found with oxide on it. Generally, the critique included relatively small fit and finish issues, though given Buck's reputation such matters warranted on the spot correction.

The tip provides for a wire cutter plate, and includes an integral screwdriver tool. Also obvious in the above photo is the *Phrobis dolphin* located between the stone and rear strap snap. All Phrobis M9s feature this marking.

Figure 99: (Reverse view) The scabbard features a sharpening stone, flanked by two integral strapping loops.

Aside from the wire cutter, a significant feature integral to the scabbard is the sharpening stone, obviously intended to provide the soldier a convenient means of repairing the bayonet edge, and while it does in fact serve its intended purpose it does so, at best, very poorly. Actually, in this author's opinion, the stone's principle shortcoming, functionally, is the length, as it is much too short to achieve a full throw to the edge. However, in a pinch it will do.

Figure 100: Front view of M9 wire cutter plate. When the bayonet blade is fitted over the plate stud a scissor configuration is formed. With one hand holding the bayonet handle and one grasping the sheath, cutting wire can be accomplished by pulling each device toward the other just as if using pruning shears or bolt cutters.

From an operational point of view, the stone is subject to loss and breakage, which is the precise reason early models came equipped with a protective strap that secured over the stone via a snap. This method did a good job of keeping the stone in place, but breakage continued to be problematic.

The multipurpose qualities of the M9 are, in large part, possible because of the scabbard's design, which includes integral strapping loops that allow for numerous suspension configurations, as well as wear with a wide variety of individual load bearing equipment systems.

Military specifications require that the scabbard be designed in such a way as to facilitate rapid removal of the tool with one hand, but not otherwise distract the soldier from the task at hand. The specifications are satisfied nicely using two rather simple mechanisms.

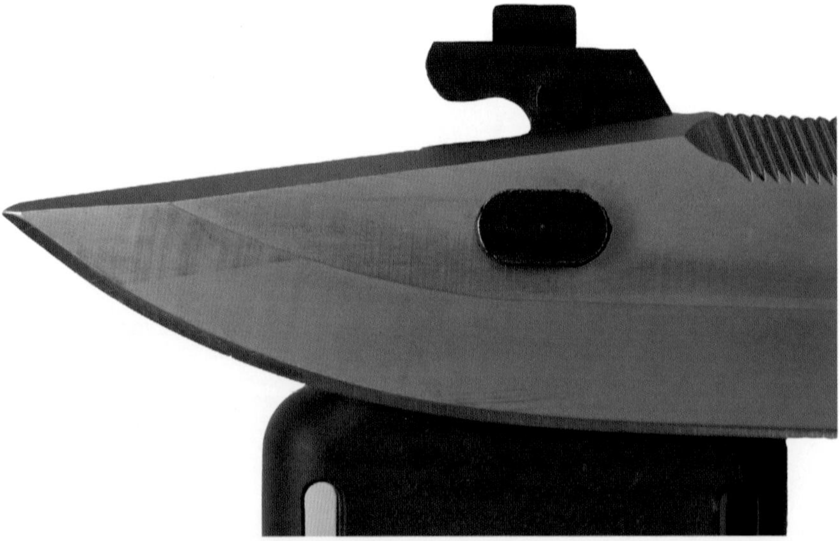

Figure 101: The feature sought after by the Army for at least eighty years: a wire cutter feature integral to the bayonet.

Figure 102: The sharpening stone is glued into a recess in the scabbard's reverse as shown above.

The suspension assembly is composed of a wire clamp for attachment of the weapon to the load bearing equipment's (LBE) pistol belt. The device was patented by Bianchi as a component of his Universal Military Holster, and the assembly is comprised of a plate having a *U* shaped wire spring appendage, which passes through a rolled tube integral to the top of the plate, which acts as a hinge.

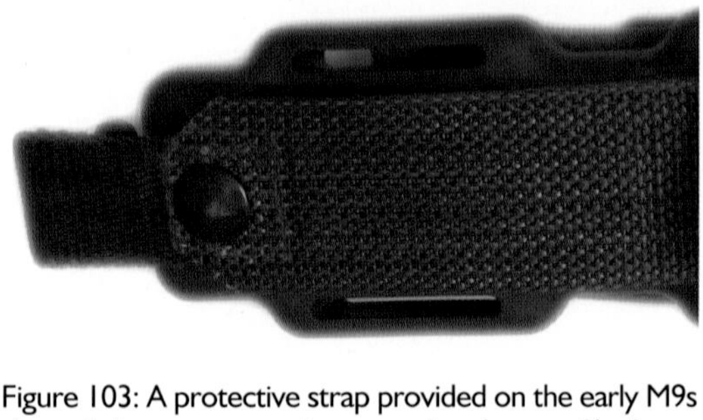

Figure 103: A protective strap provided on the early M9s intended to protect against stone breakage and/or loss.

At the bottom of the plate are two integral rolled tubes with open sides facing inwardly which accept the distal ends of the appendages, and result in the belt being clamped between the two. This arrangement allows attachment to a variety of

Figure104: The quick disconnect assembly makes it possible to rapidly remove the scabbard from the suspension unit (below) using only one hand (per MIL Specs).

Figure 105: Suspension assembly (Load Bearing) in open position.

Figure 106: View of Suspension Assembly (Load Bearing) in semi-closed position. To complete closure the two clip *legs* are squeezed and pushed between the two tabs then released, whereupon it is locked securely.

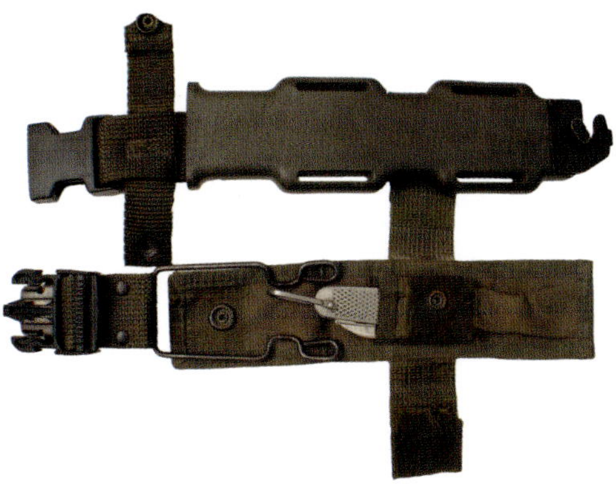

belt types and dimensions, and is easily removed or attached, but this does not satisfy the MILSPEC requirement.

The component that does satisfy the requirement, allowing the soldier to remove the bayonet with one hand and without distracting him from the task at hand, is the quick disconnect fastener. Shown below is the device as it appears upon removal of the bayonet and scabbard from the suspension assembly. By squeezing the lateral clips between the thumb and forefinger while simultaneously pulling downward, the unit may be disengaged from the load bearing equipment. It is simple, easy, and reliable.

Of interest to collectors is that the early scabbard rigs were equipped with quick disconectors manufactured by FASTEX of Des Plaines, IL, whereas the later Lancay and OKC rigs came from ITW NEXUS of Wood Dale, IL. However, FASTEX is the entity that patented the device.

The Phrobis M9P2

The next variation of the M9 was created when Buck removed its date symbol, and is identified here as the M9P2, or the *second generation,* as it is known to many collectors. Whether it is technically correct to refer to it as a generation is debatable, and as discussed earlier, P2 is the designation used here for clarity. Beyond the name, and Buck's date code, there is no difference between the two knives.

More correctly, there is no difference between the two knives structurally. As collectors know, the P1s are very rare given the low numbers produced, whereas the P2s are much more abundant, and generally referred to as the *crazy nine* because of the font used.

Figure 107: View of the M9 system minus the bayonet. Of note is the issue pocketknife in the magazine pouch.

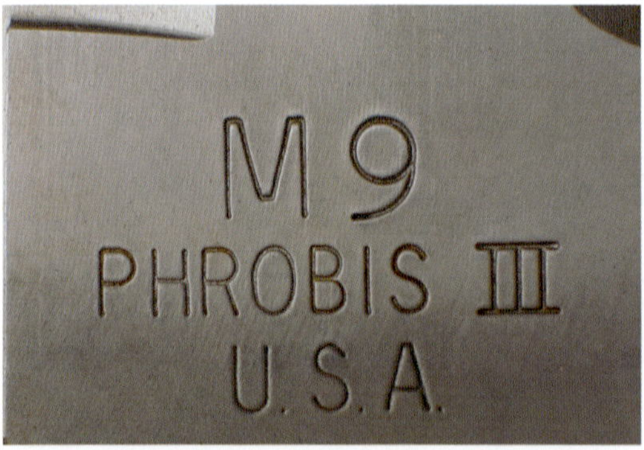

Figure 108: The P2, or Second Generation M9, as produced by Buck. Note that the only difference is the absence of the Buck chevron.

Figure 109: Note above the change from brass rivets (left) to steel rivets (right) on the suspension assembly.

While very few changes to the Phrobis generation M9s ever saw the light of day, the Army did allow a limited number of minor alterations in design, such as those demonstrated in the comparative photo in Figure 109 below. This comparison demonstrates a change from brass rivets (on the left) to steel rivets (on the right) of the suspension assembly. Exactly when this change took place is unknown, though brass was certainly used on the M9P1 and M9P2.

Figure 110: The P3, or Third Generation. Note that the crazy nine font has been replaced by a rounded number nine.

The Phrobis M9P3

At some point Buck changed the font used on their dies, as evidenced by the P3's variation of the crazy nine font, which was replaced by a more rounded number nine and a less square letter M. Otherwise, no changes have been noted.

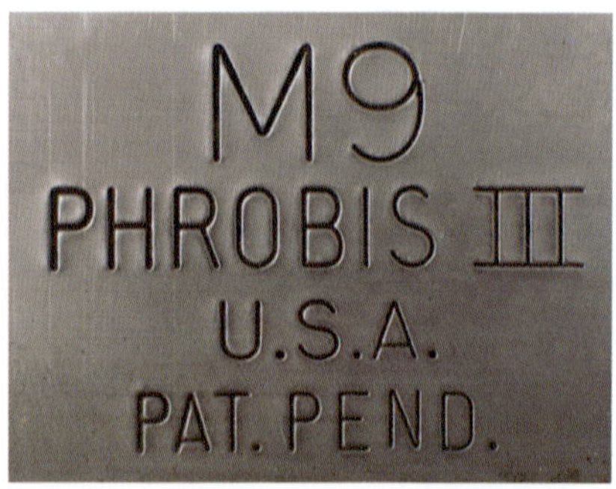

Figure 111: The P4, or Fourth Generation M9, retains the same font but has an additional line.

The Phrobis M9P4

The P4 variation differs from all previous variants, in that a Phrobis added a fourth line, proclaiming that a patent was pending. Aside from qualifying this version as a separate variant, this fourth line enables the collector to assign an approximate date to the piece, as the contract ended in 1989, and obviously this knife cannot be older than that year. Also known is that Mr. Finn applied for his patent on 13 March 1987, and received its approval on 18 April 1989.[47] Therefore, this variation was made sometime between March 1987 and 1989.

The Phrobis M9P5

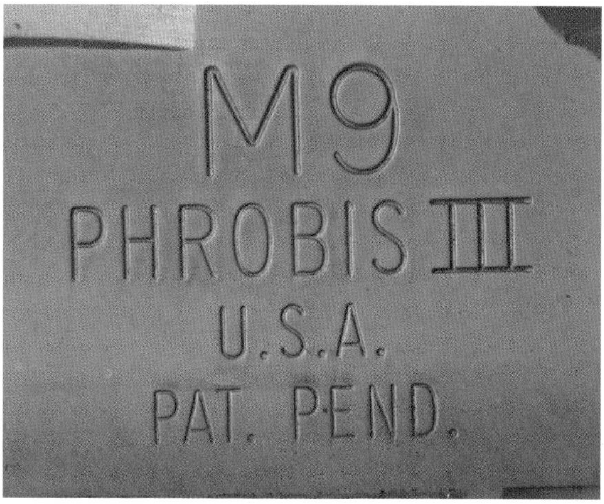

Figure 112: The P5, or Fifth Generation M9, retains the additional line, but has once more undergone a font change.

The P5 variation is described variously as being a small font, or some sources call it a narrow font. Regardless, it possesses a unique font, and is obviously of later production than the P4, as the P4 has the same font as the P3 but an additional line. So, the font on the P4 was in use prior to the additional line being added.

Having covered the entire system, discussed all the major components, as well as the peculiarities used to discriminate between variations, the only component, albeit an unofficial one, remaining to examine is the small vertical scabbard case. Know to many in the collecting community as the *magazine pouch* and to many infantrymen of the late 1980's as the *accessory pouch,* this small, relatively short lived accessory has arguably become the center of more contention than perhaps any other single aspect of the M9 system.

Human nature, being what it is, leads most otherwise reasonable people to stubbornly cling to whatever tradition they have integrated into their behavior, even to the point of including the names they assign to objects. If at this point the reader surmises that the author expects to make a case for a particular name and that because the evidence is logical others will call the pouch this or that he is completely mistaken. This author knows people much too well for that. The intention here is to simply layout the facts and present the logical conclusion. If some choose to accept it that's super, if not, the objective and the facts will in any event remain.

Generally objects are named for their function and certainly the Army is steeped in the functional tradition. It is therefore valid to ask what the function of the pouch is as well as *whose* actual, or intended, function should be the final determining factor considered when naming it. How one answers this a question will most likely determine what that person chooses to call the pouch.

As collectors, we frequently encounter many markings and objects that are new to us, outside our realm of expertise, or that defy obvious identification. Filling this knowledge void, in any field or disciple, is the function of the *popular culture* which is replete with endless answers and explanations to nearly any mystery. As such, one has the option of accepting the common dogma, or going it alone in an effort to ferret out the facts. For these latter individuals who are more difficult to convince, and when references fail, the next best approach is to simply apply some old-fashioned *cultural forensics*. That is to say, try to understand the frame of reference from whence the object in question originates.

For example, when considering bayonets, one generally associates them with infantrymen and rifles. Experienced militaria collectors, and those who study or are familiar with general military history, will quickly note that while WW2 German soldiers commonly carried both pistol and rifle, it is traditionally *not* an America Army practice to issue pistols to those assigned rifles. Within the Army, generally, the only soldiers who are issued pistols are those members of crew-served weapons teams, commanders, and other staff officers and NCOs.

Therefore, a reasonable question to ponder might be why a rifleman would have a pistol magazine anywhere, much less attached to his bayonet scabbard. For those who are novices, or just are not that familiar with the military, or the Army in particular, it is beneficial to note that the Army, for generations, has published a Modified *Table of Organization and Equipment*, or *MTO&E*.

Figure 112.1: Above: The pouch on the left is a magazine pouch containing a GP knife as issued with the M9 System. The pouch shown on the right is a standard issue magazine pouch containing one each Beretta M9 pistol magazine.

This publication is, essentially, a document that lists by line and item, the number and kind of equipment a particular unit is authorized to have, the number of rifles, bayonets, etc. Therefore, each individual soldier is assigned the type and kind of weapon, and other equipment, based on duty position (*MOS*, or job if you will) as specified by the unit TO&E. A cursory look at such a document will quickly show that no one is authorized a bayonet, unless also assigned a rifle: no rifle, no bayonet! Logic then dictates that a pistol magazine would have no relevant, or practical, use attached to a rifle component such as a bayonet scabbard.

While documentary evidence is critical in determining many facts, so too is other primary source evidence such as bona fide eye witness accounts. In this case the author can without reservation testify to relevant events during the mid-eighties, when the Army adopted the M9 bayonet, as at the time he was assigned to a mechanized infantry battalion.

Following Forces Command's, or *FORSCOM's*, decision to upgrade infantry units, M9 bayonets were shipped from depot to target installations where they were distributed directly to individual company arms rooms throughout the battalions. That is, each company's armorer, and supply representative, drew their company's allotment of M9's directly from post depot *en mass*.

There followed a command directive to provision each M9 unit with a *Knife, Pocket, General Purpose*,[48] which became integral to the *kit* being secured in what was generally known as the *accessory pouch*. It should also be noted that applicable *hand receipts* listed only the M9 system; no mention of the pouch was ever observed on any document other than the unofficial user's manual which will be addressed later.

Whether such a supply action was confined to sporadic local policy, or dictated by higher organizational command is unclear, though numerous other former infantrymen have confirmed that their units did the same, so it was at least widely practiced. Infact, an article appearing in the March 1986 edition of *Soldiers Magazine* sheds some interesting light on the subject.

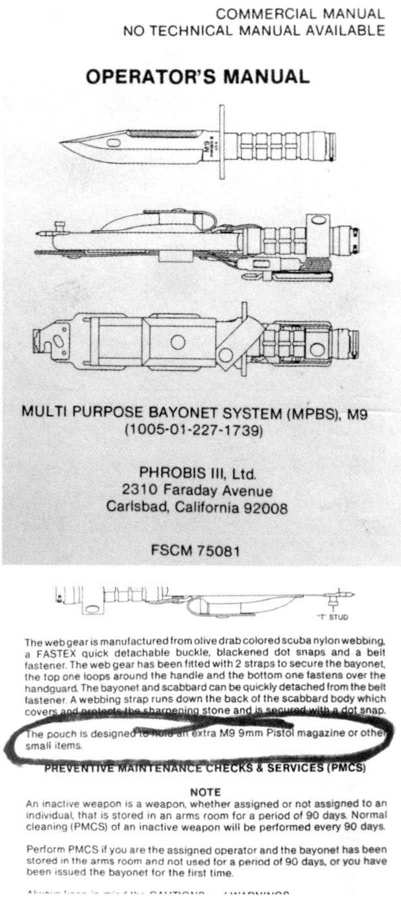
COMMERCIAL MANUAL
NO TECHNICAL MANUAL AVAILABLE

OPERATOR'S MANUAL

MULTI PURPOSE BAYONET SYSTEM (MPBS), M9
(1005-01-227-1739)

PHROBIS III, Ltd.
2310 Faraday Avenue
Carlsbad, California 92008

FSCM 75081

STUD

The web gear is manufactured from olive drab colored scuba nylon webbing, a FASTEX quick detachable buckle, blackened dot snaps and a belt fastener. The web gear has been fitted with 2 straps to secure the bayonet, the top one loops around the handle and the bottom one fastens over the handguard. The bayonet and scabbard can be quickly detached from the belt fastener. A webbing strap runs down the back of the scabbard body which covers and protects the sharpening stone and is secured with a dot snap.

The pouch is designed to hold an extra M9 9mm Pistol magazine or other small items.

PREVENTIVE MAINTENANCE CHECKS & SERVICES (PMCS)

NOTE

An inactive weapon is a weapon, whether assigned or not assigned to an individual, that is stored in an arms room for a period of 90 days. Normal cleaning (PMCS) of an inactive weapon will be performed every 90 days.

Perform PMCS if you are the assigned operator and the bayonet has been stored in the arms room and not used for a period of 90 days, or you have been issued the bayonet for the first time.

Figure 112.2: Above: The *Operator's Manual* supplied by the manufacturer, but not an official Army publication.

Major George Birdsong of the Infantry Center Small Arms Branch, Directorate of Combat Developments, said of the M9:

"...the infantry had a bayonet that any right-thinking warrior could proudly display as a symbol of his calling...The tough, quick-release sheath has a built-in sharpening stone, a detachable pouch for a pocket knife and converts for use by lefties."

If the fellows at development thought the pouch was for a pocket knife it's pretty clear that that's what it was intended for; at least from the Army's point of view. And, since this IS an Army topic, one would rationally expect others to defer to the Army.

Aside from the above, exactly how and why the pouch came to be included in the M9 MPBS kit is still very unclear. What is certain is that this author has been unable to find any Mil Spec requirement for such a pouch, no contract orders have surfaced showing requests for pouch replacements, and it is not listed as a scabbard component in any contract order or Army supply action, nor is it made mention of in the M9 patent.

Again, the only known reference found calling it a *magazine pouch* is the small Phrobis Operator's Manual. These publications were provided by Phrobis with each bayonet, but were not official Army references. Nonetheless, the publication, states that "the pouch is designed to hold an extra M9, 9mm pistol magazine *or* other small items."

This verbiage as used above has all the flavor of an after thought, and taken within such context one can easily understand Mr. Finn to mean that the pouch *could* be used for storing magazines, or other small items, or for whatever one saw fit. From such a statement it is very difficult to imagine that he had any singular premeditated intention for the pouch other than as a notions bag – a small, yet handy, nice to have accessory.

Such casual interpretations as the above seldom satisfy the critical mind which endlessly ruminate over the question of what Mr. Finn actually intended the pouch be used for? The search for that answer culminated in finally admitting that since all avenues and efforts heretofore were exhausted, and without the slightest meaningful insight, it became obvious that the simplest, best course of action was to simply ask the man himself. To this end the author wrote to Mr. Finn simply asking what he had intended when designing the pouch. Had he meant it specifically for magazine stowage, or was that just and off the cuff suggestion?

The reply came from Charles Finn with the very sad news that his father had passed away the year before. This was tragically disappointing news as this author is a long time admirer of Mr. Finn. Equally distressing was the reality that America had lost a staunch patriot, an exceptional designer, an innovative entrepreneur, and simply just a plain *good man*! And while it is not possible to say enough good things about the man himself, it is just as impossible to imagine the loss his family has sustained!

Such terrible news certainly blunted this author's desire to dig deeply into the subject, though Charles offered valuable insight into the issue by confirming that his father had indeed intended that the pouch be used to carry spare pistol magazines, and that Mr. Finn was rather adamant that the MPBS be employed as a system with all of its components.

Without doubt this information provides greater insight into the designer's intent though it does not, nor could any reasonable person expect that it would, explain what Mr. Finn's thought process had been which prompted him to arrive at such a decision. In other words, why did he design it for pistol magazines; what were his reasons and what did he base them on? While it would be supremely interesting to have these answers we are obviously left to our own devices to derive such conclusions.

Ultimately, while giving all possible respect and deference to Mr. Finn, it is necessarily tempting to surmise that the designer spent so much time working with Special Forces that his operational perspective became too focused. That is, Special Forces personnel generally carry both long and side arms. For them any extra storage for ammunition is desirable and makes absolute sense for one who is designing equipment in consideration of special, or elite, mission requirements. The same cannot be said when considering the needs of conventional forces, especially given the infantry's unique role.

Conversely, the argument could be made that Mr. Finn's operational perspective exceeds the author's estimations, in that he actually provided for both elite and conventional force requirements as evidenced by his statement that; "the pouch is designed to hold an *extra M9, 9mm pistol magazine OR other small items*." Certainly one could reasonably interpret this to mean "… Special Forces can use the pouch to store an extra M9 magazine, and all the rest can use it for other small items." Such interpretation would cover all possible circumstances and essentially make the pouch a multipurpose or universal component – very much in character with Mickey Finn's penchant for *multipurposing*.

What is certain is that this author knows of no time when the pouch was employed as, known, or ever called a *magazine pouch* within the ranks. Moreover, the Army also apparently failed to pickup on Mr. Finn's intention as evidenced by the Technical Manual, which makes no mention of any such item. To be exact, TM 9-1005-237-23&P specifically states that "The M9 Multipurpose Bayonet System scabbard consists of four major parts; the scabbard body, wire cutter plate, attaching assembly load bearing end, and attaching assembly scabbard end." Therefore, technically, officially, the pouch does not actually exist! Further noteworthy is the fact that during the first contract every system came with a pouch but all subsequent contracts omitted it.

Finally, one must concede that the pouch was designed for carrying extra M9 pistol magazines, however evidence demonstrates that such was not an Army policy, that there was no institutional requirement or need for such an item, and that the prevailing general, and unofficial, practice was to use the item as *a notions pouch*.

And so, each can make his own individual decision as to the pouch's most appropriate name. In the end though, the preponderance of evidence weighs in favor of those, and the Army in general, who refer to it as an *accessory pouch*.

8

Kentucky Calling

Production

The town of Carrollton, Kentucky, is located at the confluence of the Kentucky and Ohio rivers, just off Exit 44 of Interstate 71, and is at the midpoint between Cincinnati and Louisville. Established in 1794 as Port William, its namesake being the Maryland home of Charles Carroll, the last living signer of the Declaration of Independence; it is also home to LAN-CAY, Inc.

According to Kentucky Secretary of State Records, the business first organized in 1989 under the name LAN *CAY, Inc* though now it is listed as *inactive*. A second active name is listed as LAN-CAY, Inc.

Wife and current President, Patricia C. Brown, in an interview with a Kentucky magazine, related that in 1992 her husband, Barry Brown, closed his furniture store in Warsaw, KY, when he learned that the Defense Department routinely contracted small businesses to provide various items of supply. It was at that point that he moved to Carrollton in order to establish his new business. An examination of DoD records show that contract number DAAA09-92-C-0406 was awarded on 31 March 1992, coinciding with Mrs. Brown's account of the company's startup date.

By all accounts a practical man, Mr. Brown acquired an old manufacturing plant in the industrial section of town as the new home for LAN-CAY operations. Far from modern or stylish, the building is reputedly a spacious and accommodating facility for the twenty-some odd employees who work there.

These varied employees busy themselves turning out M9 bayonets and a number of other devices, including M19 blank firing adapters, M2 flash hiders, Gerber multi-tools, EOD pouches, and the M11 knife, as well as custom blades, and of course the M9 bayonet.

All indications are that the company has made great strides since first opening, and DoD contracts are primarily responsible for the bulk of LAN-CAY's business. Mr. Brown is obviously a very perceptive businessman, as he beat out multiple bidders in order to secure the initial M9 contract, which opened the doors to what has become, from all outward appearances, a very lucrative endeavor.

Such success, as any businessman will testify to, does not come easy or cheap. In the competition for contract number DAAA09-92-C-0406 Mr. Brown won it by offering to make each M9 unit for $46.80. Phrobis, in 1986, was costing the DoD $48.13 per unit,[49] according to the initial contract filed. Lan-Cay was, obviously, offering the M9 in 1992 at a lower price than Phrobis charged 6 years earlier. Not a bad deal for the government.

Phrobis has given the collector a nice variety of M9s with interesting anomalies to make each variation unique. Moreover, Phrobis and Buck have turned out M9s of superb quality, each exuding traditional American quality and workmanship. LAN-CAY is providing a quality product at reasonable prices, and they have every reason to be proud of their work—though it is quite utilitarian compared to the Buck and Phrobis knives.

In all fairness, the current M9 is exactly what the DoD specified, and its Spartan appearance has nothing to do with LAN-CAY; they are simply following instructions. Someone once said that the early M9s were more knife than bayonet, and that the later M9s were more bayonet than knife. That is certainly a true statement and an astute assessment of the M9 line.

At any rate, LAN-CAY, as well as the DoD, have given the collector a large number of variations primarily because the Army wanted to change the M9 design to better suit Army priorities. Such *dabbling* is responsible for so many design changes, though most were small.

In Appendix B under *classification*, there are no less than NINE variations of LAN-CAY M9s! That is a remarkable number, and a boon to the collector. If one follows the classification table the first is the *M9/G1*.

The M9/G1 – General Cutlery

The designation *M9/G1* is appropriate, as LAN-CAY subcontracted the company of General Cutlery for production of the first of its M9 blades. Presumably, during this time LAN-CAY was still in the process of bringing their machinery on line at the Carrollton plant.

While General Cutlery provided blades, LAN-CAY performed the final assembly of the units at their Kentucky plant. This arrangement continued until problems with the General Cutlery blades became known. And, while several sources mention that there were *quality control issues* with the General Cutlery blades, none have given specific details. Nonetheless, somewhere in the neighborhood of 300[50] from General Cutlery entered the logistics pipeline, and naturally that makes these particularly unique and desirable pieces for the collector.

Figure 113: Author's rendition of a 1st contract M9 by LAN-CAY subcontractor General Cutlery. These are extremely rare, as only about 300 were made.

Figure 114: The General Cutlery locking assembly should be unmarked.

Figure 115: All General Cutlery units came with the early style cutter plates.

Figure 116: General Cutlery units would have had 1992 dated FASTEX connectors.

Since apparently there was a large number of General Cutlery blades that failed to meet acceptance standards, the collector should be cautious of any specimens offered for sale. Because collectors frequently are unable to be 100% certain of a piece's origin, especially these days when *knockoffs* are so prevalent, and frankly the quality is so good, the old truisms must be relied on more now than ever. The top three being: 1) Rely on instinct; 2) The reputation of the seller; and 3) Objective details of the piece.

In the case of the General Cutlery blades one thing is certain, and that is that the locking assembly should be unmarked. If it is marked with any variation of LanCay it is not an original configuration. As well, the unit should include an early scabbard with the screwdriver at the tip of the cutter plate, and a 1992 dated FASTEX connector.

General Cutlery's participation in the realm of M9s did not end with its Lan-Cay subcontract, for as one can see from the data found in Appendix E, the company secured individual contracts beginning in May 1996, wherein under DAAE20-96-C-0224 it was to supply $91,969.00 worth of M9 scabbards. Subsequently in June 2002, per DAAE20-02-P-0136, General Cutlery again contracted to provide 2,889 scabbards at a cost of $13,428.00, making each unit's cost $4.69; seemingly a bargain price.

The M9/L1

The *M9/L1*, per specification, is no different from the General Cutlery (*M9G1*), as it is a continuation of the same contract. The difference from this point and forward is that Lan-Cay assumed production of their own blades, made at Lan-Cay on their machines, and naturally the markings are uniquely their own.

The M9/L1 is easily identifiable, in that it is three lines with LanCay stamped in all capitol letters, with the *L* and *C* being larger than the rest. Another difference collectors will notice between the early Lan-Cay and Phrobis bayonets is the finish.

Figure 117: The M9/L1 above with markings highlighted for better visibility. Easily identifiable by the three line marking having LanCay stamped in all capitol letters.

Blades continue unfinished, at this point, as specifications had yet to change, and consequently, both Phrobis and Lan-Cay finishes are the result of each company's peculiar blasting techniques. Whereas Phrobis finishes appear to be almost a white color, Lan-Cay blades are darker, and are reminiscent of a parkerized finish even though they are actually sand blasted.

At this point Lan-Cay had not received any new Mil-Specs, and therefore the early M9/L1s essentially appear no different from the earlier Phrobis models. It still has a fuller *blood groove*, and the blade remains hollow ground.

All of this would change with the new *Product Improved Bayonet* or *PIB,* but in the early days of the contract the PIB changes were still being hashed out at Rock Island Arsenal. However, change was certainly in the wind.

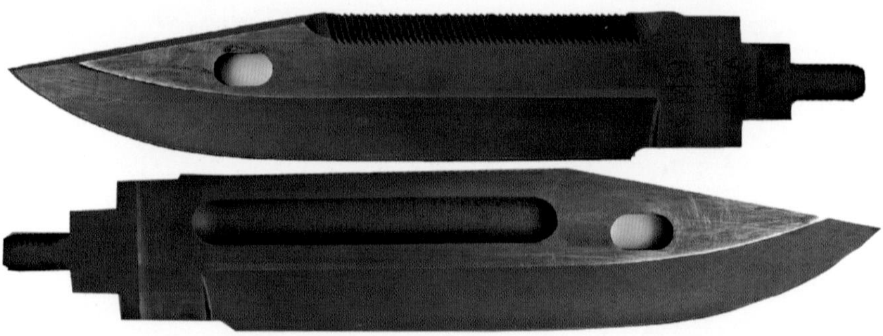

Figure 118: The M9/L1 above appears almost to be parkerized due to Lan-Cay's unique sand blasting technique.

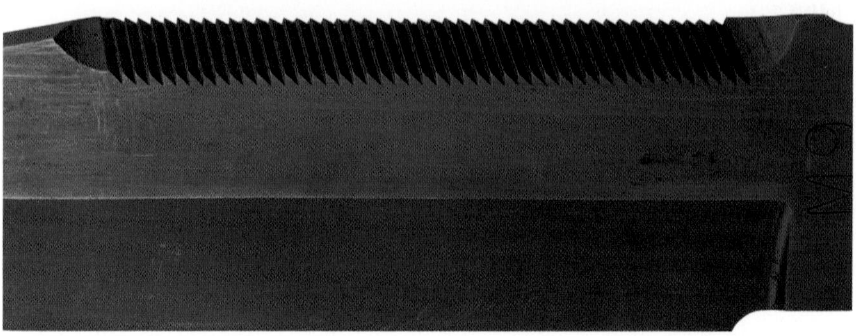

Figure 119: The M9/L1 blade configuration is unchanged from previous Phrobis blades.

Figure 120: The M9/L1's remaining components are also unchanged and unmarked as above.

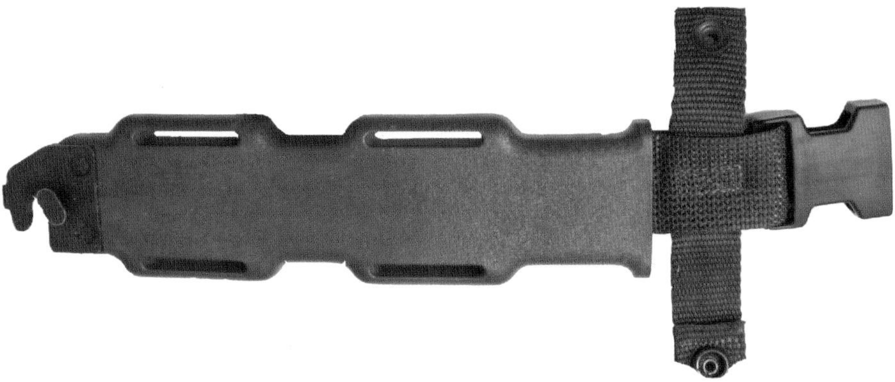

Figure 120.1: The M9/L1's scabbard is also the early design with webbing MWO.

The M9/L1-1

Ostensibly, there had been reports of blade breakage from the field, and the Army sought to rectify the situation by modifying the blade design. For whatever reason attention focused on the fuller as the culprit, and through the issuance of an *Engineering Change Proposal* or *ECP*, the contract depth changed to one-half that of the original. In actuality, the problem appears to have been a tempering glitch, and nothing to do with the fuller.

In the end, the Army decided to eliminate the fuller altogether, but by the time word of the decision reached the people on the ground an estimated 350 blades had made their way into the system.[51] These blades were identical to all before with the exception of having a half, or *shallow*, fuller. The greater impact is that, once again there was produced a rare variation of M9, and a boon to collectors. Obviously, genuine M9s with a half fuller are extremely rare, and command top dollar!

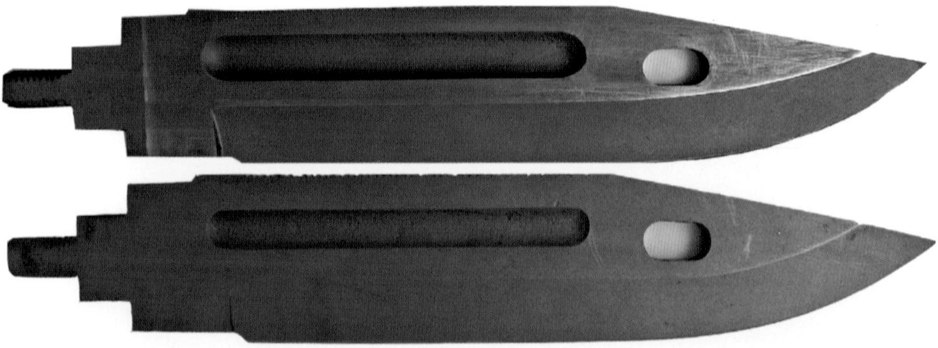

Figure 121: Fullers for comparison: top photo is a full fullered M9/L1; bottom photo shows the M9/L1-1 with its reduced depth fuller.

Having said that, over the past few years quite a number of shallow fullered M9s have appeared on the market, all in near mint condition, and marked as shown in Figure 122B, which is where the real problem lies—the marking. The blades in question carry a hyphenated Lan-Cay mark, which is totally inconsistent with what one of these 350 originals should bear. This would not be possible, as the *shallow fullered* M9s were part of the first contract, and Lan-Cay did not change its name from LanCay until the second contract. Moreover, while there actually was some temporal overlapping of the two contracts, there was not enough to account for this entirely different marking.

In fact, one prominent source lists these blades as *late production*, placing them just before the current M9 production model. While the source does not explain the position, ***it*** is correct in that these blades are without a great deal of doubt reworks that were somehow channeled into the civilian market.

The upshot here is that these very rare M9/L1-1 variations should, in every other respect, have the same appearance as the M9/L1s. An original *shallow fullered* M9 would be marked as shown in Figure 122A. Therefore, to maintain *tidiness*, this variation is designated M9/L1-1, as the first variation of the first contract, and those marked as shown in Figure 122B do not fit into this collection, as they are not original military issue, nor of a variation that was used to fill a military contract.

It goes without saying, that when the Army finally made the decision to eliminate the fuller there were blades already at some stage of completion, and Lan-Cay had little choice but to set them aside. Not only that, but also this M9/L1-1 *wanna be* has a flat-ground blade, whereas the later variation M9/L1-2 retains the traditional hollow-ground edge. While it does occasionally happen, usually companies do not change so quickly from one machining style to another and then back again.

Finally, it appears that after the second contract was well underway, and the company's name changed, the decision was made to sell them. The finishing process would no doubt resume, and therefore result in contemporary markings. In fact, all of these variations encountered by this author also carry the Lan-*Cay* marking on the butt of the pommel. Originals obviously would have unmarked pommels.

Figure 122 (A and B): The M9/L1-1 marking would be LANCAY if production were proceeding consistent with the first contract as pictured on the left. Blades marked as in photo B were obviously made after the company changed names, which was during the second contract.

The M9/L1-2

Process would dictate that had attention been focused on the fuller as the weak spot, and efforts to ameliorate the flaw included decreasing the fuller, then finally eliminating it altogether, that the shallow fuller would continue as a variation devoid of the feature. That is what process would dictate; that is what reasonable people do, and that is what this author has done from a nomenclature perspective.

Gleefully leaving the shallow fullered blade behind, attention is directed to the *Non-fullered* M9, which is known here as the M9/L1-2, or the second variation of the first contract. This blade—actually the entire rig—is different only in two respects.

Figure 123: The M9/L1-2 marking is LANCAY, consistent with first contract markings, and yet must by virtue of process be placed after the M9/L-1.

First, and most obvious, it is devoid of a fuller. No fuller. Not apparent, and frankly this author has no idea how it would be, is the fact that at this point all Lan-Cay blades were changed from forge cut to laser cut.

How many of this variation were actually produced is unknown, though the first contract stipulated that it would conclude on 09 March 1993.[52] As we see, though, production ran well into the second contract, and it is at this point that things get very complicated, because the entire process seems to have existed within a complete state of flux; at least to *this* researcher it does!

On 14 September 1994, the Army awarded contract DAAA09-94-C-0571 to Lan-Cay for 104,111 M9 bayonets, all with PIB changes. These changes included adding a black oxide finish and moving the saw teeth further forward on the spine, which eliminated the traditional cut-out, while rounding the base of the saw teeth. And, as mentioned earlier, the fuller was eliminated completely. Lastly, the scabbard design underwent modification to its current form.

The M9/L1-3

Certainly, a second contract would have come as good news to the company, but the problem was the first contract—it was still in production. For the second contract, machinery would have to be set up in order to perform the new operations as called for by contract DAAA09-94-C-0571.

The apparent solution was to produce the needed number of blades with then current machine settings, which were IAW[53] the second contract, in order to satisfy the remaining first contract requirements, but to give them the sandblasted finish instead of the oxide coating. No doubt, this would have required the approval of Rock Island, but because it was a sensible solution to a difficult situation, it likely was fairly easy and expeditious. The result was second contract blades, PIB, having a first contract finish.

What came from this minor wildfire, and sources vary somewhat, was that on or about late April 1995 Lan-Cay satisfied contract DAAA09-92-C-0406 with the shipment of a final 1,090 bayonets. For the collector this is yet another niche to fill in the M9 line—the third variation of the first contract.

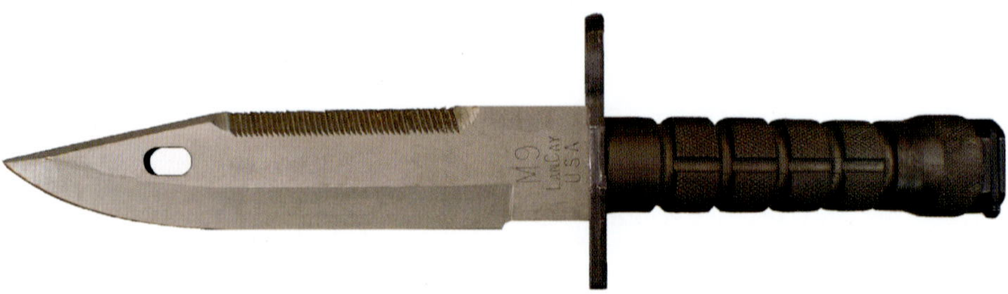

Figure 123.1: The M9/L1-3 is a PIB blade with bead blasted finish; 1,090 of these bayonets were used to complete contract DAAA09-92-C-0406.

The M9/L2

And so, at this point Lan-Cay's problems, real or imagined, were resolved: changes were finally written into the Mil-Specs, the contract awarded, and Lan-Cay completed making the necessary production changes. With all these issues at rest, M9/L2s should be flooding from the factory. Well, that would be true, except that apparently there was the small issue of product profitability remaining to deal with.

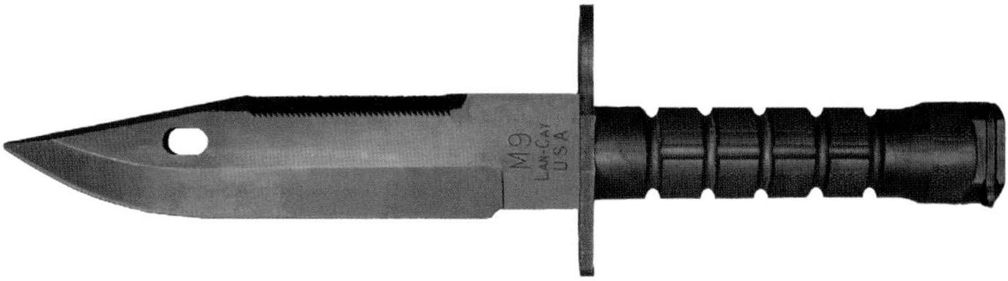

Figure 123.2: The M9/L2 is a PIB blade with an oxide finish and the full compliment of improvements.

The M9/L2-1

The second variation to the second contract involves a change from hollow to flat ground blades. It is merely the author's assumption, though a good one, that in an effort to strengthen the blade the Army decided the M9 blade ought be a flat rather than a hollow grind.

Figure 123.3: The M9/L2-1 is exactly the same as the M9/L2, but the blade is hollow ground.

The M9/L2-2

As it turned out, Lan-Cay previously submitted a *Request for Variance* authorizing use of the 200 rejected blades whose points were a hair under specs. For whatever reason, no action on the request had been forthcoming, leaving Lan-Cay little choice, save stowing the blades on the shelf until approval came. When finally the approved request arrived the first contract had ended, leaving specifications of the second contract in effect.

How Lan-Cay and the Army actually handled the administrative mechanics of the issue is unclear, but we do know that the Request for Variance of the 200 blades received approval from Rock Island. Given the time frame, Lan-Cay was obliged to use these blades as part of the second contract. As such, this variation is essentially a first contract blade

Figure 123.4: The M9/L2-2 is a first contract blade with an oxide finish.

given the black oxide finish of the second contract. The scabbard should likewise be of the PIB style, with the lock stamped to read Lan-Cay. Needless to say, one of these knives would be a very rare find—perhaps the rarest!

The M9/L3

This is the third major iteration of the **Lan-Cay** M9, as well as a return to forging instead of cutting the blanks with a laser. Whereas the preceding variations referred to particular contracts this does not. It is merely the last in the series, based on design implementations.

Having said that, though, it is quite common among collectors to refer to the *third contract* as the one in which Lan-Cay and the Ontario Knife Company shared a 25,000-unit award—each supplying 12,500 M9s. Actually, as listed in Appendix E, one can see that Lan-Cay was awarded four contracts between the second and contract number DAAE20-99-D-0134. That would make the third contract actually the Seventh contract.

Figure 124: Oxide coated, flat ground, rounded teeth bases and elimination of the spine step are all incorporated into the current version of the M9.

Nevertheless, the M9/L3 variation is the current issue M9 with all of the product improvements. It is truly a no frills weapon, starkly utilitarian, though well suited for its intended purpose.

Figure 125: Current Lan-Cay marking.

Figure 126: Current Lan-Cay marking on the locking assembly and as it has appeared since the second contract.

The M9/O1

The M9/O1 simply differentiates Lan-Cay's version from Ontario Knife Company's, as both firms split the contract, with each being awarded allocations for 12,500 units. The Ontario M9 is rather easily distinguished from all others by its lighter green color. Reminiscent of *Chicom green*[54] it apparently meets specs, though how is anyone's guess.

The M9/L3 and M9/O1 are at the top of the M9 evolutionary tree, and represent the erstwhile final refinement. Yet, when one compares just the blades of this chapter, much less all of the Phrobis pieces, it is so clearly obvious that the weapon has been transformed from a magnificently sleek and superbly finished blade rivaling many custom ground blades, to a rudimentary slab of sharpened steel!

Too severe? Perhaps, but we are all entitled occasional lapses of perspective. Nonetheless, both the M9/L3 and M9/O1 are fully capable of executing their missions, just as their predecessors were, though much less impressive from an aesthetic perspective.

Figure 127: Current Ontario Knife Company locking assemblies are unmarked as above.

Figure 128: Just like its Lan-Cay counterpart, the OKC M9 is oxide coated, flat ground, rounded teeth bases, and without the spine step.

Figure 129: Current Ontario Knife Company M9.

Figure 130: Current Ontario Knife Company M9 is easily distinguished from all others by its lighter green color.

Figure 131: Comparative view: Top M9 is the latest iteration, below it a first run piece.

Figure 132: Above: simple is frequently very effective, though a matter of perspective.

Scabbards

One may wonder why the topic of scabbards appears at the end of the chapter instead of being included with each variation's section; and that would be a logical question to ask. The answer, quite simply, is that this author can accurately associate very few scabbard variations with a specific bayonet variation.

The essential problem here, and with the M9 in general, is twofold. First, it is a modular system, and parts are both readily available and easily interchanged from one unit to another. From a user's point of view this is a wonderful feature, but for historians and collectors it is no less than a vexation, precisely because one can seldom be certain what the original configuration should be, and hence what configuration any one scabbard should possess!

For instance, once the PIB specifications were implemented subsequent production units possessed discrete features, which one can reliably say belong to a specific unit. Particularly maddening is the period of change over from Lan-Cay's first to second contract, as quantitatively there were four variations entering supply channels at nearly the same time. In such a case, is it possible for one to say with complete confidence which scabbard belongs to which variation? Not likely.

The leftover first contract blades entered the system during the time that the PIB scabbard should have been in issue, the emphasis on *should*. The unanswerable question is was it? No one can say, even though many collectors DO, and if they are comfortable with that delusion so be it; this author is not!

The second troubling complication for collectors, and those writing to collectors, is the very nature of Army maintenance. Interchanging, or more accurately replacing, parts is a natural function of the maintenance system, and if, for example, the cutter plate of an early unit needs replacing it will get the type that's available in the system. Armorers do not try to match parts; they simply install whatever is available and if old stock is on hand that is what they use. Sometimes, if it is a critical safety issue units will retrofit, or perform *MWOs*,[55] though such with regards to the M9 is unlikely.

9

Separate Identity
The Marine's Search for a Multipurpose Bayonet

Figure 133: No introduction required! (Marine Corps Photo)

The United States Marine Corps is one of the world's most, if not the most, unique and famous of all military organizations. The *Corps* possesses a blend of history, traditions, ethos, and symbolism which has, in a very short couple hundred years, congealed in such a rare way as to give it a fame literally known the world over. And, while many nations have armed units called *Marines,* when one speaks of *The Marines* it is the United States Marines that first comes to mind!

Such fame and reputation brings with it a tremendous individual and organizational responsibility, one that every Marine zealously accepts, being ever mindful of his particular role in perpetuating the Corps, its traditions, and reputation. At the organizational level, the same *espirit de corps*[56] and ethos permeates the leadership and guides Marine Corps policy. Everything about Marines and the Marine Corp is unique, from their dress down to the very way in which they think!

It is in this same vein, a sheer pleasure to observe the way in which Marines problem solve, how their solutions are generally so typically Marine! This author's impression of the *Marine process* is that they appear almost unconsciously to follow a simple, uncomplicated, and focused formula. One that is, apparently, not accessible to their sister services, who too often become engrossed in analyses, assessments, and matrices to the point that the original problem often simply evaporates! Perhaps this same phenomenon has for so long caused the Corps to balk at the M9. They test it, try to like it, and yet, always find it somehow unacceptable within the parameters of the *formula.*

Before going too far, let us be clear that while this text is about the M9, and its iconic representation of the American Soldier, an exploration of its connection with, and to, the Marines is an essential part of that whole. Therefore, while one runs the risk of critics misconstruing the thesis, there actually is no inconsistency in the contention that the M9 has symbolically come to emblematize the American Soldier, exactly because the operative noun here is *soldier*, not *Marine!* For, as any Marine will quickly tell you, they are not soldiers they are Marines! And, while both share an immutable vocation and camaraderie, among the group known as soldiers, Marines have their own separate identity!

Intimately connected to this identity are icons, or symbols, and while most organizations have them, the Marine Corps has amassed an impressive collection over the past two hundred plus years. For instance, Iwo Jima is symbolic of the Marines in World War II, and of course,

Figure 134: Among the group known as soldiers, Marines have a separate identity! (Marine Corps Photo)

the *Eagle, Globe and Anchor* immediately conjures up more general images of the Marine Corps. However, somewhere in the mix is the equivalent of the M9, and the reason that this underlying connection to the Marine's M9 experience is separately explored in its own chapter.

Figure 134.1: Note the EGA stenciled on the left breast pockets. (Marine Corps photo)

The Marine Corps and Army have traditionally worked very closely on new weapons development, as the mission of both is similar, and naturally, similar missions require similar tools. And, while each service routinely carries out its own research and development, the Army produces the bulk of weapons and materiel. Having said that, it is not in the least unusual for the Marines to develop a piece of equipment so impressive that the Army adopts it as well. The best example that comes to mind is the M16A2 rifle.

Figure 135: The M16A2—what the rifle always should have been. (Marine Corps Photo)

For many years, shooters in both the Army and Marine Corps bemoaned the M16's shortcomings. Most agreed that it was a good weapon when employed in certain environments, but that many of its features were simply inadequate for the line soldier, and particularly deficient where long-range shooters were concerned.

At 55 grains, the standard M196 ball ammunition proved itself far too light and unstable for precision long-range[57] engagements, where ideally weight and velocity should combine to produce stability, and ultimately accuracy and penetration. Unfortunately, even with the proper ammunition, the rack weapon's[58] sights were not fully, or easily, adjustable, and therefore ammunition upgrading alone would offer no appreciable overall advantage.

The Marine Corps obviously saw the value and potential of the M16, and rather than develop a completely new rifle, they initiated an aggressive program to improve it, focusing on the redesign of its intrinsic areas of weakness.

Some refinements were nothing short of profound, while others were just nice to have, specifically ergonomic hand guards to replace the old triangular ones whose smooth surface made a sure grip difficult, especially when wet or muddy. Worse was the hand guard retaining ring, as it was undersized with such restrictive access that even small fingers had trouble manipulating it. This situation made it difficult for the firer to disengage the retaining rings, and thus a terribly frustrating disassembly task. The A2 version included an improved conical retaining ring, enabling a firm purchase with plenty of room for one's fingers and making it much easier to remove the round, ribbed hand guards.

Concerning accuracy, the M16A1, despite its miserably inadequate sights, is a reasonably precise shooter up to 300 or 400 meters, a range at which an able infantryman can place three

Figure 136: The improved M16A2 above sports adjustable sights, a 68 grain round, heavy barrel with a 1:9 right hand twist, and is more than capable of bringing pure *scunion*[59] at 500 meters! Also note the improved conical hand guard retaining rings. (Marine Corps Photo)

Figure 137: A heavily modified rifle (fore end grip, Picatinny Rail System, sling adapter). (Marine Corps photo)

rounds within a four to six inch group. In fact, as service rifles go, the M16A1 is amongst the world's most accurate; however, the M16A2 is simply a menace at, and beyond, 500 meters!

The accuracy issue, not surprisingly, involved three critical components: the barrel, sights, and the ammunition. Original Army specs called for a rifle that weighed no more than five and a half pounds with a twenty-round magazine. Given such constraints, it is not surprising that the M16A1 barrel was intentionally very lightweight. However, all is compromise, and in this case, the lower mass results in weakness, and in particular the phenomena of *barrel lash*.[60]

The M16A2 is fitted with a newly designed barrel that is much heavier and thicker beyond the front sight post, which ameliorates a good amount of lash. And, while this author is no mechanical engineer or physicist, he has noted a distinct reduction in barrel lash with this configuration, which can only improve long-range accuracy.

In any case, barrel lash is not the only shortcoming the heavier barrel ameliorates. The A2's thicker barrel is essential in order to accommodate the new heavier 68-grain bullet of the SS109 cartridge. Stability is further enhanced by the new bore, which was changed from a one in seven (1:7) to a one in nine (1:9) right hand twist. The resulting faster spin, coupled with a lower velocity[61] of the heavier projectile, increases the stability of the round and results in an appreciable increase in accuracy and range, as well as penetration and stopping power.

Finally, the Marines put it all together in a neat package by lengthening the stock and incorporating fully adjustable rear sights, with large sure grip windage and elevation knobs and an *L-shaped, flip up*, long and short-range sight aperture, as well as a three round burst selector and a brass deflector.

Figure 138: The OKC3S easily adapts to the new MOLLE load bearing system. (Marine Corps photo)

These relatively simple design changes truly transformed the M16A1 rifle from an impotent, short-range brush gun into a very accurate, hard hitting, long range infantry rifle. The Marine's transformation of the M16A1 so impressed Army Leadership that they pushed through its adoption as the standard Army long arm in the late 1980s!

A decade or so later, and a war not in the jungles, but the desert of Iraq, has naturally led to even further modifications, resulting in today's M16A4, and its stubby brother the M4A4. Today this *toy from Mattel* stands as the U.S. Army's longest serving standard infantry *rifle*, now nearing its phenomenal fiftieth birthday!

While the Army was rediscovering the rifle range and K-D targets,[62] the Marines were stroking their chins and *eyeballing* the Army's new M9 bayonet. Neither the Army nor Marine Corps had ever been very enthusiastic when it came to the M7, and the Marines surely began thinking that maybe the flatfoots had stumbled onto something with their Rambo knife!

The 1991 M9B1

As always, and in good Marine fashion, Headquarters Marine Corps tasked its 2d Marine Division in 1991 to conduct field trials of the M9 with the intent of replacing their aging and much-beguiled M7. Chosen to supply the hardware for this trial was Buck knives, who contracted and produced a total 5000 prototype M9 bayonets for use as test pieces.[63]

Figure 139: One of the 5000 vintage 1991 USMC M9 bayonets; note *plus sign* (+) on ricasso.

By this time, the Kentucky firm of Lan-Cay undertook production of the Army M9, and coincidentally happened to be the same company that not long before underbid Buck Knife for the same Army contract. This turnabout seems all the more ironic in that Buck Knife, who had originally manufactured the M9 bayonet for Phrobis in 1987, should now secure the Marine's open bid to produce 5000 of the weapons.

The 1991 model sports easily recognizable obverse ricosso markings deeply and clearly struck in a narrow, tall font in a three-line configuration that reads *M9 - USMC, BUCK +, USA*. Note here Buck's use of symbols, in this case a *plus sign* (+) to denote the date of manufacture. See Appendix B for the entire list of Buck symbols.

Of interest to the collecting community is that with the adoption of the OKC3S, this lot of 5000 M9/1991 bayonets has been *DXed*,[64] having completed matriculation through the *Defense Reutilization Management Office* (*DRMO*)[65] process, and is currently on the civilian market. This relatively small surplus event has afforded an excellent opportunity for collectors to secure a somewhat rare variation of the M9!

Figure 140: Buck uses a variety of symbols to denote dates of manufacture: here the plus sign denotes manufacture in 1991.

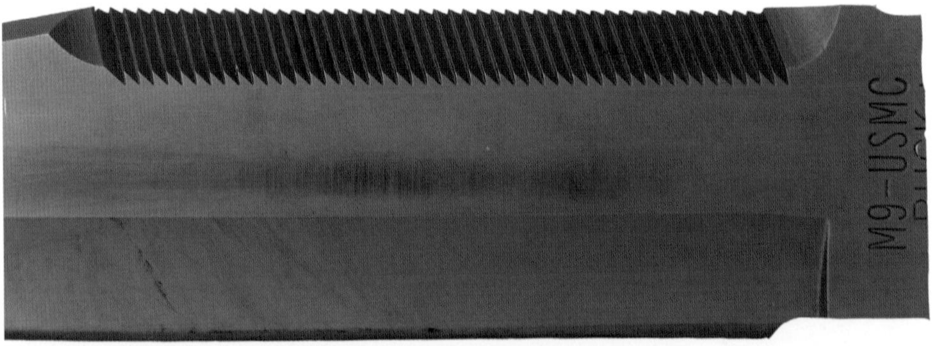

Figure 141: The M9B1 retains the saw-toothed edge on the spine of the blade.

Like the Army version, the M9/B1 design retained most of the original features as the photo below shows. The blades continue to include the saw-toothed edge for cutting wood and thin metal such as that found in aircraft construction.

While the actual design changes of the PIB (product-improved bayonet) remained on the event horizon in 1991, the evaluations and reports responsible for the decision to initiate such design modifications were well known throughout the DoD. That the Marines were unaware of such issues is highly unlikely, and yet the Marine research and development command[66] appeared unconcerned over the purported deficiencies of the early M9 models, as evidenced by their inclusion in the M9B1's design.

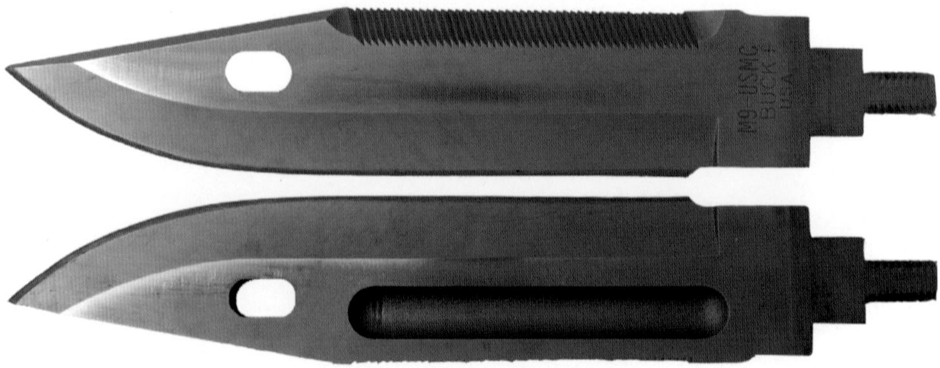

Figure 142: Aside from the unique ricasso stamping M9B1 blades appear much the same as all of the early M9s.

Again, the M9B1 is little different from the standard M9, as has been noted previously, though some small variations do exist. Aside from the obvious ricosso markings, the next most readily apparent difference is the hex nut used to secure the bayonet latch assembly to the M9's handle.

The M9B1, with its singular hex nut, necessitates the carrying of a hex wrench if one is to disassemble it in the field. The Army models included a single slot, enabling the soldier to use the scabbard's flat-tipped screwdriver feature should situations necessitate disassembly of the bayonet. On the other hand, it is entirely possible that Marine designers did not intend for field stripping of the bayonet, thereby eliminating the need for a tool with which to accompvlish disassembly.

Figure 143: Buck used a standard hex nut to secure the latch assembly, whereas the Army screw head is both hex and slotted for a flat tip screwdriver.

Figure 144: The standard hilt at the top is carbon steel that has been parkerized per PIB specification changes, whereas the bottom photo shows the USMC M9B1 hilt unchanged from earlier models.

Figure 145: Yet again, there was no change in the bayonet's hand guard or handle from earlier models.

Finally, the scabbard remained unchanged from the early design. It must be pointed out that at this point in history, and while the Army had adopted the M9 some years prior, the Marine Corps had yet to get on board. It was clear that they wanted a change from the M7, but it was not at all clear what Headquarters Marine Corps perceived such a change to be.

Figure 146: Early M9 bayonet scabbard configuration.

Taken in the above context, one should view the 1991 trial as the Marines taking a good hard look at the bayonet, but not necessarily committing to its adoption regardless of the evaluation outcome. Another point to consider is that at the time the Marines issued two blades to their fighters, the M7 bayonet and the K-Bar; one a fighting knife, the other a field utility knife.

Given those points, one can well imagine the Corps looking at the M9 and mentally considering whether this Multipurpose Bayonet System was worth the loss of their venerable near sacred K-Bar! Exactly because the K-Bar is one of the Marine icons spoken of at the start of this chapter, even the thought of its elimination would have been very unsettling to the many in the Corps, to say the least. Therefore, given those terms the M9 indeed had a great deal to prove before there was even the smallest possibility of its adoption.

The 1993 M9B2, 3, and 4 Series

In 1993, the Marines gave the M9 yet a second look, but this time they changed more than the latch assembly nut. For this evaluation Buck Knives provided three M9 variations, all constructed of stainless steel and having tangs of three differing designs. Modifications of this sort lead one to believe that there was a concern over the strength of the standard tangs, or it may have simply derived from differing opinions as to the method of attaching the handle.

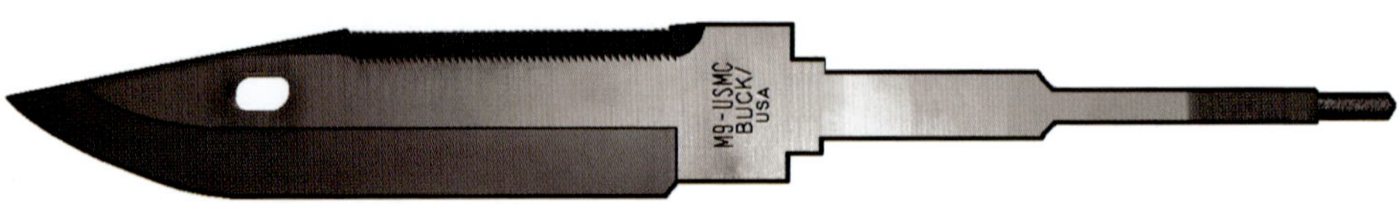

Figure 146.1: M9B2 tang featuring a threaded tip to secure handle and latch.

As is Buck's practice, all test piece ricassos were stamped with the lettering *M9, USMC, BUCK /, U.S.A.*, where the forward slash reveals the year of manufacture to be 1993 in a rather tall and comparatively narrow font. It is unfortunate the author was unable to secure photos of these very interesting and rare test examples, nor to locate the contract. All information contained herein is either direct author observation or secondary source material.

Nevertheless, the first type featured a permanent configuration, having its locking assembly riveted in place by means of actually peening the tang's end, which effectively prevents fieldstripping, as the attachment is essentially permanent. If there ever had been a debate as to whether or not to provide for field disassembly this feature effectively squelched it.

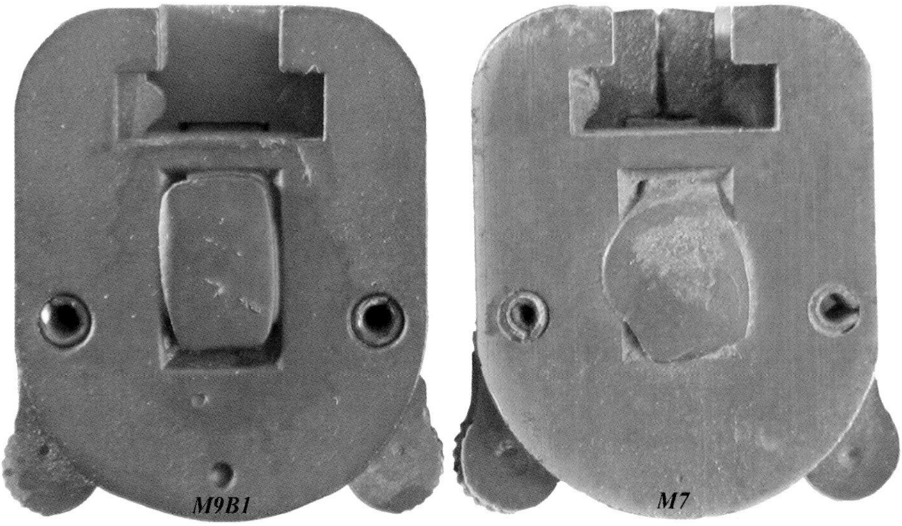

Figure 146.2: M9B1 (left), instead of a securing nut, the tang tip is peened over as on the M7 (right).

A second variation featured a flat tang, being integral to the blade, and a threaded male end onto which one screwed a barrel nut. The barrel nut is the female end, or likened to an inverted screw, as it is tubular with internal threads, which allow for screwing it onto the tang, thereby effectively securing the latch assembly to the handle.[67] Unlike the standard tang, which is short and threaded to accept a cylindrical extension, this second style does not lend itself well to expedient repair should the need arise.

The final configuration is simply the standard design, whereby the integral tang has been lengthened and the tang extension shortened. The logic to this arrangement is fleeting, except perhaps to lend to the mechanism a degree of reparability.

This cohort of test pieces is another excellent example of the applicability of nomenclature. As such, they have been designated M9B2, M9B3, and M9B4 respectively. It is unknown how many copies Buck actually produced, though some sources put the number at 175 each of the M9B2 and M9B3 for a total of 350. Production numbers for the M9B4 are unknown.

Figure 147: A marine in Iraq equipped with one of the 1991 Buck M9s prior to replacement by the OKC3S. (Marine Corps photo)

Eickhorn's USMC Bayonet, XM9/2000

By the fall of 2001, the M9 bayonet had been in the Army's inventory for nearly fifteen years, had performed well, was popular amongst the soldiers, and was by all indications going to be the official bayonet for a very long time. Yet, despite a recognized need for something else, the Marine Corps' official bayonet remained the M7!

Moreover, it was obvious to all involved that the Marine Corps simply was not interested in, nor sold on the M9. True, the Marines had looked at it, they had evaluated it, they had even modified it, and yet after nearly fifteen years they continued to use their old bayonet, rather than accept the M9! There can be no doubt that the M9 was lacking something. The M9's failure after evaluation by the *marine formula* is a strong indicator of its lack of some quality that the Marines Corps valued so highly they were willing to take nothing rather than something which failed to satisfy their apparently elusive requirements.

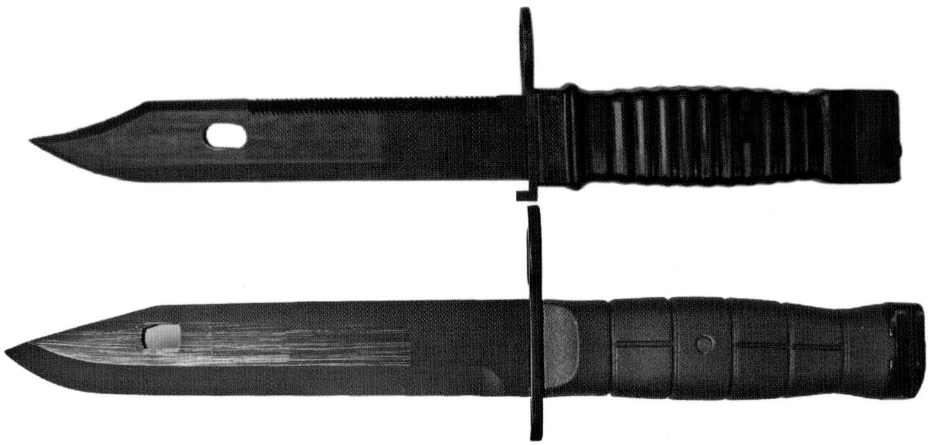

Figure 148: Comparison of Eickhorn's Stoner KCB (top) and the proposed USMC XM9/2000 (bottom).

The Eickhorn XM9/2000

It is within this context that on 25 September 2001, the *Marine Corps Test and Evaluation Command* managed, in what can only be seen as an act of sheer desperation, to send concerned sectors of American industry absolutely ballistic!

In an obvious effort to obtain an acceptable bayonet, *Marine Corps Systems Command* negotiated with, and settled upon an Eickhorn design that, ostensibly, met all Marine Corps requirements. Below is the controversial solicitation:

"The Marine Corps Systems Command (MARCORSYSCOM) intends to negotiate and award on a sole source basis...with Eickhorn*Solingen for Bayonets. A *firm fixed price* (*FFP*), Indefinite Delivery / Indefinite Quan-Tity ...is the contract type anticipated to be utilized for this effort; and award will be based upon the Acquisition of Commercial Items procedures in Federal Acquisition Regulation... Eickhorn*Solingen, Lohodorfer Str 72 D-42699, Federal Republic of Germany, is the only known source cap-Able of delivering bayonets with the Marine Eagle, Globe and Anchor Markings at a rate of 5,000 per month beginning 30 days after acceptance of the first 50 Limited Production Units. The 50 Limited Production Units will be delivered within 30 days after receipt of contract award. The Eickhorn *Solingen Bayonet 2000 will replace the M7 Bayonet throughout the Fleet Marine Force... Award is anticipated to be made on or about 16 October 2001."

Note 22 is modified to read:

"However, all responses to this notice received by 12 October 2001 will be considered by the Govern-ment", in lieu of the fourth sentence in Note 22..."

According to the solicitation competitors had just three weeks to submit their proposals if they expected to compete with the Eickhorn bayonet for contract consideration. On the face of this, it appears that the Marine Corps had already made up its collective mind. The whole situation gave the appearance that the Marines were taking no unnecessary chances, no matter how unfair, on some third party spoiling their plans! Moreover, while this author seldom criticizes, or has reason to, the Marine Corps, this whole affair just seems, on the face of it, very much not like the Marines!

What occurred next was that a large sector of the American cutlery industry, to their credit, apparently shared the same sentiment and wasted little time letting the Marines, DoD, and Congress know about it! And, whatever the dynamics of the Eickhorn-Marine Corps deal, those in the industry with a dog in the hunt threw a living fit that could have been heard in the Halls of Montezuma! Without the slightest exaggeration, the resulting firestorm was obviously just awful, because MARCORSYSCOM spent, for a bureaucracy, relatively little time reversing its decision!

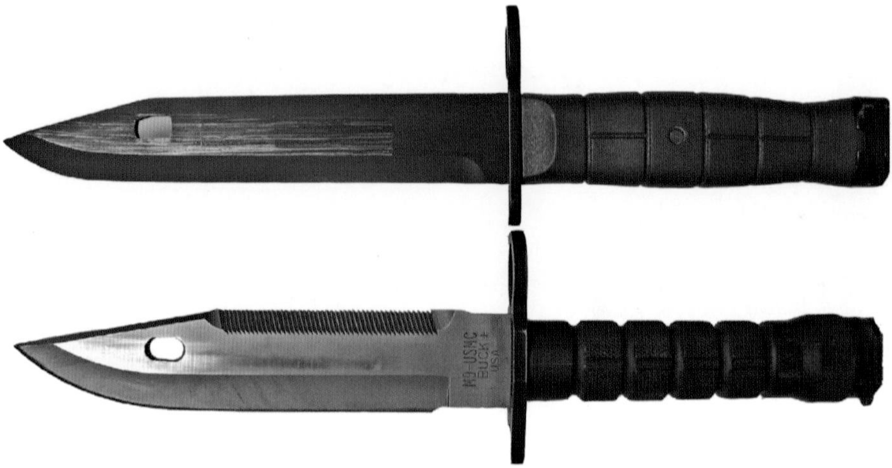

Figure 149: Side by side comparison of Eickhorn's proposed USMC XM9/2000 (top) and the M9 MPBS (bottom).

On October 18, 2001, twenty-three days after the initial announcement, Marine Corps Systems Command, via the Commerce Business Daily, rescinded the egregious solicitation:

"This Commerce Business Daily (CBD) Modification Notice hereby rescinds the Marine Corps Systems Command announcement of 25 September 2001 regarding Bayonets 2000. Due to industry response, the Government no longer intends to pursue this requirement on a sole source basis to Eickhorn Solingen. Additional information regarding the Marine Corps Systems Command's revised acquisition strategy for Bayonets will be issued in the CBD in the near future."

The Marine Corp's response is nothing short of a tap-dance, usually done by higher bureaucratic echelons, but it nevertheless gave them some badly needed time to strategize a way out of the industrial siege and an opportunity to actually *get it right*, unless the whole purpose was to cause just such an uproar from the beginning.

Of course, what followed one could interpret as a small propaganda blitz featuring Major James Riordan, director of Combat Equipment and Support Systems at the Marine Corps Systems Command in Quantico, VA, who offered this explanation in an interview that ran in *National Defense Magazine:*

"'What the Marines want to do,' Riordan said, 'is replace their 1960s-era M7 bayonet, which is primarily a stabbing weapon, with a new version, having a cutting edge that also can serve as a combat knife. Right now, Marines who need a combat knife and a bayonet have to carry around two blades, which is awkward,' Riordan explained. 'The service wants to fix that problem, and it wants to do it quickly,' he said. Last fall, the Marines announced plans to award a sole-source contract to the German-based company, Eickhorn-Solingen. The firm was 'the only known source capable of delivering bayonets with the Marine eagle, globe, and anchor markings at a rate of 5,000 per month beginning 30 days after acceptance of the first 50 limited production units,' the notice said."

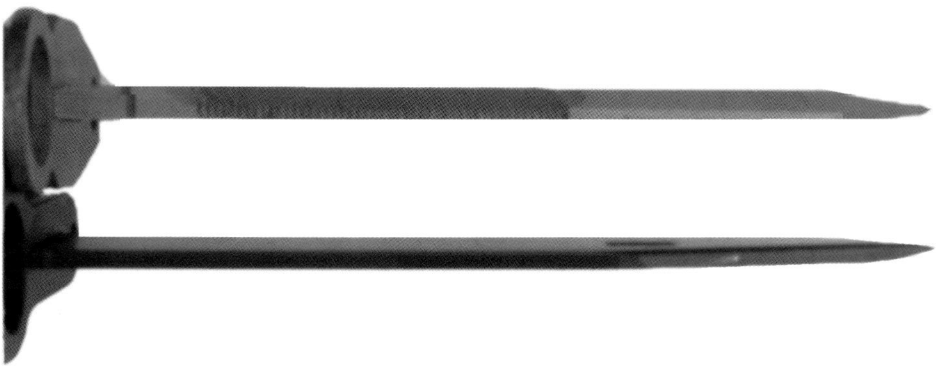

Figure 150: The M9 MPBS (top) is obviously much thicker and more robust than Eickhorn's proposed USMC XM9/2000 (bottom), and one has to wonder how it would hold up in the prying role.

The only known source! The statement leaves one desperately struggling to maintain even the most elemental composure from disbelief! Such an excuse is not even within the realm of believability, and is so obviously a heaping, helping of rhetorical spin! Assuming that there was a requirement for five thousand units per month, any number of U.S. companies could easily have fulfilled it. On the other hand, why would the Marine Corps NEED that many each month? There was no conflict at the time. In fact, to satisfy contract DAAE20-99-D-0135, OKC was turning out four thousand complete units per month, AND still producing their civilian lines! To insist that Eickhorn was the only known source is pure rubbish!

The more about this situation that is known the less it actually makes sense, particularly as there simply is no *known* reason that the Marine Corps could not have just as easily issued a solicitation for what they wanted from the beginning. That was what they did in the end; and in any event, no great disaster befell anyone!

Perhaps the Marines were working off the assumption that the only company regarded by the DoD to have the manufacturing capacity to provide an off the shelf bayonet was

Eickhorn. It would not be the first time that a vague, twisted, or misguided bureaucratic requirement was responsible for the demise of an otherwise worthwhile effort.

Whatever the Marine Corps' actual predicament was, it must be said that, in all honesty, the Solingen bayonet XM9/2000 was/is little better than the M7. In fact, Eickhorn has been hawking one variation or another of the *KCB* since at least the 1960s. The first that comes to mind is the project wherein Eickhorn provided a similar variation for the U.S. Army's Stoner System program, and while it is quite a somewhat rare knife, it is just another KCB playing dress up!

The overriding fact is that the KCB is essentially no more than an AK clone, and while there's no shame in some good old fashioned *industrial innovation,* it is little better than its Russian counterpart. Probably its greatest detraction, in this author's opinion, is its redesigned square handle, which feels entirely alien to the hand while offering much less purchase than that of the M7.

In the case of Eickhorn's XM9/2000, it is the first of the KCB line that actually approaches an effort to move away from their proprietary design. And, it must be said, though grudgingly so, that it is just ever so slightly a refreshing design that has naturally retained the traditional features common to all of the KCB variants while incorporating Marine Corps specifications.

Figure 151: The M9 (bottom) scabbard seemingly dwarfs that of the XM9/2000 (top).

How well the XM9/2000 actually met specs is unknown, but this author is most struck with the piece's relatively comfortable handle, and to a lesser extent the blade. The favorableness of the blade is its distinctly knife feel, though it is noticeably thin and seems comparatively frail. One cannot help seriously doubting its performance when used to pry objects, or other rugged tasks. Moreover, as demonstrated in Figure 151, the M9 appears very beefy when compared to the XM9/2000, and one can have little doubt that the M9's blade probably outperforms the Eickhorn in just about every field task, with the possible exception of slicing or skinning.

A noticeably narrow affair, the blade comes with a decent edge. This is truly fortuitous, since the honing strip glued to the scabbard can best be described as a lame attempt exclusively to fulfill a specification, though without actually providing any true functionality! Half-assed immediately comes to mind, as the strip is obviously too narrow, and too short to actually work an edge; but that's just one man's opinion!

Figure 151.1: The XM9/2000's *honing strip*—inadequate beyond description!

Otherwise the scabbard seems solid, and it adequately secures the knife inside via a friction brake located just within the scabbard throat, as well as a very functional wire cutter, and the obligatory flat tip screwdriver appendage. The scabbard is of a good diameter for using as a wire cutter handle, and feels comfortable and solid in the hand, offering a sure-grip traction surface with which to secure a firm purchase.

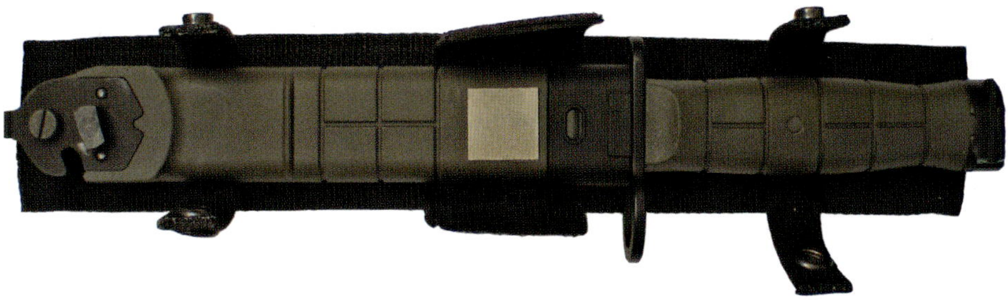

Figure 151.2: The XM9/2000's attachment system allows removal of the MPBS from the carrier, though with three straps and one button snap (attached between scabbard and carrier) it is not quick and must be distracting.

Finally, the black nylon webbing that constitutes the carrier is also of issue, in that it requires significant attention in order to detach the MPBS. This situation arises primarily due to the three straps and one button snap, which attaches between scabbard and carrier, and is far from being quick to release. Moreover, the system is at least distracting when compared to the single *squeeze and pull* motion required to remove the M9. Aside from that, it is quite capable of adequately securing the weapon to the soldier, whether attached to traditional or modular load bearing equipment.

In the final analysis the XM9/2000 is, in the author's opinion, a barely adequate weapon that is clearly inferior to the M9 at nearly every turn! Moreover, in its historical context, it is absolutely not worth the grief that would have resulted had the Marine Corps chosen to fall on its preverbial sword in order to obtain it, and it would have been a flagrant waste of public funds! For, if the desire was an *adequate* bayonet, the M7 more than satisfied the need.

Again, the Marines wisely chose to resolicit, though there remains that nagging feeling that this whole affair was more a maneuver than an actual pursuit.

Figure 152: Side by side comparison of the M9 MPBS wire cutter configuration (left) and Eickhorn's proposed USMC XM9/2000 wire cutter configuration (right).

Finally, the OKC3S

The entire Marine search experience brings to light a myriad of valuable lessons concerning acquisition, though perhaps the whole affair is simply another example of one generation cursed to reinvent the wheels of their ancestors. Whatever the case, the foremost take-away lesson of it is that open and fair competition is the surest means of procuring the very best product at an optimum price. In fact, the OKC3S is

Figure 153: The Corps' long search finally ended with the adoption of the OKC3S. (Marine Corps photo)

an excellent example of American industry's ability to provide the best products in the world when given the opportunity to do so.

Another valuable lesson, which doubtfully bureaucrats will ever learn, is that in most circumstances doing nothing is preferable to doing *something* for its own sake! Within this context, all indications are that the Marine Corps knew the M9 simply was not what they wanted, and they wisely abandoned acquisition of it. Their mistake lay in the apparently hasty decision to contract with Eickhorn, who offered the only feature the M9 did not: the Marine Corps emblem!

Admittedly, details of behind the scenes considerations and negotiations are unknown, which leaves open the possibility that Eickhorn was the only viable option. However, given the facts of the events heretofore described, it is supremely difficult to put forth any postulation other than that the Marine Corps wanted their own unique bayonet emblazoned with their unique emblem. Such is especially tempting to believe, as so many pieces of Marine Corps equipment compliment the Corps' unique and separate identity! Moreover, while it is doubtful that anyone involved would ever admit to such motivation, given the obvious superiority of the M9, one can arrive at no other logical conclusion! In all simplicity, it is a case of, as the Army would say, *good concept, poor execution*!"

In deference to, and defense of, the Marine Corps, one might use the esoteric argument that had the Marines not engaged the Eickhorn contract in the way that they did, that the competition responsible for the development of the OKC3s would never have occurred, and therefore the Marines would never have adopted the OKC3s. As it is, such a thing is not possible to know, yet there does seem to be a very serendipitous quality to the whole affair, and in the end, everything did, as they say, *work out for the best.*

Why Not the *M10*?

As nomenclature is a recurring theme throughout this work, now is a good time to explore the nomenclature of the OKC3s as a preventative measure in combating *collector legend,* which will no doubt rear its creative head at some point. The two salient questions are: what does OKC3s mean, and why is not this bayonet an M10, or an *M*-something?

The answer to both is quite simple, and straightforward. OKC is, of course, the initials of the Ontario Knife Company, and 3s represents the 3d pattern. As to why the Marine Corps did not assign it a model number is also straightforward, though perhaps not so simple.

The short answer is that Mil-Standard 1461A, dated 15 May 1987, says so. Specifically, it directs that:

"Items adopted or proposed for adoption for Army (or Marine in this case) use but accommodated by commercial or foreign-government designation shall not be retype designated in accordance with the system contained herein unless an approved Requirements Document (see 4.2.4.3.1) indicates that some change in design, function or interchangeability is necessary for Army (Marine) applications. A *Commercial Nondevelopmental Item* (*NDI*) maybe assigned a designation when approved requirements exist and the responsible requesting activity has a military identification to distinguish between like items already in use."

Where the word *Army* appears in the above text, *Marines* has been inserted to maintain clarity, since the quote is from the Army version of the Military Standards, which are

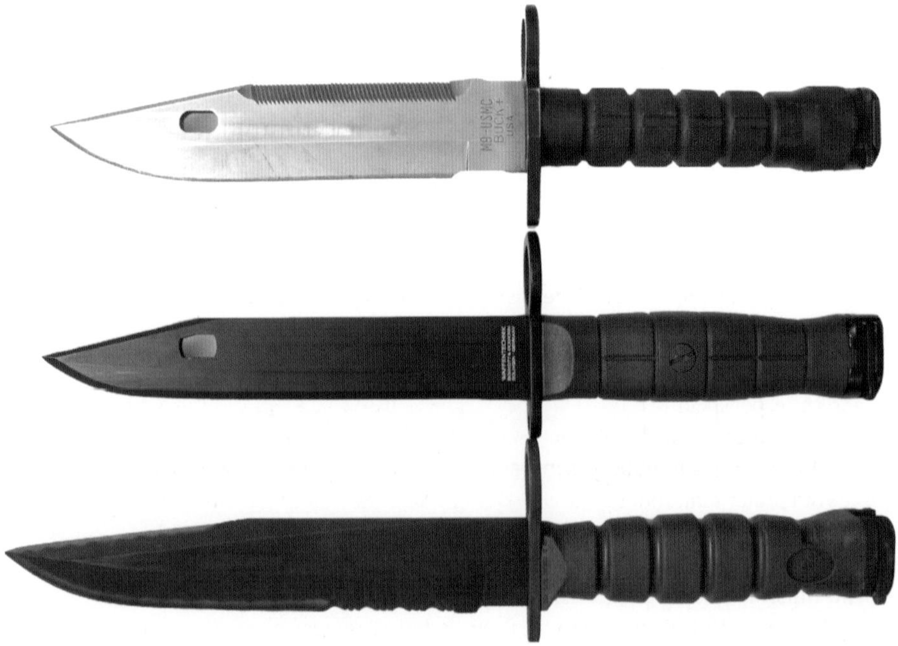

Figure 154: For comparison, from top to bottom, the M9, the XM9/2000, and the OKC3s.

dictated by the Department of Defense and applicable to all branches. So, in essence what we have here is a case wherein DoD has decided that off the shelf materiel will maintain its commercial identity so long as it is functionally unique.

Ontario Knife's Bayonet OKC3s (M9/O1)

In terms of selection, there occurred a robust competition at Quantico conducted, and monitored, by the Instructor Trainers of the Marine Corps Martial Arts Center of Excellence. These top-notch fighters evaluated a wide variety of designs submitted by seventeen companies, some of which had provided knives to the Corps during and since WWII.

The list is impressive, and includes the Ontario Knife Company—ultimately the contract winner—and Lan-Cay Inc., who submitted something in the neighborhood of four different designs demonstrating the technique known as the *shotgun approach*, though in fairness others did the same. Camillus Quality Knives, who first gave the Marine Corps one of its most famous icons, the Ka-Bar, as well as Buck, who had provided them the M9 nearly a decade before. Other competitors were Gerber Legendary Blades, Advanced Machining, TiKnives Inc., Berrizargo, S.L., Capco, Saber Tech LLC, Queen Cutlery, Mission Knife and Tool, Knives of Alaska, Schrade Cutlery, Benchmade Knives, TTF Inc., and finally, the ever pervasive Eickhorn GMBH.

So what is the OKC3s exactly? Well, the standard objective answer is that it is a bayonet/fighting knife that has a non-reflective phosphate finished, 8 by 1-3/8 by .2 inch thick blade which, with scabbard, weighs 1¼ pounds, and that is produced from high

Figure 155: An absolutely wicked blade having two extremely sharp edges including the false edge.

carbon steel and includes a razor sharp edge on both the blade and false edge, along with an area of serration.

The knife, per specifications, has been temperature tested at -25 to +135 degrees Fahrenheit without any indication of breakage. Its grip is composed of the non-slip synthetic material *DYNAFLEX*, which is a rubbery, semi-soft material, with an ergonomically grooved surface that is ovoid rather than round, with the design intention being prevention of repetitive-stress injuries and hand fatigue, especially during training. It also has a *positioning access point* for rapid redirection of the blade during conditions of reduced visibility.

The finish is deeply parkerized, which does not scratch off when removed from the sheath like some. But what is truly striking is the presence of the blade, in that it appears much more massive than it actually is, even though it is quite large and menacing to be sure. It also comes sharpened with a razor's edge much like the early Phrobis M9s, but with the additional advantage that the false edge also has just as fine an edge, giving it a point easily equal to that of the best lance.

Figure 155.1: The OKC3s compared to the KaBar; similar but not comparable.

All in all, it requires little to imagine the brutish destruction this point is capable of visiting on nearly any object were it thrust with even modest force, not to mention its machete effect when slashing! It has, in fact, been credited with piercing ballistic body armor, which is a phenomenal accomplishment, and yet easily believable.

For those accustomed to the KaBar, there is a substantial similarity but no real comparison, as the KaBar is *slight* in comparison. That is, it is much lighter and smaller, but the OKC3s seems to embrace the hand as much as the hand embraces it! Similarly,

Figure 156: Well-placed serrations give the OKC3s the ability to cut through a variety of materials.

there is a balance and stability to the OKC3s, whereas the KaBar feels as though it requires a firm grasping lest it fall from the hand! Holding the OKC3s the first time is truly a phenomenal sensation! So much so, that one must experience it first hand, because it is as incredible as it is subjective!

The other observation of the two is that of orientation, in that, whereas the KaBar's point sweeps upward, the OKC3s points exactly ahead. It is straight, and the mind seems aware of it, as if being aimed wherever the eyes travel.

Interestingly, the ripping edge is in the form of serrations similar to those on a bread knife, rather than the saw toothed configuration of the M9, though it proved easily capable of cutting through an ammo can with no appreciable dulling, and with less than maximum effort. It is also interesting that the serrations are located on the main edge rather than the spine, though this configuration takes clear advantage of the point and main edge, as follow on sawing is much easier. This is also an obviously well designed feature.

Admittedly, it took a while to notice the absence of a cutter plate attached to the scabbard, doubtless because the whole wire cutter issue has been so pervasive up to this point. No doubt, the Marines quickly saw the silliness of that whole idea, and opted to address capabilities which are actually mission pertinent. In that same vein one will note that the aperture located in the M9's lower guard is not present in the OKC3s' guard, probably because if one wanted or needed to attach a lanyard there is no better place than the muzzle ring.

Figure 157: For comparison, from top to bottom, the M9, the XM9/2000, and the OKC3s.

For detail's sake one will observe that both the obverse and reverse ricassos bear the appropriate markings, but significantly that the actual nomenclature is OKC3s, which came as a bit of a surprise. So much so in fact that a call was placed to MARCORSYSCOM with the explanation that, or so the author was told, since the knife was actually designed and developed by Ontario Knife that it is known by their model designation, which is the third pattern.

Figure 158: For comparison, from top to bottom, the M9, the XM9/2000, and the OKC3s.

Next to the blade, the single most impressive feature of the knife is its handle, and the incredible comfort level it affords the hand when grasped which, as observed previously, exceeds even that of the KaBar. It is easily the most comfortable grip of any knife this author has ever experienced; at once pleasant to hold while offering total hand to grip security even when wet. It is very easy to recognize that the designer of this feature knew knives as well as he knew hands, and was supremely skilled at communicating the two!

Again, it is interesting to note that attachment of the latch plate to tang is accomplished by riveting, a feature that seems to keep resurfacing relative to the Marine mindset, and as observed in the 1993 trials. Obviously, this is not a weapon easily taken apart, nor one that is subject to loosening should a screw work itself loose.

Figure 158.1: Note the ease with which the OKC3s attaches. (Marine Corps photo)

Finally, the feature that gives all Marines that warm fuzzy like nothing else can is the *Eagle Globe and Anchor* icon. Prominently molded into the obverse grip, the logo is simply executed, as well as complimented on the reverse by an identical oval featuring the USMC initials.

Admittedly, this evaluation is superficial, but all indications are that Ontario Knife has come up with exactly the bayonet the Corps has always wanted!

The OKC3s scabbard possesses a weight to noise reduction comparable to the M7, and it is compatible with current issue modular load bearing equipment. In addition to two fastening straps, the knife secures to the scabbard by means of an integral stainless steel spring/friction device just inside the scabbard throat.

For maintenance of the knife's edge, there is an integral ceramic-coated aluminum honing rod located on the back of the scabbard, where a thick webbed strap protects it during stowage. Finally, the tip of the scabbard is open to facilitate drainage, and its color matches the Marine Corps' other *coyote tan* gear.

Figure 159: Scabbard for the OKC3s, sleek, simple, quiet, and well thought out.

Even after as brief and superficial an evaluation as has been undertaken here, it is obvious that the OKC3s is indeed a superior edged weapon within the realm of military bayonets and fighting knives. Its clever and practical design, coupled with extraordinarily quality materials and workmanship, makes it a weapon in no danger of serious competition!

Figure 160 & 161: To remove webbing simply slip off the elasticized end piece; on the right the Ceramic and aluminum honing stone attached to back of sheath and protected by heavy webbing.

Having said as much, one must concede that to compare the OKC3s to the M9 is an exercise in gross unfairness! The M9 is a superior weapon, but one born of the Cold War mindset, and developed in a technologically bygone era. Just as importantly, the Marines and Ontario Knife have the distinct advantage of significant knowledge gained from years of M9 testing and field observations, an advantage the designers of the M9 did not have. Moreover, when viewing the two from such a perspective, one could validly argue that the OKC3s has actually evolved from the M9.

Whatever one's postulations and observations, it is abundantly clear that the Marine Corps has, yet again, appropriated a superior weapon for its infantrymen. Moreover, they have accomplished it while simultaneously acquiring yet another symbol of their unique and separate identity!

Figure 162: Part of the whole - yet uniquely separate.... *Semper Fi!* (Marine Corps photo)

Appendix A: Glossary of Terms

AAR After Action Review a critique following any operation
ACAT Acquisition category
ACIE Army Clothing and Individual Equipment
Acq Acquisition
ADA Air Defense Artillery
ADACS Automated Data Collection System
AEC Army Evaluation Center
AI Additional Issue
AIT Advanced Infantry/Advanced Individual Training (Army)
ALMC U.S. Army Logistics Management College
AMBL Air Maneuver Battle Lab
AMC U.S. Army Materiel Command
AMDBD Army Medical Department Board
AMEDD Army Medical Department
AMEDDC&S U.S. Army Medical Department Center and School
AMMO Ammunition
AMRDEC Aviation and Missile Research and Development Center
AMSAA U.S. Army Materiel Systems Analysis Activity
AMSEC Army Modeling and Simulation Executive Council
AMSO Army Modeling and Simulation Office
Ao Operational Availability
AP Acquisition Plan
APA Army Procurement Appropriation
APB Acquisition Program Baseline
APG Aberdeen Proving Ground
APM Assistant Product Manager

AR Army Regulation
ARDEC Army Research, Development, and Engineering Center
ARL U.S. Army Research Laboratory
ARNG Army National Guard
AROC Army Requirements Oversight Council
ARPA Advanced Research Projects Agency
ARTEP Army Training and Evaluation Plans
ARTY Artillery
ASSY Assembly
ATACMS Army Tactical Missile System
ATC Aberdeen Test Center
ATE Automatic Test Equipment
ATEC Army Test and Evaluation Command
ATTC Aviation Technical Test Center
AUTIP Army User Test Instrumentation Program
AVN Aviation

BCIS Battlefield Combat Identification System
BDAR Battle Damage Assessment and Repair
BDE Brigade
BDU Battle Dress Uniform
BFV Bradley Fighting Vehicles
BFVS Bradley Fighting Vehicle System
Blade Spine Typically the thickest part of the blade. On a single-edge flat-ground knife, blade spine always refers to the outermost back of the blade. Technically, the spine is the fullest, thickest part of the blade, where the main bevel meets the false edge bevel.
Blood Groove A groove in the knife blade that makes it lighter and stiffer, also referred to as the *fuller*. A popular misconception holds that the blood groove's purpose is to break the vacuum when the blade is being extracted from a victim's body. In fact, no such vacuum occurs.
BN Battalion
BOI Basis of Issue
Bolster The metal material at the blade end of the knife handle; today these are usually of nickel silver or a mild stainless steel. In older less expensive knives they were often made of iron or mild steel.
Bowie Knife A large, fixed blade knife with a blade length from 6 to 14 inches. Invented by Rezin Bowie, but made famous by his brother, Jim, who died at the Alamo.
Box magazine Bundles of ammunition contained within a housing, usually a rectangular box shaped structure, that is inserted into a rifle, or pistol, usually from beneath via the magazine well.
BSA Base Support Agreement
BTRY Battery

CAC Combined Arms Center (TRADOC)
CAS Close Air Support

CASCOM Combined Arms Support Command
CATD Combined Arms Test Directorate
CBR Chemical, Biological, Radiological
CCRB Course Content Review Board (USMC)
CG Commanding General
CGS Command and General Staff
CHEM Chemical
CIE Clothing and Individual Equipment
CIO Chief Information Officer
CLIN Contract Line Item Number
Clip Clips are bundles of ammunition that are loaded through the top of weapons as a means of inserting the ammunition into the weapon's internal magazine. They may also be used to insert ammunition into external box magazines.
Clip Point Blade A blade on which the back line breaks and slants downward to produce a finer and more useful point.
Close Operations Major committed combat elements, usually comprised of maneuver, close combat and close air support, indirect fire support and counter-fire, combat support and combat service support, and command and control. Infantry and armored units apply direct combat power with short-range weapons assisted by attack helicopters and conventional artillery.
CMD Command
CO Commanding Officer
COC Chain of Command
Cohort A group of soldiers who entered the Army together and remained as an integral unit throughout their enlistment.
Cold War The period of 1945 to 1989 when the world was essentially polarized around either the United States (the West) or the Soviet Union (the East). The war was essentially a stand-off between the two.
COM/INT Communications/Intercept
COMARLANT Commander, U.S. Army Forces, Atlantic
Commercial off–the-shelf (COTS) An item that is sold, leased, or licensed to the general public; offered by a vendor trying to profit from it; supported and evolved by the vendor, who retains the intellectual property rights; available in multiple, identical copies; and used without modification of the internals.
CONUS Continental United States
Cosmoline
CoS Chief of Staff
COSCOM Corps Support Command
CP Command Post
CSA Chief of Staff, Army
CSM Command Sergeant Major
CSS Combat Service Support
CTC Combat Training Center
CWO Chief Warrant Officer
CY Calendar Year

D&O Doctrinal and Organizational
DA Department of the Army
DAB Defense Acquisition Board
DDJC Defense Distribution Center San Joaquin
DDSP (USN) Defense Distribution Depot Susquehanna, Pennsylvania
DDR&E Director of Defense Research and Engineering
DEFCON Defense Readiness Condition
DEL Delivery
DEPSECDEF Deputy Secretary of Defense
DEW Directed Energy Weapon
DIA Defense Intelligence Agency
DIR Director
DLA Defense Logistics Agency
DoD Department of Defense
DOD Department of Defense
DODD Department of Defense Directive
DODI Department of Defense Instruction
DRMO Defense Reutilization Management Office
DRT Design Review Team
DS Direct Support
DSARC Defense System Acquisition and Review Council
DS/GS Direct Support/General Support
DSA Defense Supply Agency
DSN Defense Switched Network
DSNET Defense Secure Network
DSS Direct Support System
DT&E Developmental Test and Evaluation in OSD
DTC U.S. Army Developmental Test Command
DTG Date Time Group
DX Literally Direct Exchange; used when an item is turned in and a new item is issued on a one-for-one basis. Also a military colloquialism denoting something that is gotten rid of: "He was worthless so I *DXed* him!"

E-date Test end date
ECP Engineering Change Proposal/Package
Edge The cutting surface of the blade
EDP Expeditious Discharge Program; a discharge program initiated in the early 70s giving unit commanders authority to discharge soldiers rapidly and with a minimum of paperwork or review.
End users Individuals who will be using the system in the operational environment.
EIA environmental impact assessment
En bloc magazine A weapon's ammunition feed mechanism capable of containing multiple rounds and contained within the receiver mechanism—not removable
ENG Engineer
ENGR Engineer

ENL Enlisted
EPLRS Enhanced Position Location Reporting System: EPLRS provides battlefield situational awareness to both the user and to their higher headquarters. This information greatly enhances the command and control of tactical units by providing commanders with the location of friendly units, a dynamic representation of the Forward Line of Troops, and abbreviated SITREPs for conditions and identification of adjacent equipped units.
ERDEC Edgewood Research, Development, and Engineering Center
Ergonomic Product designs that accommodate the structure, contours, and natural grip of the human hand.
Ethereal Intangible; spiritual
EXP Experiment
Eyeball To ***Eyeball***, or to look intently for the purpose of evaluation.

F&AO Finance and Accounting Office
FA Field Artillery
FAR Federal Acquisition Regulation
FAR Functional Area Review
FAS Field Artillery Section
FAST Forward Area Support Team
FAT First Article Testing. A contractor's sample that exists before production begins and is representative in all respects to the article which will be produced.
FDTE Force Development Test or Experimentation
Flat Ground The surface of the blade is flat from, or near, the back of the blade to the beginning of the sharpening bevel. Most production pocket knives are flat ground, while most handmade hunting knives are hollow ground.
Flatfoots Army infantry
FMF Fleet Marine Force
FM Field Manual
FOB POINT OF ORIGIN
FOF Force-on-Force
FOIA Freedom of Information Act
FORSCOM Forces Command
FOUO For Official Use Only
FTX Field Training Exercise
FUE First Unit Equipped
Fuller See Blood Groove
FY Fiscal Year

GAO General Accounting Office
GI *Government Issue*; only soldiers are *G.I.s*, therefore only soldiers are *issued.*
GMT Greenwich Mean Time
GO General Officer
GPS Global Positioning System

GS General Support
GSA General Services Administration

HAC House Appropriation Committee
HAZMAT Hazardous Material
HE High-Explosive
HET Heavy Equipment Transporter
HHC Headquarters and Headquarter Company
Hollow Ground The concave region of the blade surface is ground on a round surface (the face of a wheel.) This forms a hollow just above the beginning of the sharpening bevel and just below the back of the blade.
Hone As a noun: a fine stone used to put a finished edge on a knife or razor.
As a verb: the action of finishing the edge of a knife.
HMMWV High Mobility Multipurpose Wheeled Vehicle
HQ Headquarters
HQDA Headquarters, Department of the Army
HSC Health Services Command
Hundred MPH Tape Pronounced hundred mile an hour tape: a green duct type tape used wherever two objects meet, a hole or tear exists, or anywhere a GI can stick it to accommodate his purpose.

IAW In accordance with
ID Infantry Division
IG Inspector General
INSCOM Intelligence and Security Command
ISDN Integrated Services Data Network
ITAB Information Technology Acquisition Board

JAG Judge Advocate General
JCS Joint Chiefs of Staff
JIM Joint Improvement Modernization
JITC Joint Interoperability Test Command
JT&E Joint Test and Evaluation
JTF Joint Task Force

K Thousand
K-D targets Known Distance: A traditional bull's eye set at 500 meters as opposed to the man sized-type silhouette set at various distances.

LAN Local Area Network
LCC Life-Cycle Cost
LINES Line System or Linear Infighting Neural Override Engagement
LNO Liaison Officer
LOE Letter of Execution
LOG Logistics

LOI Letter of Instruction
LOS Line-of-Sight
LTC Lieutenant Colonel (Army)
LtCol Lieutenant Colonel (USMC)
LWL Land Warfare Laboratory
LR Letter Requirement

M9ophile A person who loves to collect M9s
MACE Martial arts Center of Excellence (USMC)
MACOM Major Army Command
MACP Modern Army Combatives Program
MAINT Maintenance
MAP Materiel Acquisition Process
MARCORSYSCOM Marine Corps Systems Command
MCC Marine Corps Commandant
MCMAP Marine Corps Martial Arts Program (MCMAP
MCO Marine Corps Order
MDAP Major Defense Acquisition Program
MEDCOM Medical Command
MGySgt Master Gunnery Sergeant (USMC)
MI Military Intelligence
MIL Military
MILES Multiple Integrated Laser Engagement System
MILPERCEN Military Personnel Center
MILPO Military Personnel Office
MILSPEC Military Specification
MIL-STD Military Standard
MILSTRAP Military Standard Transaction Reporting and Accounting Procedures
MILSTRIP Military Standard Requisitioning and Issue Procedures
MIPR Military Interagency Procurement Requisition
mm Millimeter
MOA Memorandum of Agreement
MOPP Mission Oriented Protective Posture
MOS Military Occupational Specialty
MOT&E Multi-Service Operational Test and Evaluation
MOUT Military Operations Urban Terrain
MP Military Police
MPBS Multipurpose Bayonet System
MRE Meals, Ready to Eat (combat rations)
MSE Mobile Subscriber Equipment - Similar to a cell phone
Msg Message
MTOE Modified Table of Organization and Equipment
MVA Modern Volunteer Army
MWO Modification Work Order

NAF Non Appropriated Funds
NATO North Atlantic Treaty Organization
NBC Nuclear, Biological, and Chemical
NCO Noncommissioned Officer
NG National Guard
NIST National Institute of Standards and Technology
NLT Not Later Than
Nomenclature A system of words used in a particular discipline; terminology.
NRDEC Natick Research Development and Engineer Center
NSN National Stock Number
NTC National Training Center
NUC Nuclear

OCONUS Outside Continental United States
OKC Ontario Knife Company
OPCON Operational Control
OPFOR Opposing forces
OPORD Operation Order
OPS Operations
OPSEC Operations Security
OPTEMPO Operational Tempo
OPTEVFOR Navy's Operational Test Evaluation Force
ORSA Operations Research Systems Analyst
OSD Office of the Secretary of Defense
OSHA Occupational Safety and Health Administration
OT Operational Test
OT&E Operational Test and Evaluation
OTA Operational Test Agency
OTC U.S. Army Operational Test Command
OTECC Operational Test and Evaluation Coordination Committee
OTRR Operational Test Readiness Review
OTSG Office of the Surgeon General

PA Pattern of Analysis or Physician Assistant
PAM Pamphlet
PAO Public Affairs Officer or Office
Parity In the Cold War a state of homeostasis; no stronger or weaker than the opposing side.
PC Personal Computer
PCS Permanent Change of Station
PEO Program Executive Officer
PER Personnel
PERSCOM Personnel Command
PI Product Improvement
PIB Product Improved Bayonet

Picatinny Rail The Picatinny Rail System
PIP Product Improvement Program
PLUGGER PLGR - Precision Lightweight GPS Receiver
PLL Prescribed Load List
PLRS Position Location and Reporting System
PLS Palletized Load System
PM Project Manager
Product Manager
Program Manager
Preventive Maintenance
PMCS Preventive Maintenance Checks and Services
PMO Program, Project, or Product Management Office (or Officer), or Provost Marshall's Office.
POC Point of Contact
POI Program of Instruction
POL Petroleum, Oils, and Lubricants
Pommel The end of a knife's handle. A metal cap over the pommel, called a butt cap. There are many different forms of pommels.
Proponent Agency The agency responsible: Ordnance for weapons, JAG for legal.
PUB Publication
PVT Production Verification Test or Private

QA Quality Assurance
QC Quality Control
Qty Quantity
Quillion/Quillon The guard which protects the hand from injury.

R&A Review and Analysis
R&C Review and Comment
R&D Research and Development
RAM Reliability, Availability, and Maintainability
Reverse The opposite side of the knife than the obverse side.
RC 1- Reserve Component
2- Remote Control
RCAS Reserve Component Automation System
RDA Research, Development, and Acquisition
RFV Request For Variance
RIA Rock Island Arsenal (Illinois).
Ricasso Flat area above and behind the hollow or flat ground region of the blade.
RM Resource Management
RMP Risk Management Plan
Rockwell Hardness The C scale, which is used for measuring the hardness of tool steels, is measured by pressing a diamond into the steel for a measured distance.
ROK Republic of Korea (South)
RRAD Red River Army Depot (Texarkana, Texas)

SA 1- System Assessment
2- Secretary of the Army
SAC Senate Appropriation Committee
SATCOM Satellite Communications
Satin Finish A finish that is not mirror-polished; lines from the fine abrasive gives a satin appearance.
SAW Squad Automatic Weapon
SECARMY Secretary of Army
SECDEF Secretary of Defense
SEDS Simulators, Emulators, Drivers, and Stimulators
Serrated Scallops in the edge which allow a sawing action; ideal for cutting things like seat-belts and plastic rope.
SFQC Special Forces Qualification Course (*Q-Course*)
SGM Sergeant Major
SIDPERS Standard Installation/Division Personnel System
Sheath Device for carrying a knife, tool, etc., on a belt, pack, or anywhere there is a strap.
SIG Signal
SIGSEC Signals Security
SIR Serious Incident Report
SITREP Situation Report
SLAD Survivability/Lethality Analysis Directorate (of ARL)
SLGR "SLUGGER"; Small Lightweight GPS Receiver; predecessor of the PLUGGER.
SMA Sergeants Major Academy
SMART Simulation and Modeling for Acquisition, Requirements, and Training
SME Subject Matter Expert
SMI Soldier Machine Interface
SO Special Operations
SOF Special Operations Forces
Soldier "To soldier"; the act of soldiering - to do those things that soldiers do.
SOP Standard Operating Procedure
SSAC Source Selection Advisory Council
SSC Soldier Support Center
STD Standard (Type Classification)
STEP Simulation, Test, and Evaluation Process
STRATMOB Strategic Mobilization Logistics Base, Gooseneck, SC
Stripper clip A flat metal strip into which a bundle of ammunition is placed that the firer inserts into a special notch on the top of the rifle's receiver in order to push the ammunition off of the clip and into the weapon's internal magazine, or used to load a box-magazine.
Sutler A sutler is a civilian who sells provisions to an army in the field, in camp, or in quarters.

T&E Test and Evaluation
TACCS Tactical Army Combat Service Support Computer System
TACFIRE Tactical Fire Direction System

TARDEC U.S. Army Tank Automotive Research, Development, and Engineering Center
TACSAT Tactical Satellite
TACSATCOM Tactical Satellite Communications
TACSIM Tactical Simulation
TAG The Adjutant General
TAMCN Table of Authorized Materiel Control Number
TBA To Be Announced
TBD To Be Determined
Tae kwon do A Korean art of self-defense; a style of karate.
TDA Table of Distribution and Allowances
TDAP Test Development and Acquisition Plan
T-date test start date
TDP Test Design Plan
TDY Temporary Duty
T&E Test and Evaluation
TELECON Telephone Conversation
TEMA U.S. Army Test and Evaluation Management Agency
TEXCOM Test and Experimentation Command
TF Task Force
TGT Target
TM Technical Manual
TN Technical note
TOC Tactical Operations Center
TOE Table of Organization and Equipment
TOPM Test Operating Procedures Manual
TOPS Test Operating Procedures
TOW Tube launched, Optically tracked, Wire guided missile
TRAC TRADOC Analysis Center
TRADOC U.S. Army Training and Doctrine Command
TRTC Tropic Regions Test Center
TSG The Surgeon General
TSM TRADOC System Manager

UIC Unit Identification Code
URD User Requirement Document
USAARMC&S U.S. Army Armor Center and School
USAARMCOM U.S. Army Armament Command
USADASCH U.S. Air Defense Artillery School
USAES U.S. Army Engineer School
USAEUR U.S. Army Europe
USAFAS U.S. Army Field Artillery School
USAHSC U.S. Army Health Services Command
USAIB United States Army Infantry Branch
USAIC United States Army Infantry Center
USAICS U.S. Army Intelligence Center and School

USAINSCOM United States Army Intelligence Command
USAIS United States Army Infantry School
USAISC U.S. Army Information Systems Command
USAKA U.S. Army Kwajalein Atoll
USAMSAA U.S. Army Materiel Systems Analysis Activity
USAR U.S. Army Reserve
USAREC U.S. Army Recruiting Comand
USAREUR U.S. Army, Europe
USARJ U.S. Army, Japan
USARPAC U.S. Army Pacific Command
USARPAC United States Army Pacific Command
USARSO U.S. Army, South
USASDC U.S. Army Strategic Defense Command
USASOC U.S. Army Special Operations Command
USATRADOC U.S. Army Training and Doctrine Command
USAWESTCOM U.S. Army Western Command
USC United States Code
USCENTCOM U.S. Central Command
USEUCOM U.S. European Command
USSOCOM United States Special Operations Command

VEH Vehicle
VIP Very Important Person
VTC Video Teleconferencing
VV&A Verification, Validation, and Accreditation
Vendor A commercial enterprise whose purpose in producing a product is to offer it for sale in the marketplace, and not in response to specific program needs. The vendor may also be a contractor or subcontractor who is under contract to modify a commercial item in response to unique program requirements.

WAN Wide Area Networks
WARM Wartime Reserve Mode
Waterbury Buckle A 1-1/2 inch Classic Side Release Buckle; quick disconnect buckle which secures the bayonet scabbard to the web belt.
WESTCOM Western Command
WO Warrant Officer
WPN weapon
WRAP Warfighting Rapid Acquisition Program
WRGSA War Reserve general Supply Activity, Cp Carroll, S. Korea
WSMR White Sands Missile Range (NM)

XO Executive Officer

YPG Yuma Proving Ground

Appendix B: Nomenclature

M9 Characteristics

	RICOSSO MARKINGS	FONT/REMARKS	FINISH	FULLER	GRIND	STEP	TANG	GUARD	LATCH	DATE	QTY	HI $
M9P1	M9, Phrobis III, U.S.A. >	Flat "M" CRAZY 9	BEAD	FULL	HOL	YES	ROD	DOL/OPENER	DOT	1987	1034	$1,500.00
M9P2	M9, Phrobis III, U.S.A.	Flat "M" CRAZY 9	BEAD	FULL	HOL	YES	ROD	DOL/OPENER	DOT	1987-89	U	$450.00
M9P3	M9, Phrobis III, U.S.A.,		BEAD	FULL	HOL	YES	ROD	DOL/OPENER	DOT	1988-89	U	$350.00
M9P4	M9, Phrobis III, U.S.A., PAT. PEND.	NARROW	BEAD	FULL	HOL	YES	ROD	DOL/OPENER	DOT	1989	U	$350.00
M9P5	M9, Phrobis III, U.S.A., PAT. PEND.	WIDE	BEAD	FULL	HOL	YES	ROD	DOL/OPENER	DOT	1989	U	$350.00
M9B1	M9-USMC, BUCK +, USA	SHARP TOP "M"	BEAD	FULL	HOL	YES	ORIG	OPENER	DOT	1991	5000	$500.00
M9B2	M9-USMC, BUCK /, USA		BEAD	FULL	HOL	YES	RIVET	OPENER	DOT	1993	175	$2,000.00
M9B3	M9-USMC, BUCK /, USA		BEAD	FULL	HOL	YES	THREAD	OPENER	DOT	1993	175	$2,000.00
M9B4	M9-USMC, BUCK /, USA		BEAD	FULL	HOL	YES	SH-ROD	OPENER	DOT	1993	U	$2,500.00
M9G1	M9, LANCAY, USA	GENERAL CUTLERY	SAND	FULL	HOL	YES	ROD	OPENER	BLANK	1992	300	$1,500.00
M9L1	M9, LANCAY, USA		SAND	FULL	HOL	YES	ROD	BLANK	DOT	1992	104,111	$450.00
M9L1-1	M9, LANCAY,USA		SAND	HALF	FLAT	YES	ROD	BLANK	DOT	1992-93	350	$1,500.00
M9L1-2	M9, LANCAY,USA		SAND	NONE	HOL	YES	ROD	BLANK	DOT	1993	U	$350.00
M9L1-3	M9, LANCAY,USA	2d Contract blade	SAND	NONE	FLAT	NO	ROD	BLANK	U	1995	1090	$1,000.00
M9L2	M9, LAN-CAY,U S A		OXIDE	NONE	FLAT	NO	ROD	BLANK	DOT	1994	104,111	$300.00
M9L2-1	M9, LAN-CAY,USA	Early 2d Contract	OXIDE	NONE	HOL	NO	ROD	BLANK	DOT	1995	U	$1,000.00
M9L2-2	M9, LANCAY,USA	1st Contract blade	OXIDE	FULL	HOL	YES	ROD	BLANK	U	1995	200	$1,000.00
M9L3	M9, LAN-CAY,USA		OXIDE	NONE	FLAT	NO	ROD	BLANK	L-C	1999	12,500	$100.00
M9O1	M-9, ONTARIO KNIFE CO., USA		OXIDE	NONE	FLAT	NO	ROD	BLANK	U	1999	12,500	$100.00

U = Unknown
LC = LAN-CAY

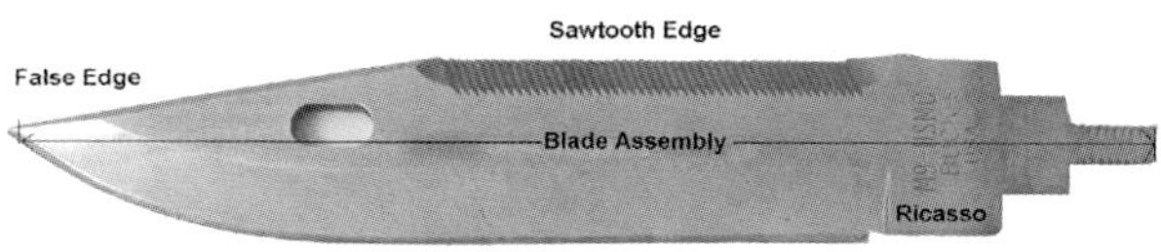

Handle

Tang

Handguard
(QUILLON)

Latch Assembly

Cap Screw

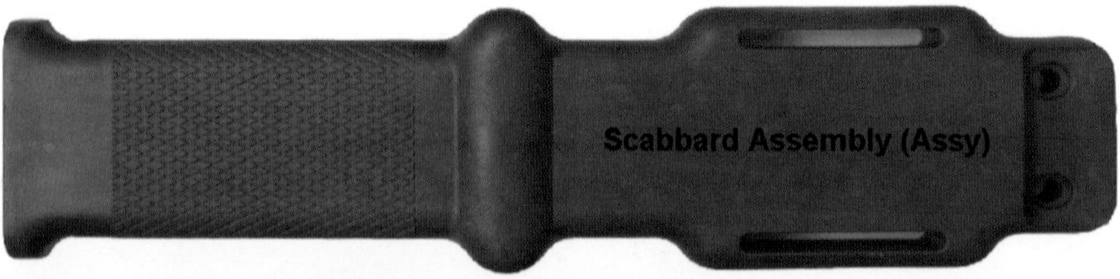

Attaching Assy Scabbard

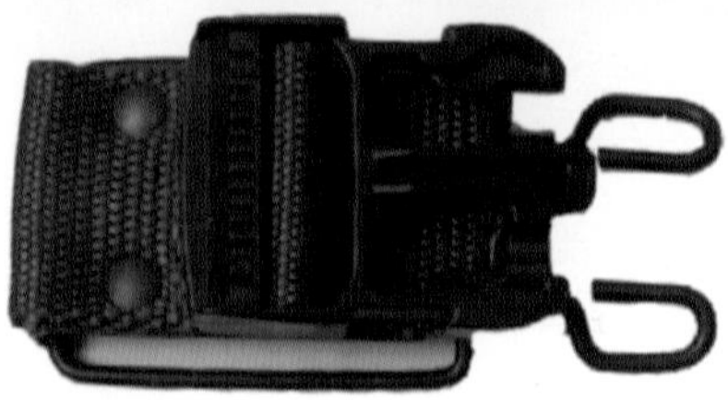

Attaching Assy, Load Bearing

Wire Cutter Plate

Cap Screws

Scabbard Assy

Attaching Assy Scabbard

Accessory Case

Attaching Assy Load Bearin

Wire Cutter Plate

Cap Screws

Cap Screws

Buck Date Symbols

Year	Symbol	Year	Symbol
1986	<	1995	⊂
1987	>	1996	⊃
1988	∧	1997	∩
1989	∨	1998	∪
1990	X	1999	⊏
1991	+	2000	⊐
1992	—	2001	⊓
1993	/	2002	
1994	\	2003	T

Appendix C:
M9 Variations

Figure 167

M9P1
Marking: M9, Phrobis III, U.S.A. >
Finish: Bead blasted
Fuller: Full
Grind: Hollow
Step: Yes
Guard: Dolphin, Bottle openers
Latch: Dot
Date: 1987
Quantity: 1034

Figure 168

M9P2
Marking: M9, Phrobis III, U.S.A.
Finish: Bead blasted
Fuller: Full
Grind: Hollow
Step: Yes
Guard: Dolphin, Bottle peners
Latch: Dot
Date: 1987-1989
Quantity: ?

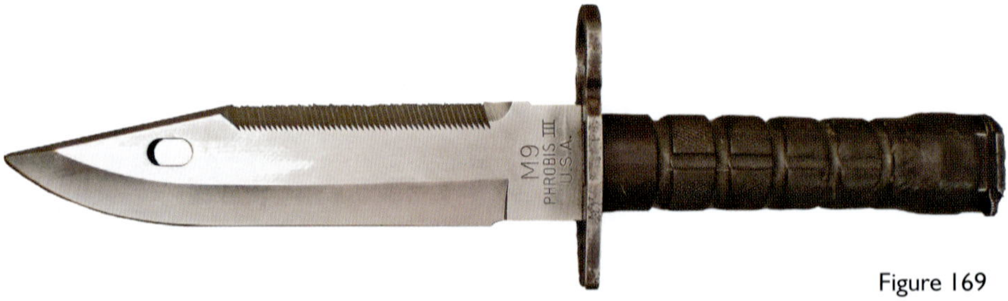

Figure 169

M9P3
Marking: M9, Phrobis III, U.S.A.
Finish: Bead blasted
Fuller: Full
Grind: Hollow
Step: Yes
Guard: Dolphin, Bottle openers
Latch: Dot
Date: 1988 - 1989
Quantity: ?

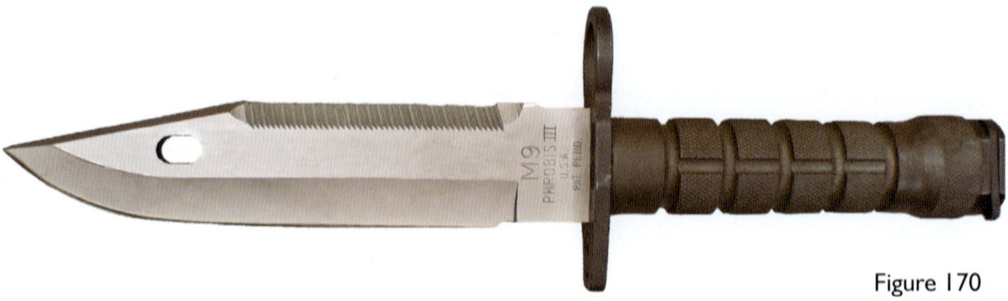

Figure 170

M9P4
Marking: M9, Phrobis III, U.S.A. – Narrow Font
Finish: Bead blasted
Fuller: Full
Grind: Hollow
Step: Yes
Guard: Dolphin, Bottle openers
Latch: Dot
Date: 1989
Quantity: ?

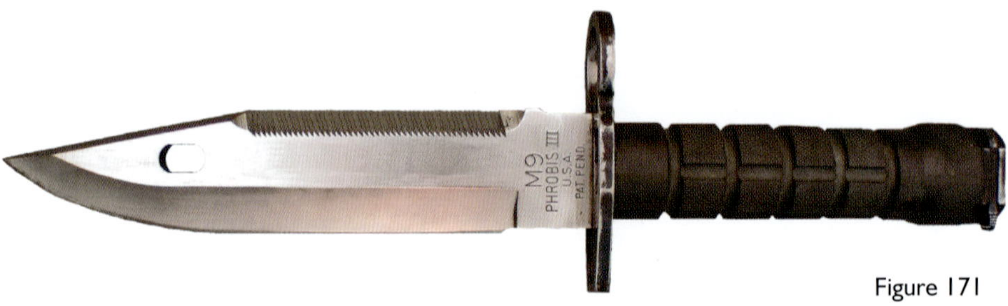

Figure 171

M9P5
Marking: M9, Phrobis III, U.S.A. – Wide Font
Finish: Bead blasted
Fuller: Full
Grind: Hollow
Step: Yes
Guard: Dolphin, Bottle openers
Latch: Dot
Date: 1987
Quantity: ?

Figure 172

M9B1
Marking: M9-USMC, BUCK +, USA
Finish: Bead blasted
Fuller: Full
Grind: Hollow
Step: Yes
Guard: Bottle openers
Latch: Dot
Date: 1991
Quantity: 5000

Figure 173

M9B2
Marking: M9-USMC, BUCK /, USA
Finish: Bead blasted
Fuller: Full
Grind: Hollow
Step: None
Guard: Bottle openers
Latch: Dot
Date: 1993
Quantity: 175

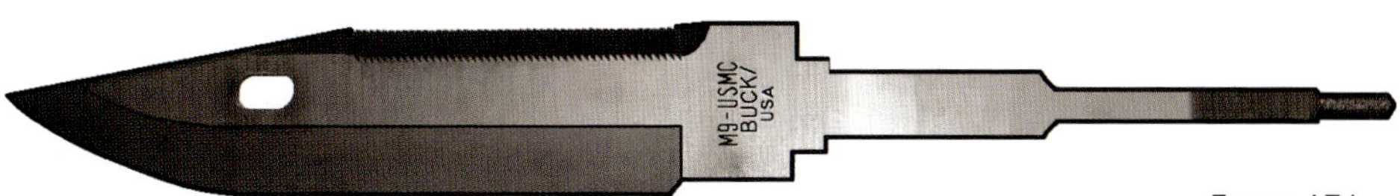

Figure 174

M9B3
Marking: M9-USMC, BUCK /, USA
Finish: Bead blasted
Fuller: Full
Grind: Hollow
Step: None
Guard: Bottle openers
Latch: Dot
Date: 1993
Quantity: 175

Figure 175

M9B4
Marking: M9-USMC, BUCK /, USA
Finish: Bead blasted
Fuller: Full
Grind: Hollow

Step: None
Guard: Bottle openers
Latch: Dot
Date: 1993
Quantity: ?

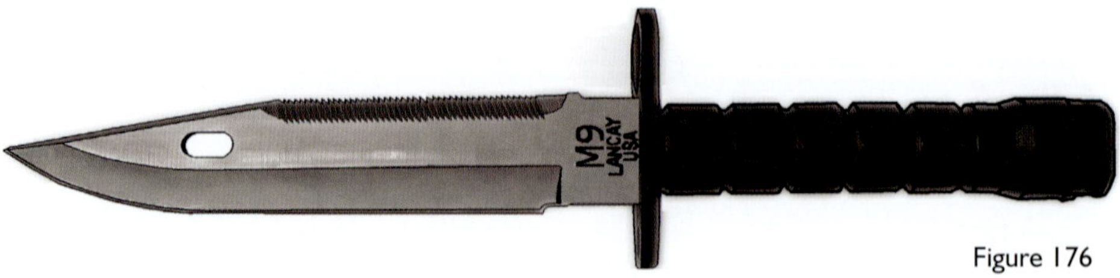

Figure 176

M9G1
Marking: M9, LANCAY, USA
Finish: Sand blasted
Fuller: Full
Grind: Hollow

Step: Yes
Guard: Plain
Latch: Blank
Date: 1987
Quantity: 300

Figure 177

M9L1
Marking: M9, LANCAY, USA
Finish: Sand blasted
Fuller: Full
Grind: Hollow

Step: Yes
Guard: Plain
Latch: Dot
Date: 1992
Quantity: ?

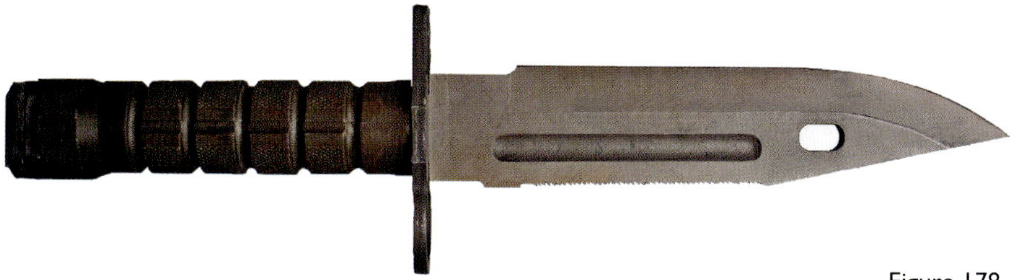

Figure 178

M9L1-1
Marking: M9, LANCAY, USA
Finish: Sand blasted
Fuller: Half (Narrow)
Grind: Hollow
Step: Yes
Guard: Plain
Latch: -
Date: 1992-1993
Quantity: 350

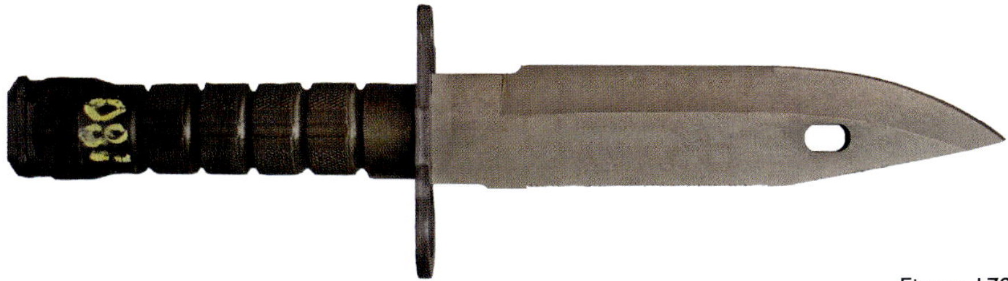

Figure 179

M9L1-2
Marking: M9, LANCAY, USA
Finish: Sand blasted
Fuller: None
Grind: Hollow
Step: Yes
Guard: Plain
Latch: Dot
Date: 1993
Quantity: ?

Figure 180

M9L1-3
Marking: M9, LANCAY, USA
Finish: Sand blasted
Fuller: None
Grind: Flat
Step: No
Guard: Plain
Latch: Dot
Date: 1995
Quantity: 1090

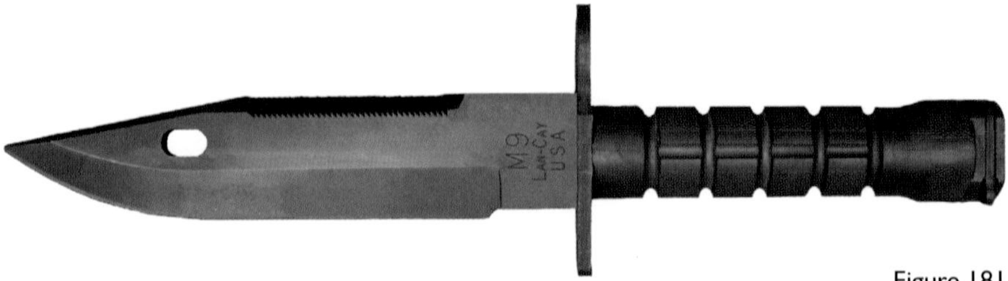

Figure 181

M9L2
Marking: M9, LAN-CAY, USA
Finish: Oxide
Fuller: None
Grind: Flat
Step: No
Guard: Plain
Latch: Dot
Date: 1994
Quantity: 104,111

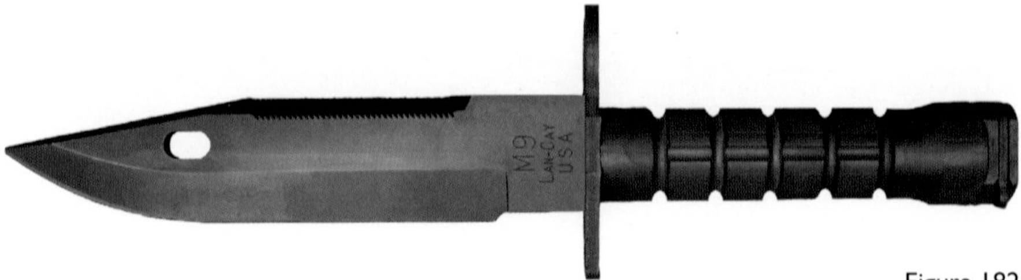

Figure 182

M9L2-1
Marking: M9, LAN-CAY, USA
Finish: Oxide
Fuller: None
Grind: Hollow
Step: No
Guard: Plain
Latch: Dot
Date: 1995
Quantity: ?

Figure 183

M9L2-2
Marking: M9, LANCAY, USA
Finish: Oxide
Fuller: Full
Grind: Flat
Step: Yes
Guard: Plain
Latch: -
Date: 1995
Quantity: 200

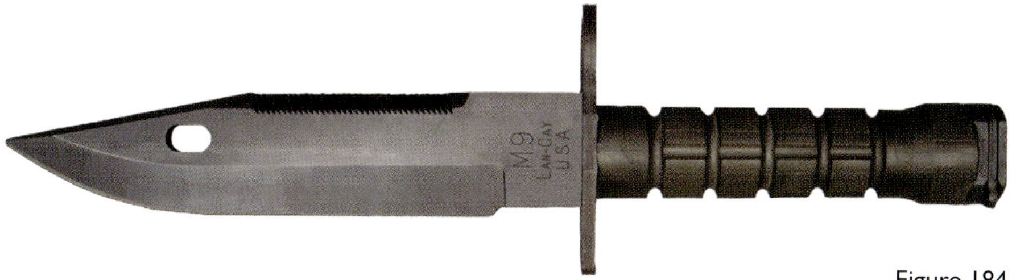

Figure 184

M9L3
Marking: M9, LAN-CAY, USA
Finish: Oxide
Fuller: None
Grind: Flat
Step: None
Guard: Plain
Latch: LAN-CAY & Dot
Date: 1999
Quantity: 12,500

Figure 185

M901
Marking: M9, ONTARIO KNIFE CO., USA
Finish: Oxide
Fuller: None
Grind: Flat
Step: None
Guard: Plain
Latch: Dot
Date: 1999
Quantity: 12,500

Appendix D: Scabbard Variations and Characteristics

Type 1

Figure 186: Front of an original scabbard featuring BRASS attaching assembly rivets, making these rather rare, as they were issued with the M9P1 (Chevron M9s), but may also have been used with the M9P2s, as the exact date of the change over from brass to steel rivets is unknown.

Maker: Phrobis
Attaching Assembly Scabbard: Early Long Webbing
Attaching Assembly LBE: Early Assembly Rivets Attaching Assembly LBE: Brass
Loops: 4
Stone: Yes
Marking: Dolphin Below stone
Stop: None
Driver: Tip
T-Stud Angle: 45 Degrees
Pouch: Yes
Date: 1987

Figure 187: Rear of an original scabbard featuring the long webbing, stone, and dolphin marking.

Type 2

Figure 188: Front of an original scabbard featuring STEEL attaching assembly rivets, which make it rather rare.

Maker: Phrobis
Attaching Assembly Scabbard: Early Long Webbing
Attaching Assembly LBE: Early Assembly
Rivets Attaching Assembly LBE: Steel
Loops: 4
Stone: Yes
Marking: Dolphin below stone
Stop: None
Driver: Tip
T-Stud Angle: 45 Degrees
Pouch: Yes
Date: 1987-1989

Figure 189: Rear of an original scabbard featuring the long webbing, stone, and dolphin marking.

Type 3

Figure 190: Early scabbard by Buck as used with the 1991 USMC contract and 1993 USMC prototype M9s.

Maker: Buck
Attaching Assembly Scabbard: Early Long Webbing
Attaching Assembly LBE: Early Assembly
Rivets Attaching Assembly LBE: Steel
Loops: 4
Stone: Yes
Marking: None
Stop: Round type
Driver: Tip
T-Stud Angle: 180 Degrees
Pouch: Yes (1991)
Date: 1991, 1993 (USMC)

Figure 191: Rear of scabbard featuring the long webbing and stone, but devoid of markings.

Type 4

Figure 192: Front of the standard scabbard, but with the new webbing MWO and issued with the first Lan-Cay contract bayonets (M9L1).

Maker: LanCay
Attaching Assembly Scabbard: Improved Webbing
Attaching Assembly LBE: Improved Assembly
Rivets Attaching Assembly LBE: Steel
Loops: 4
Stone: Yes
Marking: LANCAY below stone
Stop: None
Driver: Tip
T-Stud Angle: 45 Degrees
Pouch: No
Date: 1987

Figure 193: Rear of an original scabbard featuring the long webbing, stone, and dolphin marking.

Type 5

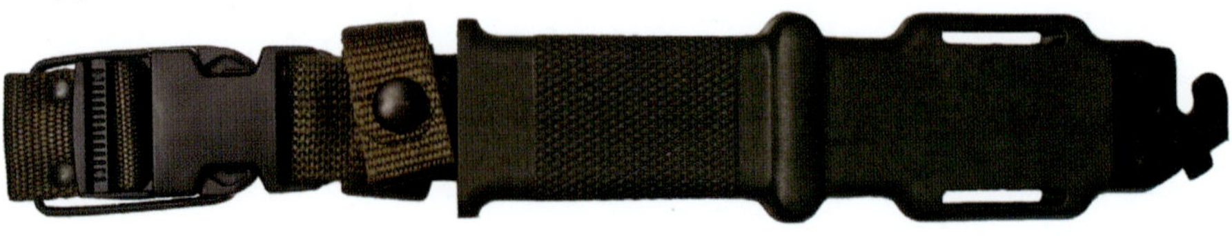

Figure 194: Front of an original scabbard featuring STEEL attaching assembly rivets, which make it rather rare.

Maker: LAN-CAY
Attaching Assembly Scabbard: Improved Webbing
Attaching Assembly LBE: Improved Assembly
Rivets Attaching Assembly LBE: Steel
Loops: 2
Stone: Yes
Marking: LAN-CAY below stone
Stop: Yes
Driver: Side
T-Stud Angle: 45 Degrees
Pouch: No
Date: 1987-1989

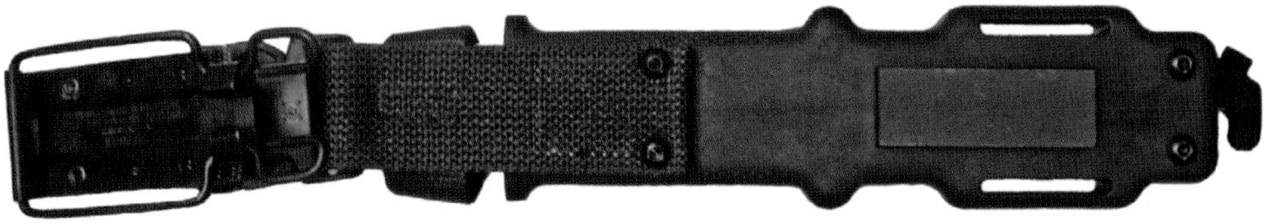

Figure 195: Rear of an original scabbard featuring the long webbing, stone, and dolphin marking.

Type 6

Figure 196: Front of an original scabbard featuring STEEL attaching assembly rivets, which make it rather rare.

Maker: LAN-CAY
Attaching Assembly Scabbard: Improved Webbing
Attaching Assembly LBE: Improved Assembly
Rivets Attaching Assembly LBE: Steel
Loops: 2
Stone: No
Marking: LANCAY below former stone depression
Stop: Yes
Driver: Side
T-Stud Angle: 45 Degrees
Pouch: No
Date: 1987-1989

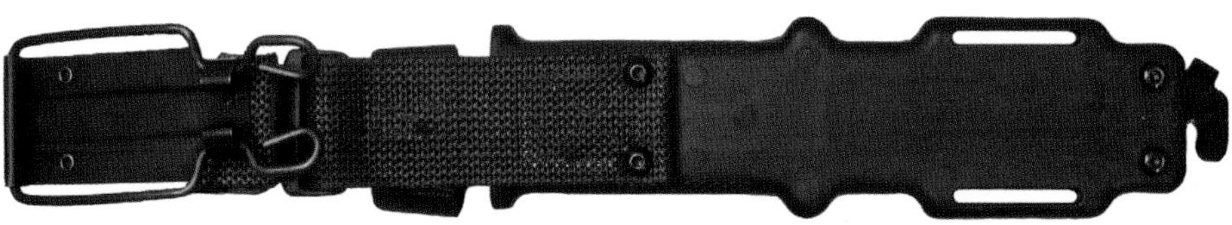

Figure 197: Rear of an original scabbard featuring the long webbing, stone, and dolphin marking.

Type 7

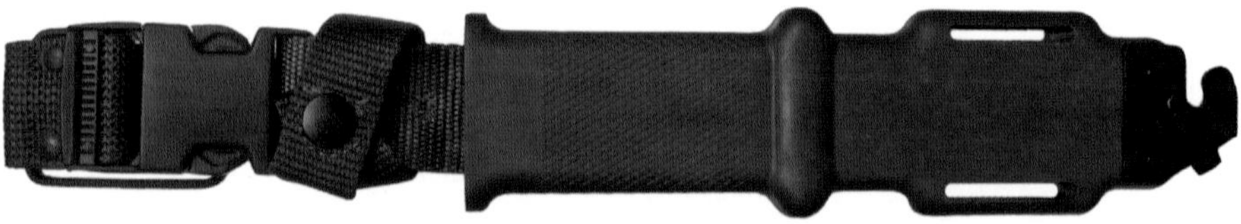

Figure 198: Front of an original scabbard featuring STEEL attaching assembly rivets, which make it rather rare.

Maker: Ontario Knife Company
Attaching Assembly Scabbard: Improved Webbing
Attaching Assembly LBE: Improved Assembly
Rivets Attaching Assembly LBE: Steel
Loops: 2
Stone: NO
Marking: None
Stop: Yes
Driver: Side
T-Stud Angle: 45 Degrees
Pouch: Yes
Date: 1987-1989

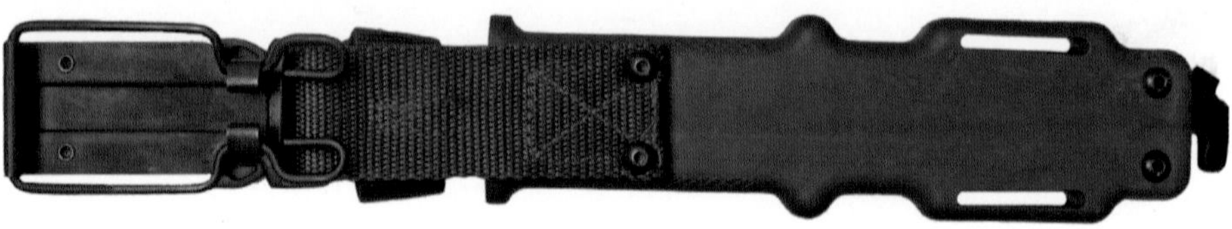

Figure 199: Rear of an original scabbard featuring the long webbing, stone, and dolphin marking.

Appendix D - Scabbard Variations

	Type 1	Type 2	Type3	Type 4	Type 5	Type 6	Type7
Maker	Phrobis	Phrobis	Buck	LANCAY	LAN-CAY	LAN-CAY	Ontario Knife Co.
AAS	Early/Long	Early/Long	Early/Long	PIB	PIB	PIB	PIB
AAL	Early	Early	Early	PIB	PIB	PIB	PIB
Rivets	Brass	Steel	Steel	Steel	Steel	Steel	Steel
Loops	4	4	4	4	2	2	2
Stone	Yes	Yes	Yes	Yes	Yes	No	No
Marking	Dolphin	Dolphin	None	LANCAY	LAN-CAY	LANCAY	None
Stop	No	No	Round Type	None	Yes	Yes	Yes
Driver	Tip	Tip	Tip	Tip	Side	Side	Side
T-Stud	45 Degrees	45 Degrees	180 Degrees	45 Degrees	45 Degrees	45 Degrees	45 Degrees
Pouch	Yes	Yes	Yes,1991	No	No	No	No
Date Range	1987	1987-1989	1991, 1993	1987	1987-1989	1987-1989	1987-1989

AAS: Attaching Assy Scabbard

AAL: Attaching Assy LBE

PIB: Product improved

Figure 200: Matrix of scabbard variations.

Appendix E:
M9 Contracts and Production Data

The following are tabulated summaries of M9 contracts from the inception of the bayonet until the present. Ideally, the actual documents would have been placed here for the reader to peruse at his leisure. However, given the actual size of the contract pages and their sheer volume that was not even a remote possibility.

What we have is the essential production facts that could be gleaned from the original contracts, recognizing that associated with each document were undoubtedly scores of memos containing comments, factoids and other historical tid-bits; all a part of the "story" of the event – particulars that we probably will never know.

As any researcher will readily attest primary source documents are the best, most reliable tool when one is attempting to paint a picture of the past, however incomplete they maybe. Never the less, much can be learned from these extracts and they are always a good reference to have at hand. For those who would like to have copies of the contracts in their entirety they are downloadable in PDF from the Rock Island Arsenal website, and the data base at the Commerce Business Daily website (http://www.fbodaily.com).

Contracts before 1994 must be obtained the old fashioned way under the FOI Act. For those who choose this route please be prepared to be bureaucratized! Rock Island means to be helpful but it so huge and there are so many different activities on it that it will take a very long time to get those documents.

Additionally, agencies will copy "files" for you under the FOI Act. If your contract is in a "file" you will receive ALL the documents in that file (unclassified) and be charged for each one. That could be fifty pages, or five hundred, and you won't know until it's time to pay! A less costly, though admittedly less complete alternative is the U.S. National Archives website (http://www.archives.gov/research) where contract abstracts can be obtained and downloaded. Less information, less frustration and less cost!

A final note on the original contracts. Only the first four or five pages are actually useful information for the collector. The remaining, which can run as high as sixty pages, are copies of laws and acts that apply to contracts in general such as equal opportunity awards for small businesses and minority owned businesses and the like. Generally, for collectors that isn't pertinent information and it can be found in the U.S. Code in any event.

AWARD DATE	CONTRACT Nr. ORDER Nr.	NOUN	NSN	QTY
15 October 1986	DAAA21-87-C-0001	Bayonet, Knife, M9	1095-01-278-1174	325,000
31-Mar-1992	DAAA09-92-C-0406	Bayonet, Knife, M9	1095-01-278-1174	30,500
14-Sep-1994	DAAA09-94-C-0571	Bayonet, Knife, M9	1095-01-278-1174	104,111
23-Apr-1996	DAAE20-96-D-0001	Bayonet, Knife, M9//////////////	1095-01-278-1174	190,915
23-Apr-1996	DAAE20-96-D-0001	Attaching, Assy //////////////////	1005-01-278-1174	10,458
23-Apr-1996	DAAE20-96-D-0001	Strap, Web //////////////////////////	5340-01-275-5398	15,423
23-Apr-1996	DAAE20-96-D-0001	Handle, Bayonet, M9 //////////	5110-01-277-5767	1,111
23-Apr-1996	DAAE20-96-D-0001	Stone, Sharpening //////////////	5345-01-275-5395	17,123
9-May-1996	DAAE20-96-C-0224	Scabbard, Bayonet	1095-01-512-2744	
10-Jul-1996	DAAE20-96T-0246	CUTTER ASSEMBLY	1005-01-394-6125	
7-Jan-1998	DAAE20-98-C-0030	Bayonet w/ Scabb, M9	1095-01-227-1739	6,000
22-Apr-1998	DAAE20-98-P-0221	Scabbard, Bay, M9	1095-01-512-2744	
7-Feb-1999	DAAE20-99-R-0049	Bayonet w/ Scabard, M9	1095-01-227-1739	2,400
4-Mar-1999	DAAE20-99-C-0035	Bayonet w/ Scabard, M9	1095-01-227-1739	
1-Jul-1999	DAAE20-99-C-0035	Bayonet w/ Scabard, M9	1095-01-227-1739	9,000
26-Aug-1999	DAAE20-99-R-0211			
8-Jun-2006	W52H09-06-R-0212	BAYONET SYSTEM	1095-01-521-6087	
		STRAP, NYLON	8465-01-507-5635	
		SCABBARD	1095-01-507-5713	
		BAYONET, KNIFE	1095-01-507-5729	
8-Jun-2006	W52H09-06-R-0212	BAYONET SYSTEM	1095-01-521-6087	
23-Sep-1999	DAAE20-99-D-0134	M9 & COMPONENTS		
23-Sep-1999	ORDER Nr. 0001	BAYONET & SCABBARD, M9	1095-01-227-1739	12,500
	REL 001	DEL 001: 23 DEC 1999		2,000
		DEL 002: 24 JAN 2000		2,000
		DEL 003: 24 FEB 2000		2,000
		DEL 004: 24 MAR 2000		2,000
		DEL 005: 24 APR 2000		2,000
		DEL 006: 24 MAY 2000		2,000
		DEL 007: 24 JUN 2000		500
13-Apr-2001	ORDER Nr. 0002	HANDLE, KNIFE BLADE	5110-01-277-5767	600
	REL 001	DEL 001: 30 JUN 2001		600
20-Feb-2002	ORDER Nr. 0003	ATTACHING ASSEMBLY	1005-01-278-1174	4,648
	REL 001	DEL 001: 01 APR 2002		4,648
2-May-2002	ORDER Nr. 0004	STRAP, WEBBING	5340-01-275-5398	4,389
	REL 001	DEL 001: 16 MAY 2002		4,389
31-Oct-2002	ORDER Nr. 0005	BAYONET & SCABBARD, M9	1095-01-227-1739	4,509
	REL 001	DEL 001: 08 NOV 2002		500
		DEL 002: 15 NOV 2002		500
		DEL 003: 22 NOV 2002		500
		DEL 004: 02 DEC 2002		500
		DEL 005: 09 DEC 2002		255
	REL 002	DEL 001: 09 DEC 2002		245
		DEL 002: 16 DEC 2002		500
		DEL 003: 23 DEC 2002		500
		DEL 004: 06 JAN 2003		500
		DEL 005: 13 JAN 2003		509
1-Jul-2003	ORDER Nr. 0006	STATUS UNKNOWN	NO RECORD EXISTS	
	REL 001	DEL 001: 20 JAN 2004		5,600
20-Nov-2003	ORDER Nr. 0007	ATTACHING ASSEMBLY	1005-01-278-1174	4,000
	REL 001	DEL 001: 20 JAN 2004		400
		DEL 002: 27 JAN 2004		400
		DEL 003: 03 FEB 2004		400
		DEL 004: 10 FEB 2004		400
		DEL 005: 17 FEB 2004		400
		DEL 006: 24 FEB 2004		400
		DEL 007: 02 MAR 2004		400
		DEL 008: 09 MAR 2004		400
		DEL 008: 16 MAR 2004		400
		DEL 008: 23 MAR 2004		400

UNIT PRICE	CONTRACT VALUE	FIRM	ORIGIN	DEST	REMARKS
$49.56	$15,641,000	PHROBIS	PIC		PICATINNY
$46.80	$1,427,400.00	LANCAY			END DATE 09 MAR 1993
	$390,871.00	LANCAY			(PIB) Product Improverd
///////////	///////////////////	BUCK	//////////	////////////	END DATE:28 FEB 2000
///////////	///////////////////	//////////	//////////	//////////	NOT AWARDED
///////////	///////////////////	//////////	//////////	//////////	NOT AWARDED
///////////	///////////////////	//////////	//////////	//////////	NOT AWARDED
///////////	///////////////////	//////////	//////////	//////////	NOT AWARDED
	$91,969.00	Gen Cutl'y Inc			
$41.00	$246,000.00	LanCay			
	$51,759.00	Lancay			
		LanCay			SOLE SOURCE
	$145,920.00	LanCay			
		LanCay			36,000 OPTION
					(ECP) L9S2030
					Stone deleted
		OKC			SOLE SOURCE
	$1,655,758.50	LANCAY			
$44.00	$550,000.00	LANCAY	RIA	RRAD	P00001: ECP L2S3082
	$88,000.00			RRAD	dtd 09MAY2003 ADDS
	$88,000.00			RRAD	ERGONOMIC HANDLE
	$88,000.00			RRAD	
	$88,000.00			RRAD	
	$88,000.00			RRAD	
	$88,000.00			RRAD	
	$22,000.00			RRAD	
$1.68	$1,008.00	LANCAY	RIA	DDSC	
	$1,008.00			RRAD	
$4.40	$20,451.20	LANCAY	RIA	DDSC	
	$20,451.20			DDSC	
$2.78	$12,201.42	LANCAY	RIA	DDSC	
	$12,201.42			DDSC	
$38.75	$179,232.75	LANCAY	RIA		
	$19,875.00			DDSC	
	$19,875.00			DDSC	
	$19,875.00			DDSC	
	$19,875.00			DDSC	
	$10,136.25			DDSC	
	$9,738.75			DDSJ	
	$19,875.00			DDSJ	
	$19,875.00			DDSJ	
	$19,875.00			DDSJ	
	$20,232.75			DDSJ	
IN RIA DATA	OF THIS ORDER				Cage Code OTG33
$38.65	$216,440.00	LAN-CAY	RIA		
	$216,440.00			DDSP	ECP L9S3021 dtd
$4.50	$18,000.00	LAN-CAY	RIA	DDSP	4-Oct-99
	$1,800.00			DDSP	
	$1,800.00			DDSP	
	$1,800.00			DDSP	
	$1,800.00			DDSP	
	$1,800.00			DDSP	
	$1,800.00			DDSP	
	$1,800.00			DDSP	
	$1,800.00			DDSP	
	$1,800.00			DDSP	
	$1,800.00			DDSP	

AWARD DATE	CONTRACT Nr. ORDER Nr.	NOUN	NSN	QTY
20-Nov-2003	ORDER Nr. 0007	STRAP, WEBBING	5340-01-275-5398	1,300
	REL 001	DEL 001: 20 JAN 2004		300
		DEL 002: 27 JAN 2004		300
		DEL 003: 03 FEB 2004		300
		DEL 004: 10 FEB 2004		300
		DEL 005: 10 FEB 2004		100
20-Nov-2003	ORDER Nr. 0007	HANDLE, KNIFE BLADE	5110-01-277-5767	290
	REL 001	DEL 001: 01 DEC 2003		290
4-Aug-2004	ORDER Nr. 0008	BAYONET & SCABBARD, M9	1095-01-227-1739	10,000
	REL 001	DEL 001: 30 NOV 2004		2,000
		DEL 002: 30 DEC 2004		2,000
		DEL 003: 31 JAN 2005		2,000
		DEL 004: 28 FEB 2005		2,000
		DEL 005: 30 MAR 2005		2,000
23-Sep-1999	DAAE20-99-D-0135	BAYONET & SCABBARD, M9	1095-01-227-1739	12,500
23-Sep-1999	ORDER Nr. 0001	BAYONET & SCABBARD, M9	1095-01-227-1739	12,500
	REL 001	DEL 001: 21 DEC 1999		2,000
		DEL 002: 30 DEC 1999		520
		DEL 003: 17 JAN 2000		2,000
		DEL 004: 23 FEB 2000		2,000
		DEL 005: 24 MAR 2000		2,000
		DEL 006: 24 APR 2000		2,000
		DEL 007: 24 MAY 2000		1,979
	REL 002	DEL 001: 18 FEB 2000	1095-01-227-1739	1
29-Sep-1999	ORDER Nr. 0002	BAYONET & SCABBARD, M9	1095-01-227-1739	25,001
	REL 001	DEL 001: 30 JUN 2000		4,000
		DEL 002: 31 JUL 2000		4,000
		DEL 003: 31 AUG 2000		4,000
		DEL 004: 29 SEP 2000		4,000
		DEL 005: 31 OCT 2000		4,000
		DEL 006: 30 NOV 2000		4,000
		DEL 007: 29 DEC 2000		1,001
24-Apr-2000	ORDER Nr. 0003	ATTACHING ASSEMBLY	1005-01-278-1174	4,963
	REL 001	DEL 001: 11 SEP 2000		227
	REL 002	DEL 001: 11 Sep 2000		131
	REL 003	DEL 001: 11 Sep 2000		222
	REL 004	DEL 001: 11 Sep 2000		93
	REL 005	DEL 001: 11 Sep 2000		39
	REL 006	DEL 001: 11 Sep 2000		2,964
	REL 007	DEL 001: 11 Sep 2000		1,287
24-Apr-2000	ORDER Nr. 0003	STRAP, WEBBING	5340-01-275-5398	6,267
	REL 001	DEL 001: 25 JUN 2000		358
	REL 002	DEL 001: 25 JUN 2000		266
	REL 003	DEL 001: 25 JUN 2000		368
	REL 004	DEL 001: 25 JUN 2000		184
	REL 005	DEL 001: 25 JUN 2000		61
	REL 006	DEL 001: 25 JUN 2000		1,193
	REL 007	DEL 001: 25 JUN 2000		151
	REL 008	DEL 001: 25 JUN 2000		56
	REL 009	DEL 001: 25 JUN 2000		1,961
	REL 010	DEL 001: 25 JUN 2000		1,036
	REL 011	DEL 001: 25 JUN 2000		633
	REL 001	DEL 001: 26 JUL 2000		28
	REL 002	DEL 001: 26 JUL 2000		27
	REL 003	DEL 001: 26 JUL 2000		13
	REL 004	DEL 001: 26 JUL 2000		4
	REL 005	DEL 001: 26 JUL 2000		17
	REL 006	DEL 001: 26 JUL 2000		5
	REL 007	DEL 002: 25 AUG 2000		14
	REL 008	DEL 001: 26 JUL 2000		38

UNIT PRICE	CONTRACT VALUE	FIRM	ORIGIN	DEST	REMARKS
$3.00	$3,900.00	LAN-CAY	RIA	DDSP	
	$900.00			DDSP	
	$900.00			DDSP	
	$900.00			DDSP	
	$900.00			DDSP	
	$300.00			DDSP	
$3.50	$1,015.00	LAN-CAY	RIA	DDSP	
	$1,015.00			DDSP	
$39.90	$399,000.00	LAN-CAY	RIA	DDSP	
	$79,800.00			DDSP	
	$79,800.00			DDSP	
	$79,800.00			DDSP	
	$79,800.00			DDSP	
	$79,800.00			DDSP	
	$2,125,337.51	OKC			
$53.00	$662,500.00	OKC	RIA	RRAD	Engr chgs: stone deleted
	$106,000.00				ECP L9S3021 dtd 04OCT1999
	$275,600.00				ECP L9S3024 dtd 23NOV1999
	$106,000.00				ECP L9S3025 dtd 23NOV1999
	$106,000.00				ECP L9S3026 dtd 23NOV1999
	$106,000.00				
	$106,000.00				
	$104,887.00				
	$53.00		RIA	RIA	Marked:Jeff Windham
$43.00	$1,075,043.00	OKC	RIA	RRAD	Eng CH:Stone deleted
	$172,000.00				ECP L9S3021 dtd 04OCT1999
	$172,000.00				ECP L9S3024 dtd 23NOV1999
	$172,000.00				ECP L9S3025 dtd 23NOV1999
	$172,000.00				ECP L9S3026 dtd 23NOV1999
	$172,000.00				
	$172,000.00				
	$43,043.00				
$4.82	$23,921.66	OKC	RIA		
	$1,094.14			WRGSA	CP CARROLL, ROK
	$631.42			STRAT MOB	GOOSENECK,SC
	$1,070.04			DDSP	
	$448.26			DDSJ	
	$187.98			RRAD	
	$14,286.48			DDSP	
	$6,203.34			DDSJ	
$2.92	$18,299.64	OKC	RIA		
	$1,045.38			WRGSA	CP CARROLL, ROK
	$776.72			STRAT MOB	
	$1,074.56			DDSP	
	$537.28			DDSJ	
	$178.12			RRAD	
	$3,483.56			DDSP	
	$440.92			DDSJ	
	$163.52			RRAD	
	$5,726.12			DDSP	
	$3,025.12			DDSJ	
	$1,848.36			RRAD	
$1.70	$652.80	OKC	RIA		
	$47.60			DDSJ	
	$45.90			DDSP	
	$22.10			DDSJ	
	$6.80			RRAD	
	$28.90			DDSP	
	$8.50			DDSJ	
	$23.80			DDSJ	
	$64.60			DDSJ	

AWARD DATE	CONTRACT Nr. ORDER Nr.	NOUN	NSN	QTY
		DEL 003: 24 SEP 2000		36
		DEL 002: 25 AUG 2000		8
		DEL 002: 25 AUG 2000		58
	REL 001	DEL 001: 30 JAN 2001		4,597
2-Feb-2001	ORDER Nr. 0005	STONE, SHARPENING	5345-01-275-5395	12,144
		DEL 002: 26 JUN 2001		1,746
	REL 002	DEL 001: 22 MAY 2001		3,453
13-Feb-2002	ORDER Nr. 0006	ATTACHING ASSEMBLY	CANCELLED	4,648
	ORDER Nr. 0007	STATUS UNKNOWN	NO RECORD EXISTS	
	REL 001	DEL 001: 22 MAY 2001		866
	REL 001	DEL 001: 21 FEB 2005		1,000
	REL 001	DEL 001: 21 FEB 2005		1,750
	REL 001	DEL 001: 21 FEB 2005		1,000
	REL 001	DEL 001: 21 FEB 2005		1,500
	ORDER Nr. 0001	SCABBARD, BAYONET, KNIFE, M9	1095-00-223-7164	2,889
26-Aug-2003	DAAE20-03-P-0449	SCABBARD, BAYONET, M9	1095-01-512-2744	3,600
	REL 001	DEL 001: 14 JAN 2004		3,600
		BAYONET, KNIFE, M9	1095-00-073-9238	1,000
26-Aug-2003	ORDER Nr. 0001	SCABBARD, BAYONET, M9	1095-01-512-2744	10,418
	REL 001	DEL 001: 14 JAN 2004		10,418
9-Sep-2004	W52H09-04-C-0222	SCABBARD, BAYONET, M9	1095-00-223-7164	12,000
9-Sep-2004	ORDER Nr. 0001	SCABBARD, BAYONET, M9	1095-00-223-7164	1,800
	REL 001	DEL 001: 10 JAN 2005		1,800
		DEL 002: 10 FEB 2005		1,800
		DEL 003: 10 MAR 2005		1,800
		DEL 004: 11 APR 2005		1,800
		DEL 005: 10 MAY 2005		1,800
		DEL 006: 10 JUN 2005		1,800
		DEL 007: 11 JUL 2005		1,800
		DEL 008: 10 AUG 2005		1,800
		DEL 009: 12 SEP 2005		1,800
		DEL 0010: 11 OCT 2005		1,800
		DEL 0011: 14 NOV 2005		1,800
		DEL 0012: 12 DEC 2005		1,034

UNIT PRICE	CONTRACT VALUE	FIRM	ORIGIN	DEST	REMARKS
	$61.20			DDSJ	
	$13.60			RRAD	
	$98.60			DDSP	
	$201,762.33			RRAD	
$0.67	$8,136.48	OKC	RIA		
	$1,169.82			DDJC	Stockton, CA
	$2,313.51			DDSP	DDSP New Cumberland,PA
	$20,451.20	LANCAY	RIA	DDSP	ORDER CREATED IN ERROR
					R
IN RIA DATA OF THIS ORDER					
	$1,385.60				
	$38,910.00				
	$36,872.50				
	$58,210.00		RIA	DDSP	
	$4,515.00		RIA	DDSP	
$4.69	$13,428.00	GENERAL	RIA	DDSP	
	$32,874.00	OKC			
	$16,884.00			DDSP	THE CONTRACT TOTAL WAS INCREASED TO $48,864.
$15.99	$15,990.00				NUMBER OF SCABBARDS DOES NOT SHOW AN INCREASE IF UNIT PRICE REMAINED $4.69 TOTAL SCABBARDS WOULD BE 10,418
$4.69	$48,864.00	OKC	RIA	DDSP	
	$48,864.00			DDSP	
	$269,574.46	OKC			
$4.19	$87,294.46	OKC	RIA	DDSP	
	$7,542.00			DDSP	
	$7,542.00			DDSP	
	$7,542.00			DDSP	
	$7,542.00			DDSP	
	$7,542.00			DDSP	
	$7,542.00			DDSP	
	$7,542.00			DDSP	
	$7,542.00			DDSP	
	$7,542.00			DDSP	
	$7,542.00			DDSP	
	$7,542.00			DDSP	
	$4,332.46			DDSP	

AWARD DATE	CONTRACT Nr. ORDER Nr.	NOUN	NSN	QTY
	REL 001	DEL 001: 10 JAN 2005		1,000
		DEL 003: 10 MAR 2005		1,000
		DEL 005: 10 MAY 2005		1,000
		DEL 007: 11 JUL 2005		1,000
		DEL 009: 12 SEP 2005		1,000
		DEL 0011: 14 NOV 2005		1,000
15-Sep-2005	W52H09-05-C-0265	BAYONET & SCABBARD, M9	1095-01-227-1739	20,000
	REL 001	DEL 001: 01 NOV 2005		5,000
		DEL 003: 21 MAR 2005		5,000
25-Sep-2001	M67854-01-R-3080	BAYONET 2000		
29-Mar-02	M67854-02-R-3030	BAYONET, MULTIPURPOSE		MAX: 120,000 MIN: 5,000
21-May-02	F49642-02-t-0179			
10-Sep-03	SPO700-03-U-G842	BAYONET, KNIFE ONTARIO	1095-01-506-3424	
22-Oct-03	SPO740-04-M-2033	BAYONET, KNIFE ONTARIO	1095-01-506-3424	
12-Jan-04	SPO740-04-M-2267	BAYONET, KNIFE	1095-01-506-3424	
24-Jan-2004	SPO740-04-V-5938	BAYONET, KNIFE	1095-01-506-3424	100
26-Aug-2003	ORDER Nr. 0001	BAYONET, KNIFE	1095-01-506-3424	100
	REL 001	DEL 001: 24 JUL 2004		100
26-Aug-2003	ORDER Nr. 0001	BAYONET, KNIFE	1095-01-506-3424	1,069
	REL 001	DEL 001: 21 MAY 2004		1,069

UNIT PRICE	CONTRACT VALUE	FIRM	ORIGIN	DEST	REMARKS
	$15,190.00			DDSP	
	$15,190.00			DDSP	
	$15,190.00			DDSP	
	$15,190.00			DDSP	
	$15,190.00			DDSP	
	$15,190.00			DDSP	
	$797,000.00	OKC			
	$7,542.00			DDSP	
	$15,190.00			DDSP	
		EICKHORN			SOLE SOURCE - RESCINDED 16 OCT 2001
					20,000 TO OKINAWA
	$61,438.00	OKC			
	$59,009.00	OKC			
		OKC			
		OKC	RIA	DDSP	ACCERLERATED DELIVERY
				DDSP	
		OKC			
		OKC	RIA	DDSP	ACCERLERATED DELIVERY
				DDSP	

Appendix F: Knife, General Purpose

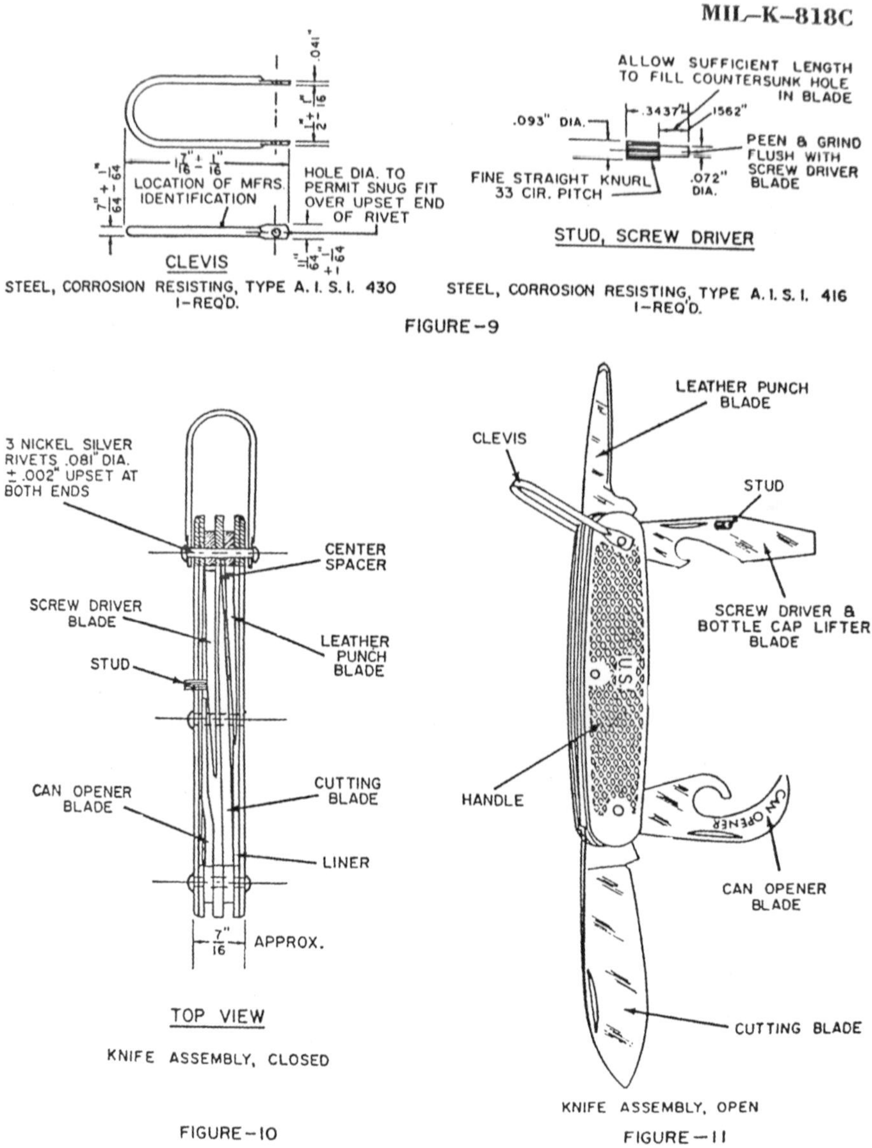

Figure 201: Typical General Purpose Knife nomenclature.

Figure 202: Typical General Purpose Knife, Army version.

The earliest mention of the GPK was found during a cursory search, and appeared in Infantry Board Report Nr. 1741 dated 23 December 1944. This report covers trials by the Infantry Board of six pocketknives in consideration for general issue of the best knife candidate. The knives tested were:

1) Experimental, Type 1, pocketknife similar to the present day GPK and described as "…entirely of polished steel except for the flat Monel metal handle sides, three brass handle spacers, and three brass rivets." It had a large blade, screwdriver, and bottle opener, can opener, and leather punch, and it had a steel carrying ring.

2) Experimental, Type 2, pocketknife which was the same as the above, except for a thumbnail notch beside the leather punch, and all blades and the blade springs had a glossy blued coating which appeared to be an oxidized finish.

3) Experimental, Type 3, pocketknife differed from the Type 1 only in that all of the steel and Monel metal parts of the knife had a dull gray coating which appeared to be parkerization.

4) Electricians Pocket Knife, TL-29, at the time standard Signal Corps issue wood handled with plated or polished steel parts. It had a large blade, a screwdriver blade with one sharpened edge, a wire-skinning notch, and a wire-scraping notch. The screwdriver blade was equipped with a lock, and it had a steel carrying ring.

5) Mountain Pocket Knife, which was a bone handled knife with all metal parts of plated or polished steel. It had five blades: a large blade, small blade, can opener, leather punch, and a Phillips screwdriver, and it had a steel carrying ring.

6) Engineer Pocket Knife, which was essentially a commercial Boy Scout knife.

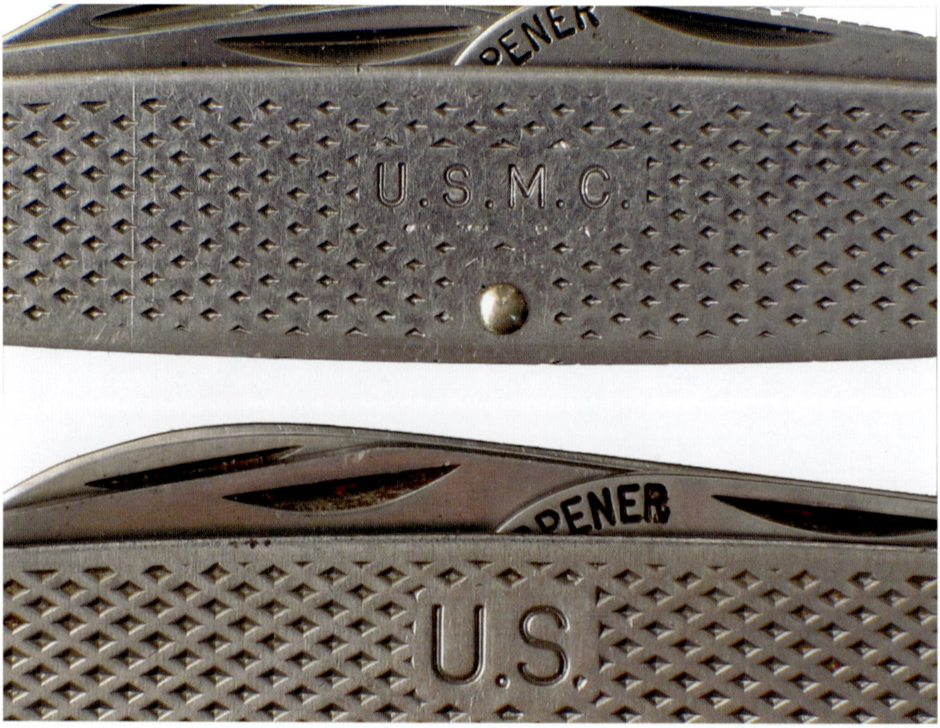

Figure 203: Subtle differences between Army and Marine Corps versions.

After conducting twenty relevant tests the Board determined that the Experimental, Type 3, pocketknife should be adopted as a general purpose pocketknife, and that one should be issued to each infantryman, and a minimum one for every twelve infantrymen—in other words one per squad.

The board also determined that the Experimental, Type 3, pocketknife was not a suitable replacement for the Electrician, TL-29 or the Mountain knife, but was equal to or superior to the Engineer knife.

The Board recommended the following changes be made prior to adoption:

1) Increased blade curvature

2) Cross hatch handles to increase grip

3) Move thumb nail nick in the can and leather pouch further from the hinge to facilitate easier opening.

4) Increase length of screwdriver blade by one half inch.

5) Strengthen the clevis at the rivet holes.

Whether the above knife was ever actually issued is unclear. However, by 28 September 1945 the Infantry Board was again testing pocketknives, as evidenced by Report Nr. 1877.

According to the report, the Board was to specifically determine the adequacy of the standard pocketknife (Type I) when compared with the stainless steel experimental knife (Type II).

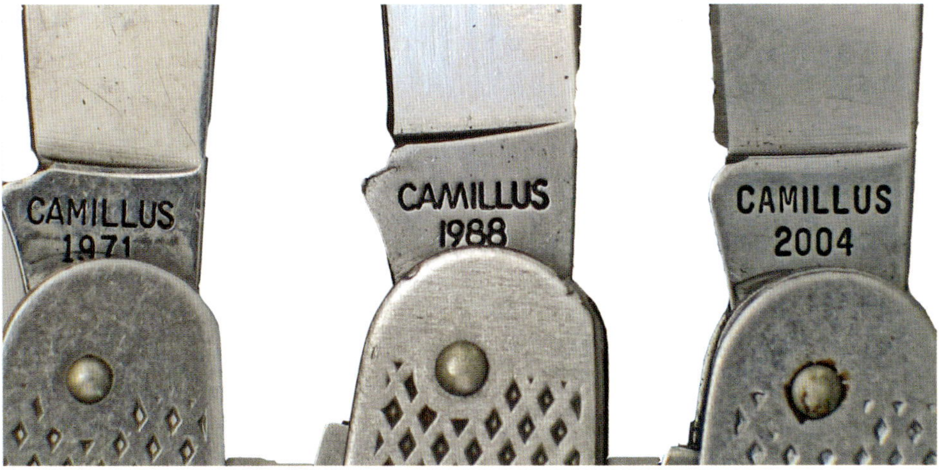

Figure 204: All General Purpose Knives bear the date of manufacture as above.

Apparently, the Type II was the *direct counterpart* of the Type I except that the blades and springs were made of stainless steel and it was not in production. The Type II knives used in the testing were hand made models; the Type Is were manufactured.

The knives were put through the same battery of tests as in the previous year, and they determined that the Type II stainless was superior to the Type I, which was regular steel with a corrosion resistant bluing, and that it (the Type II) more nearly met the established military characteristics for a general-purpose pocketknife. The fatal shortcoming of the Type I was its failure to resist corrosion, which naturally the stainless steel model accomplished easily. It was also noted that the Type I did not take and hold an edge as well as the Type II.

The recommendations of the board were that future production general-purpose pocketknives be constructed of the same materials used in the Type II. Also that the screwdriver stud of the Type II be modified, reducing the diameter of the stud to 0.090 inches and be made of stainless steel. Finally, it was recommended that pocket-sharpening stones be issued as organizational equipment on a basis of twelve per company, or one per platoon.

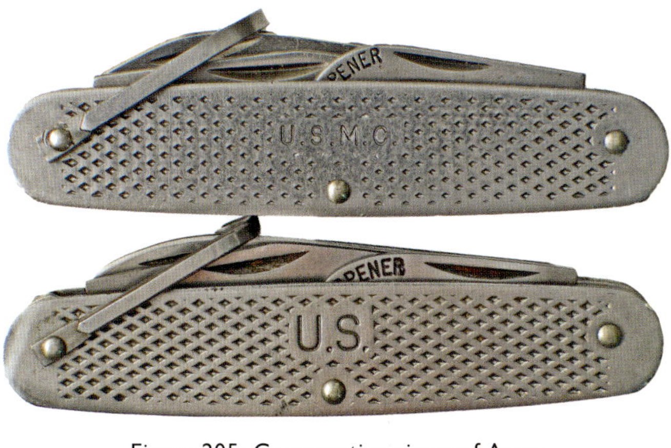

Figure 205: Comparative views of Army and Marine General Purpose Knives

Appendix G: P38 Development

The P38 is an example of the military's penchant for multipurpose equipment. While not specifically designed as such, G.I.s quickly saw its potential and have applied it to dozens of tasks for the past sixty years. Beyond that, it is also a very popular object of study for many collectors, and therefore is discussed in greater detail here for the edification of those enthusiasts.

As previously mentioned, this amazingly simple, one and one-half inch, flat piece of stamped metal was purportedly invented by the Subsistence Research Laboratory of Chicago in just 30 days during the summer of 1942. Interestingly, on July 24, 1936, the Quartermaster Corps Subsistence Research Laboratory opened in Chicago operated, obviously, by the U.S. Army.

This new laboratory was tasked to test foods and design modern packaging; to prepare drafts of proposed specifications; conduct studies, make analyses of various reserve and emergency rations and components; and to prepare information bulletins as well as coordinate with other government agencies.

The original Laboratory staff consisted of three members, two of whom were graduates of the Army's Quartermaster Subsistence School, and a civilian expert and former school instructor. Operating on the barest of budgets, and with the assistance of industrial entities the Laboratory developed *boneless beef*, and partially developed Field Rations C and D.

By September 1941 the Laboratory staff totaled thirteen, and by April 1942 its numbers had risen to twenty-two, with a proportional number of clerical and administrative personnel. The Laboratory was primarily an administrative center for the initiation, direction, and coordination of research. Such coordination involved the Army and other service branches, universities, and federal agencies, as well as many national food industries. The Laboratory's primary mission was to adapt subsistence research to military use.

Army-Navy subsistence was coordinated through a Navy liaison officer assigned to the Laboratory, while the then Army Air Corps experiments were carried out with the Aero Medical Research Laboratory in close association with the Army Veterinary Corps, who developed specifications and inspection procedures, and produced instruction manuals.

During 1940 and 1941, the Laboratory was engaged in the development of the *K ration* as well as special Army Air Corps rations, combat and emergency rations, and subsistence under all conditions. In short, the Laboratory was the central Research and Development agency for the Army, but worked closely with the other services on methods of testing, development, preservation, and production of military rations to include the packaging and associated products; to wit, the can opener.

Most P38s are constructed from stamped 1070 steel, which is tin-plated. And, according to the G.G. Greene company, the openers were produced for about a penny a piece.

Perhaps the *P38* was born in 1942 in the Subsistence Research Laboratory, but it is doubtful that the design originated there; in fact, during research for this book the author found that a number of similar designs were patented previous to 1942. Further, they are amazingly similar to the P38 of the Subsistence Research Laboratory, and most probably served as the design template for it.

A search of the German Patent office records revealed a patent issued to a Frenchman named Etienne Marcel Darque of Clichy, France, in 1913. Mr. Darque also held a U.S. Patent (Number 913,911) for his device, and is seemingly the oldest patent for such an implement.

This tool has all of the basic elements of the P38, a similar appearance, and identical function. Interestingly, it also sports the string hole used for dipping the opener into immersion heaters for cleaning! Amazing coincidence!

One must keep in mind, though, that it is altogether possible that Mr. Darque himself based his design on some earlier work yet undiscovered. What has turned up rather handily are some twenty to thirty subsequent designs based on this oldest patented pattern. Those most similar are presented here.

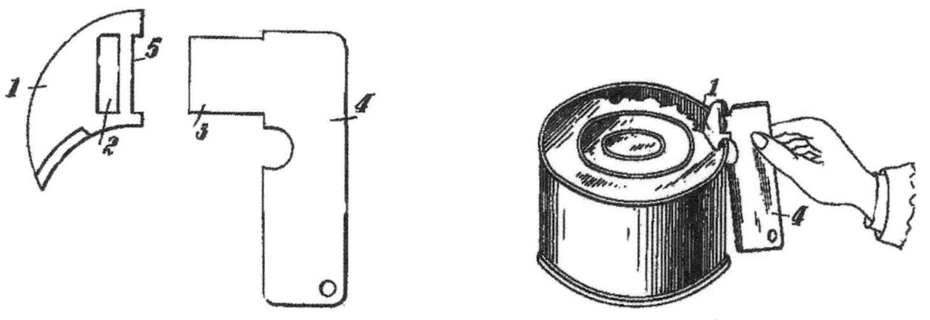

Figure 206: Patent belonging to Etienne Marcel Darque of Clichy, France, in 1913.

The next example is a design patented by one K.F. Schioniger (Patent Number 1,507,093) in August 1923. This arrangement has incorporated numerous other useful features, such as a bottle opener and flat for screwdriver. Also obvious is the basic flat, hooked opener blade. This configuration is dependent upon the same hinge as Mr. Darque's device. It is essentially this hinge that will drive the design in subsequent patents.

A few short years later, Mr. Darque's design remerged in a purer form when a Dewey M. Stremgberg patented his very P38 looking (Patent Number 1,669,311) folding can opener.

If it is indeed true that they developed this device in 30 days, it is no surprise, since there were so many examples with which to work. However, as the war drew to an inevitable close it is without any doubt that wartime contractors were biting at the bit for the day when they could return to prewar commercial activities. It is altogether reasonable then to assume that they were looking ahead to future manufacturing endeavors and products for the commercial market.

Mr. S. Bloom, no doubt having post-war profits dancing in his head, filed his patent (Patent Number 2,412,946) request on 3 July 1944. There is also little doubt that he expected to capitalize on his company's wartime production experience when America returned to normal commercial activities. With millions of Americans eager to consume the plethora of new products, this would be an advertising free-bee. G.I. consumers would already be more than familiar with his device, and ready to buy! An obvious "seller."

However, Mr. Bloom was by no means operating in a vacuum, nor was he a visionary running ahead of the corporate pack. J.W. Speaker, another wartime contractor, though somewhat slower, was not to be outdone. He filed to patent the device (Patent Number 2,143,528) shown below on 16 March 1945, just one month before the war officially ended. Interestingly, while neither one were market ready at war's end, both hit the post-war consumption frenzy. Bloom's patent received

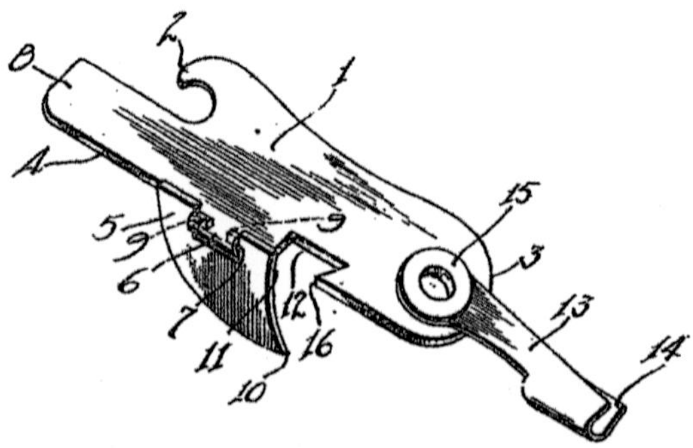

Figure 207: K.F. Schioniger in August 1923.

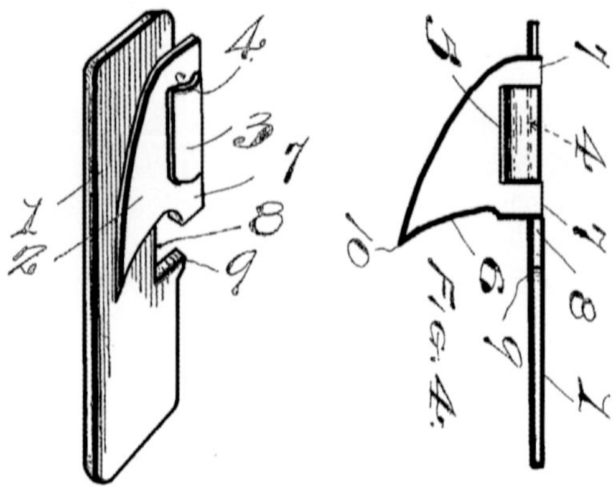

Figure 208: Patent belonging to one Dewey Strengberg of Ishpeming, Michigan, in 1927.

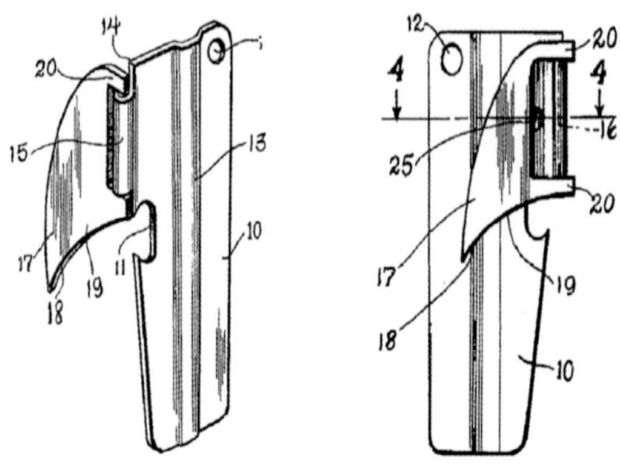

Figure 209: Bloom's patent device as it appeared on 3 July 1944.

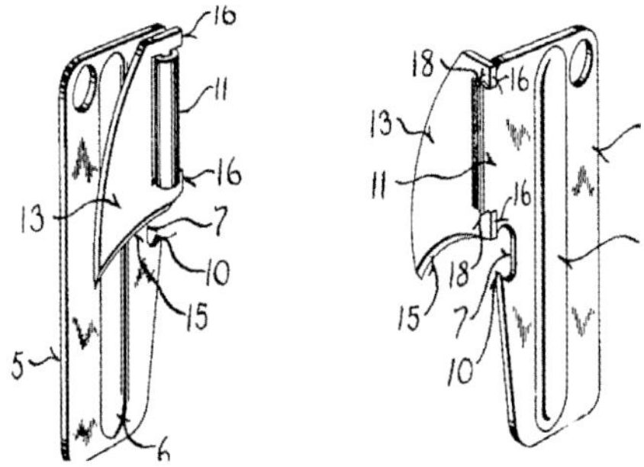

Figure 210: J.W. Speaker's patent design as it appeared on March 16, 1945.

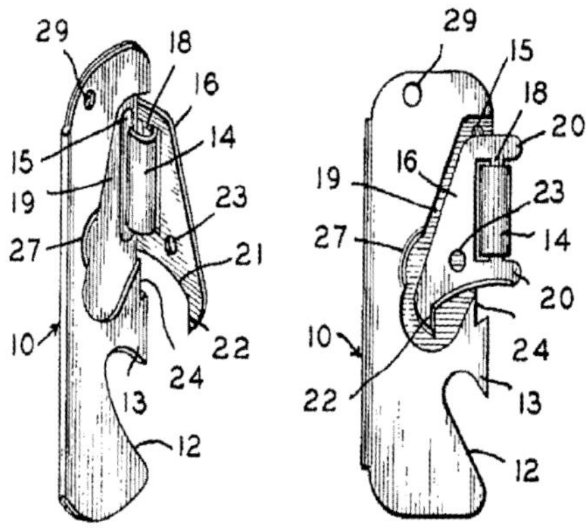

Figure 211: Combination Can and Bottle Opener as submitted by Mr. J. Kenington on 2 June 1953.

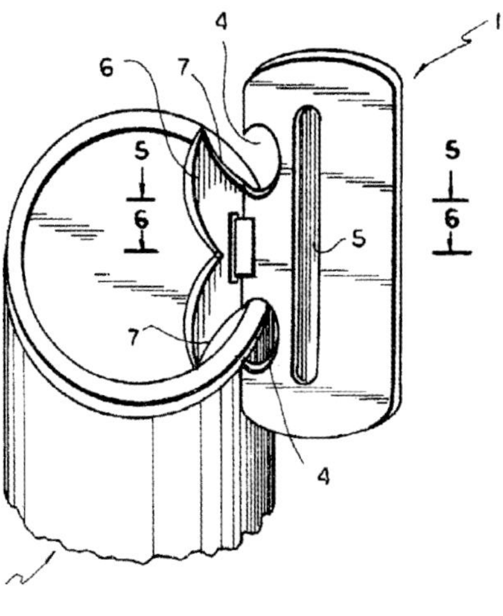

Figure 212: Aysik Biyakharov's patent design as it appeared on 17 December 1980.

approval on 24 December 1946, while Speaker's approval did not come until 11 November 1947.

Though many companies produced the P38, apparently no one else was greatly interested in commercial exploitation of the design until after the Korean War, when Mr. J. Kenington introduced his combination Can and Bottle Opener (Patent Number 2,733,505) on 2 June 1953.

The next significant design spin off (Patent Number 4,300,288) occurred when one Aysik Biyakharov of Jackson Heights, New York, filed the following patent on 17 December 1980. An odd-looking affair, it appears to be a reversible can opener, but using the old tried and true hinge of Mr. Darque.

Essentially, it is the same old reliable device, though noticeably larger. It also features a piercing blade that is actually recessed into the handle, making it less likely to catch on the lining of one's pocket. In all of the patents, the designers have gone to the trouble of pointing out that the integral hinge is a safety feature, as it allows the blade to be positioned safely out of the way to avoid unintentionally piercing the user when carried. This design has taken that idea to the next level by folding the blade into its own storage space, thus presenting a generally smooth surface.

Also obviously included is a bottle opener, which is stamped out of the body of the opener. This feature alone would dictate that the device be made larger, which it was.

The final design (Patent Number 5,189,750), and most intricate, was submitted on 2 March 1993 by one Sean Brennan of Menlo Park, California. A combination can and bottle opener, wherein the can opener swings into its stowed position and is covered by the handle of the bottle opener. A super idea, but...has anyone needed bottle openers since the appearance of the *twist-off top?*

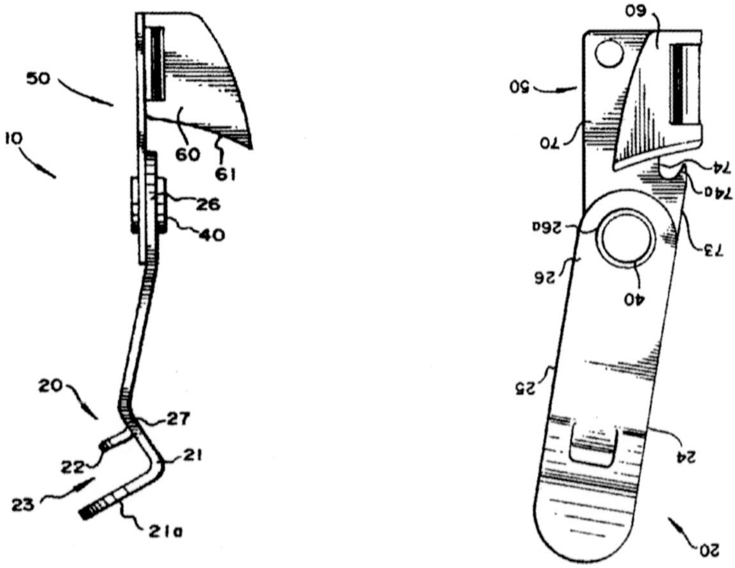

Figure 213: Sean Brennan's patent design as it appeared on 2 March 1993.

P38 Data

Date Manufacturer Markings .

1941 Bloomfield Chicago, IL None
1940s Washburn Co. Rockford, IL U.S./ANDROCK
1940s J.W. Speaker Corp. Milwaukee, WI Speaker/USA
1941's Essential Products Corp. Little Chute, WI
1943 J.W. Speaker Corp. Milwaukee, WI Speaker/USA/43
1944 J.W. Speaker Corp. Milwaukee, WI Speaker/USA/44
1948 J.W. Speaker Corp. Milwaukee, WI U.S./Speaker/USA/ 48
1949-1962 G.G. Greene Warren, PA U.S. G.G. REENE/1949
1950 Koolaire, Inc St. Paul, MN U.S./KOOLAIRE/1950
1951 Koolaire, Inc St. Paul, MN U.S./KOOLAIRE/1951
1951 Western Newell Mfg. Co. Freeport, IL U.S./WESTERN
1951 U.S.A. Tool & Metal Spec. Co. NEWELL/1951
1951 U.S.A. Tool & Metal Spec. Co.
1951 Ajax Hardware Mfg. Co, Los Angeles, CA U.S./AJAX/51
1952 Koolaire, Inc St. Paul, MN U.S./KOOLAIRE/no date
1955 U.S.A. Tool & Metal Spec. Co. U.S.A./T&M
1960 County Machine Co. Inc. Bronx, NY U.S./County Machine/1960
1961 Kay Tool & Die, Inc. Union City, TN U.S./KAY/1961
1962 Kay Tool & Die, Inc. Union City, TN U.S./KAY/1962
Mallin Hardware Shelby, OH
Shelby Corp. Shelby, OH U.S. ^/SHELBY CO.

Appendix H: The M9 Patent

United States Patent [19]

Finn

[11] **Patent Number: 4,821,356**

[45] **Date of Patent: Apr. 18, 1989**

[54] MILITARY BAYONET AND SCABBARD

[75] Inventor: **Charles A. Finn,** Oceanside, Calif.

[73] Assignee: **Phrobis III, Ltd.,** Carlsbad, Calif.

[21] Appl. No.: **25,334**

[22] Filed: **Mar. 13, 1987**

[51] **Int. Cl.**[4] **B25F 1/04**

[52] **U.S. Cl.** **7/134;** 7/151; 7/158; 30/342; 42/86

[58] **Field of Search** 42/52, 53, 86, 90; 30/340, 342, 123, 142, 143, 146, 194; 81/467, 471, 448, 477; 7/117, 125, 132, 134, 158, 166, 151

[56] **References Cited**

U.S. PATENT DOCUMENTS

57,677	9/1866	Clayton	30/342
2,688,143	9/1954	Stoa	7/156
3,201,869	8/1965	Gambino	30/342
3,842,458	10/1974	Bauer	7/134
4,458,420	7/1984	Davis	30/342
4,690,315	9/1987	Bianchi	224/252

Primary Examiner—Roscoe V. Parker
Attorney, Agent, or Firm—John E. Wagner

[57] **ABSTRACT**

A bayonet and scabbard are capable of being pivotally connected to constitute a wire or metal tape cutting implement having a recess shaped to capture the wire or tape before such cutting begins. The bayonet blade has a tang extending into the bayonet handle which is of a yield strength greater than that of the handle but less than that of the bayonet blade. A finger guard is provided with notches adjacent the blade for engaging an edge of the cap of a receptacle for removing the same.

31 Claims, 7 Drawing Sheets

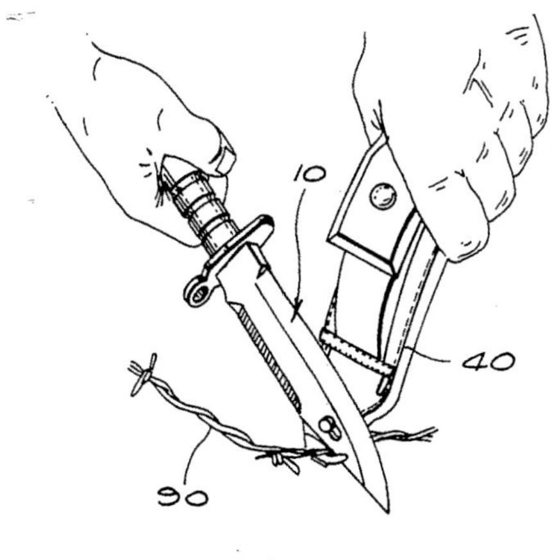

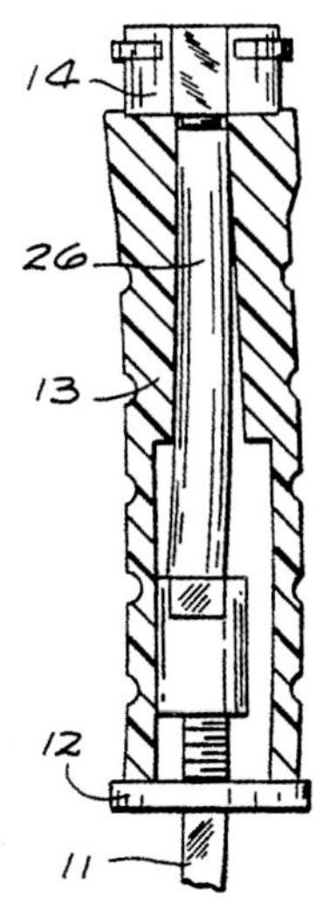

U.S. Patent **Apr. 18, 1989** **Sheet 1 of 7** **4,821,356**

FIG. 3

FIG. 1

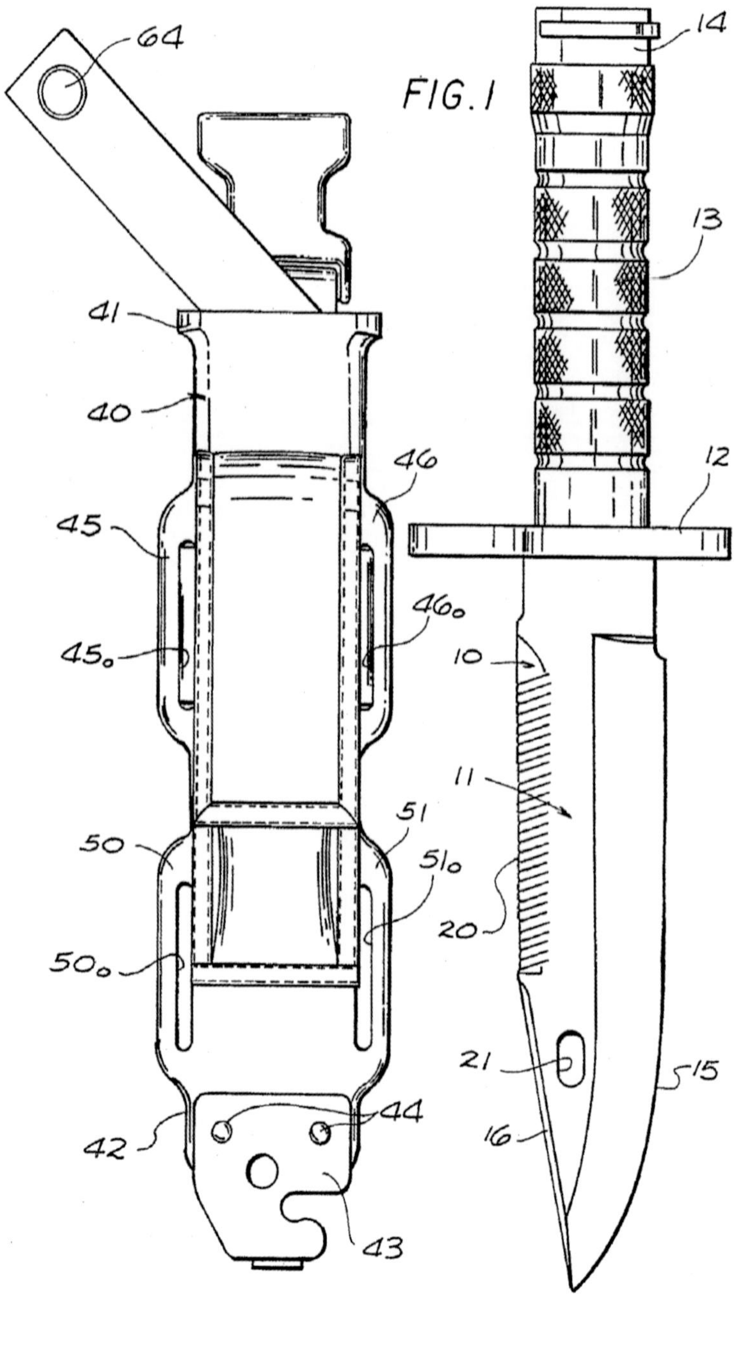

U.S. Patent Apr. 18, 1989 Sheet 2 of 7 **4,821,356**

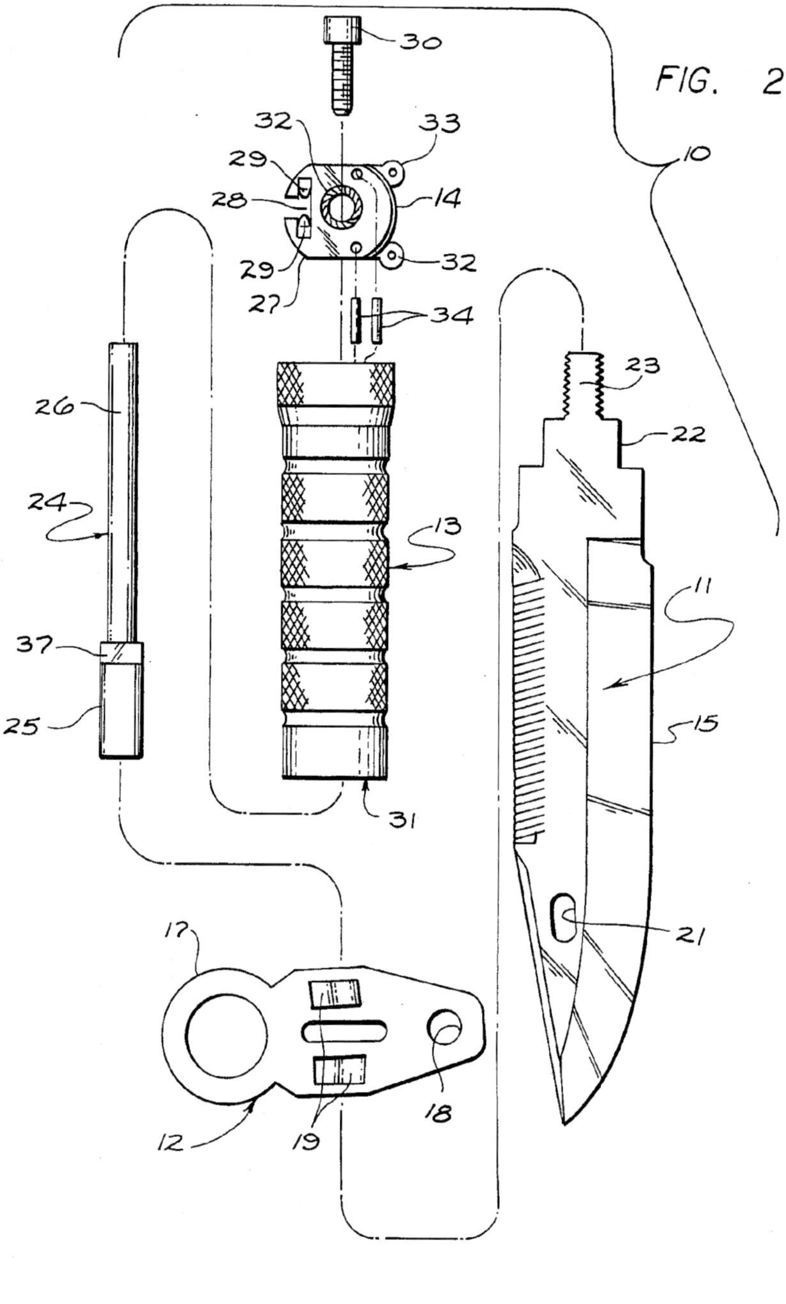

FIG. 2

U.S. Patent **Apr. 18, 1989** **Sheet 3 of 7** **4,821,356**

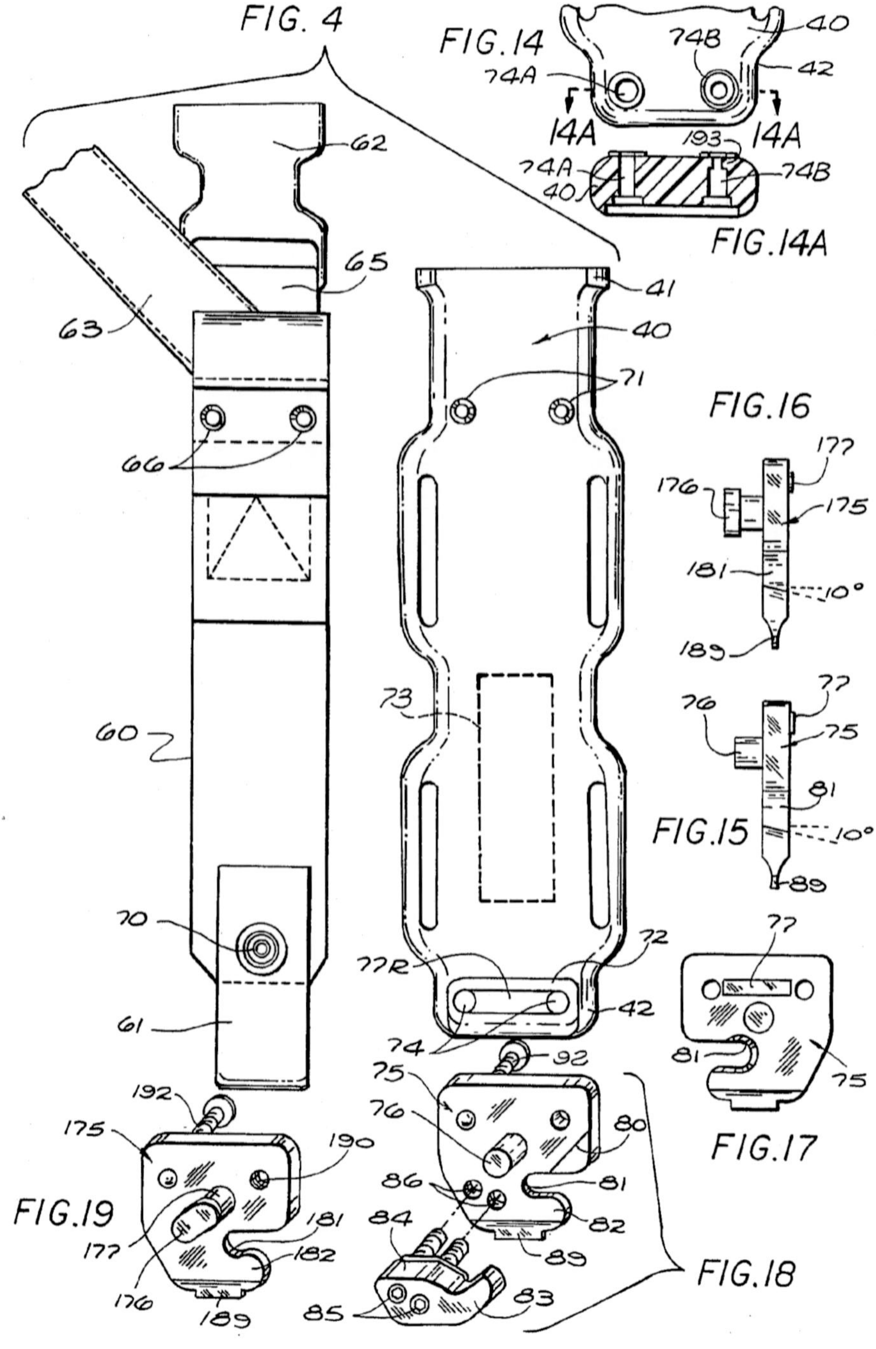

U.S. Patent **Apr. 18, 1989** **Sheet 4 of 7** **4,821,356**

FIG. 7

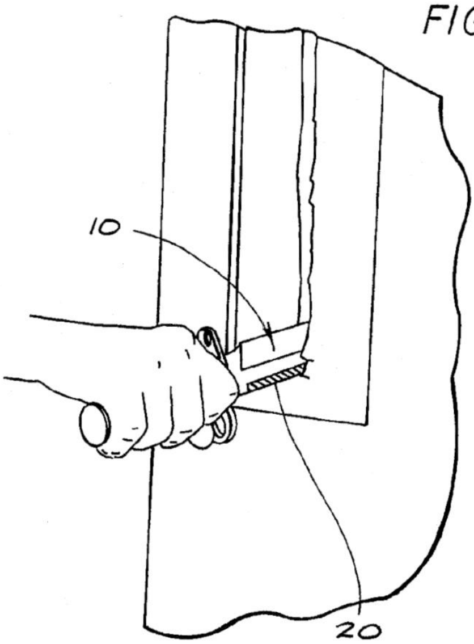

FIG. 5

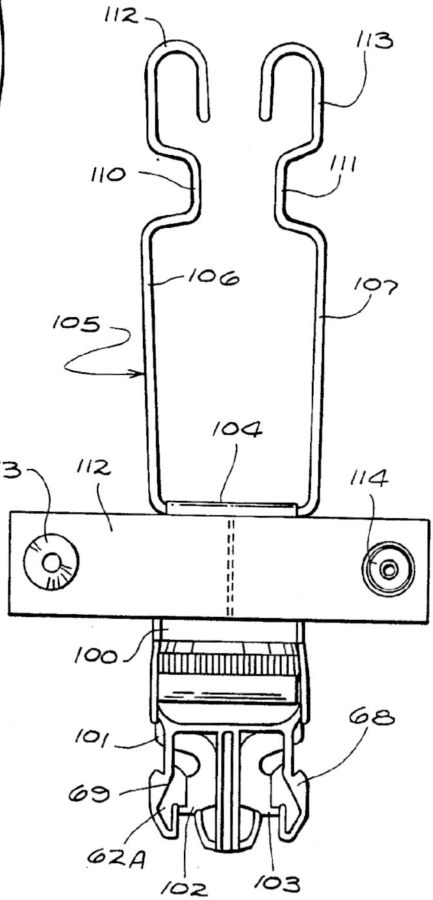

FIG. 5A

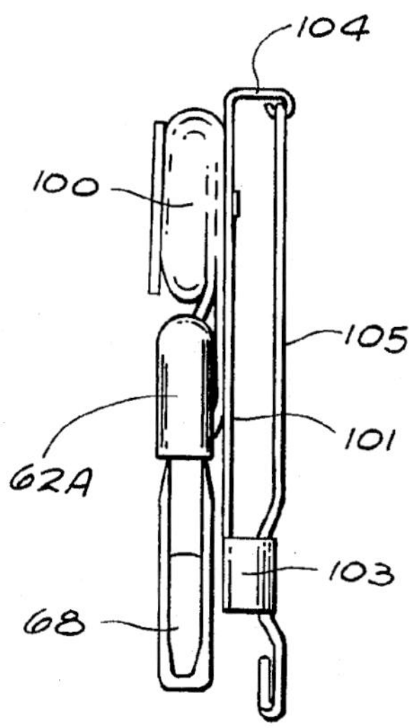

U.S. Patent **Apr. 18, 1989** **Sheet 5 of 7** **4,821,356**

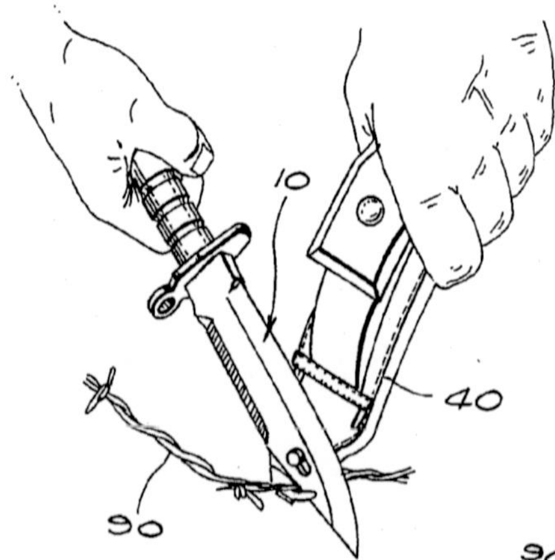

FIG. 6

FIG. 10

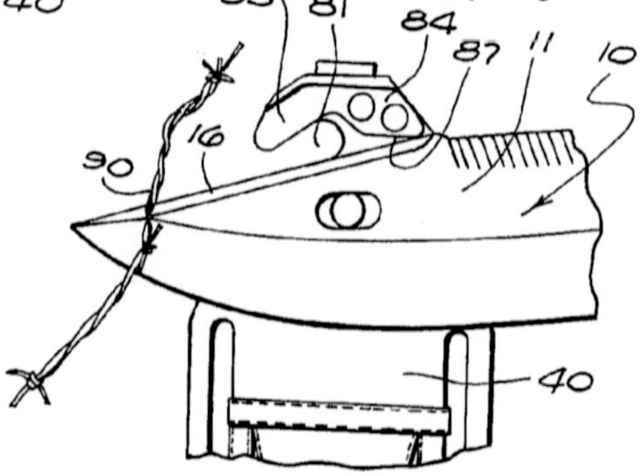

FIG. 11

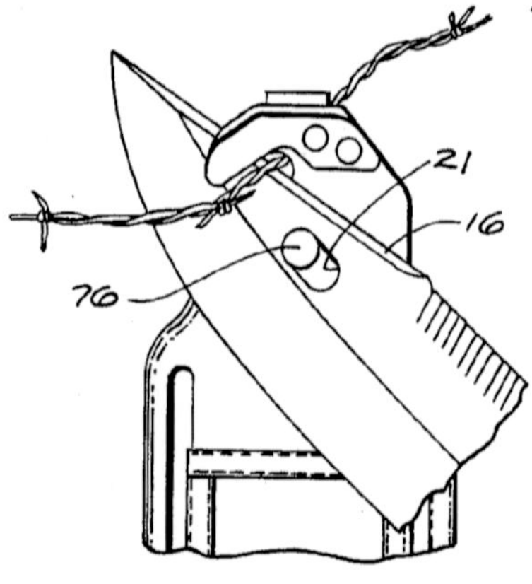

FIG. 12

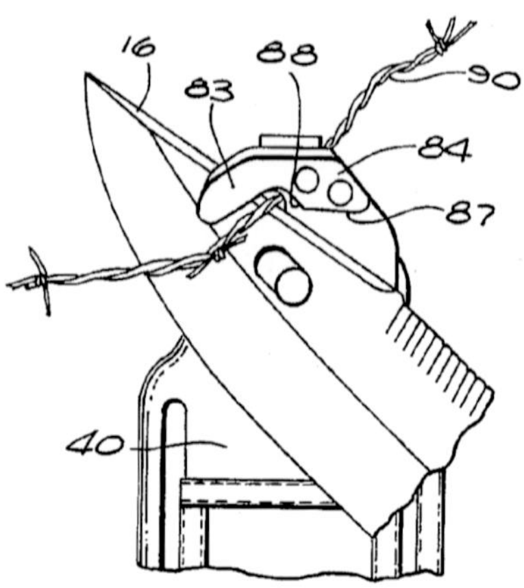

FIG. 13

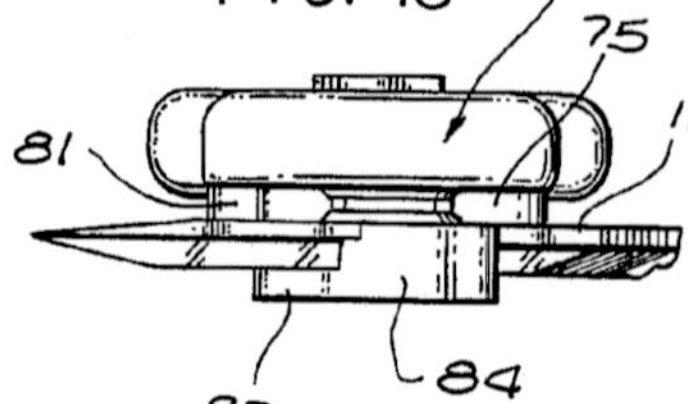

U.S. Patent **Apr. 18, 1989** **Sheet 6 of 7** **4,821,356**

FIG. 8

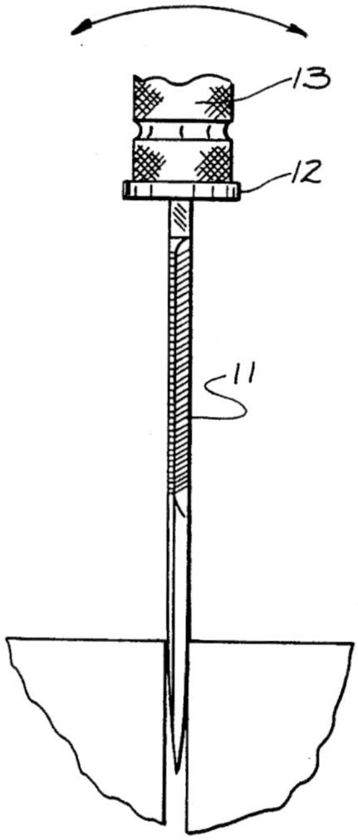

FIG. 9

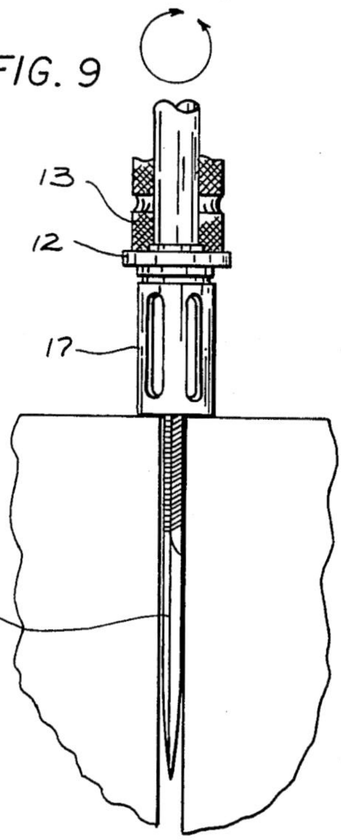

FIG. 8A

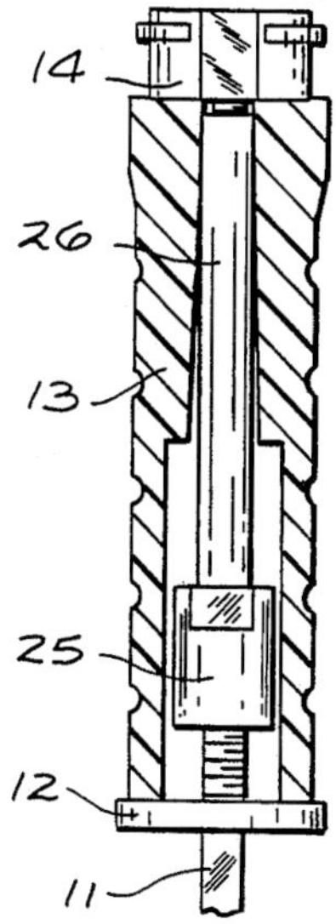

FIG. 8B

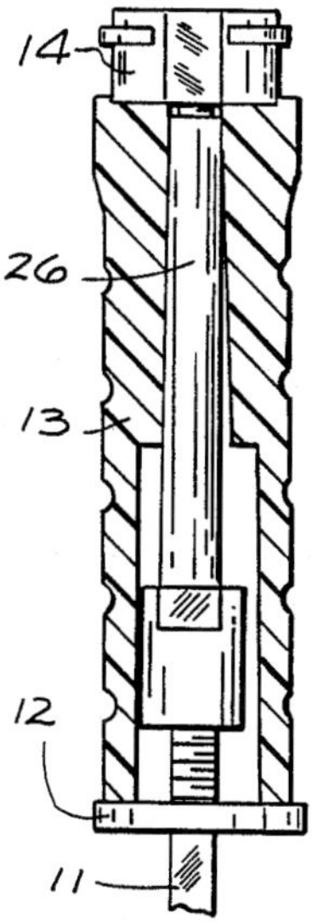

FIG. 8C

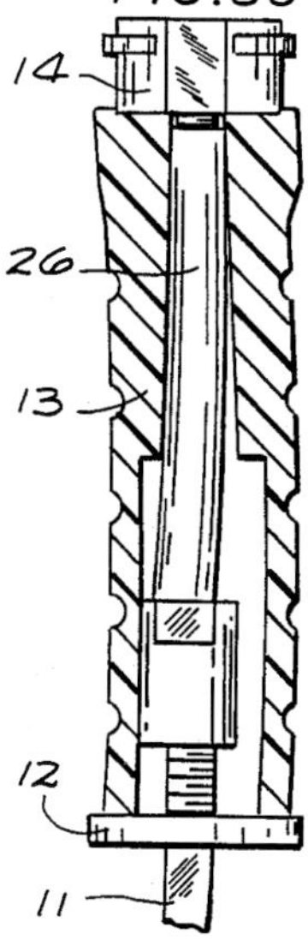

FIG. 9A

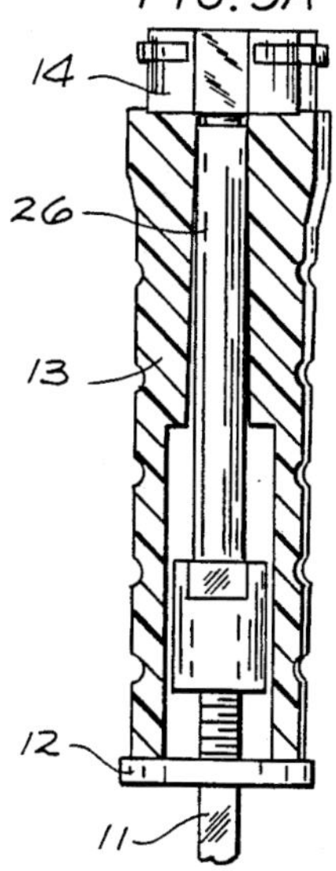

U.S. Patent **Apr. 18, 1989** **Sheet 7 of 7** **4,821,356**

FIG. 20

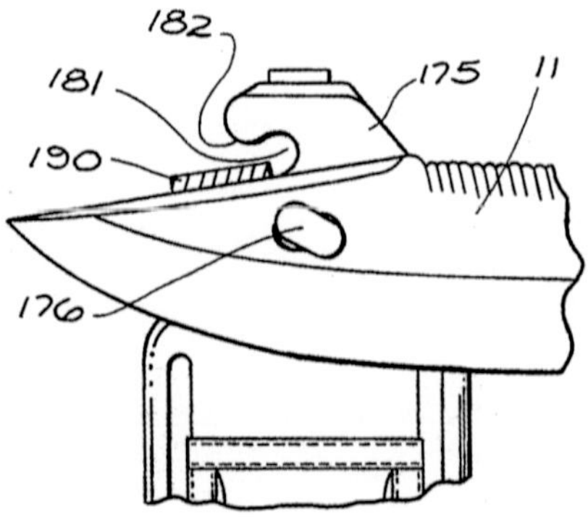

FIG. 21

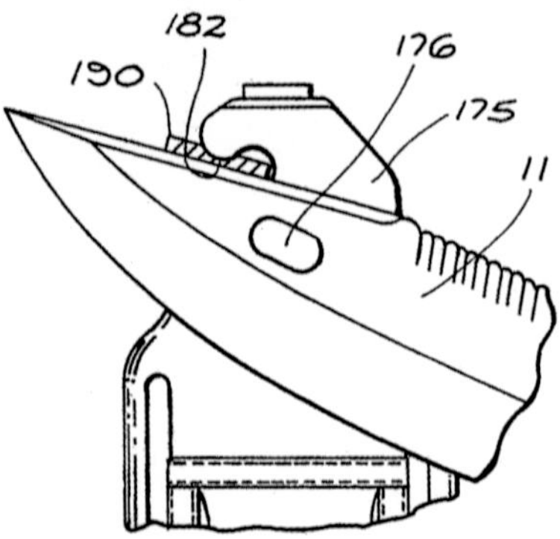

FIG. 22

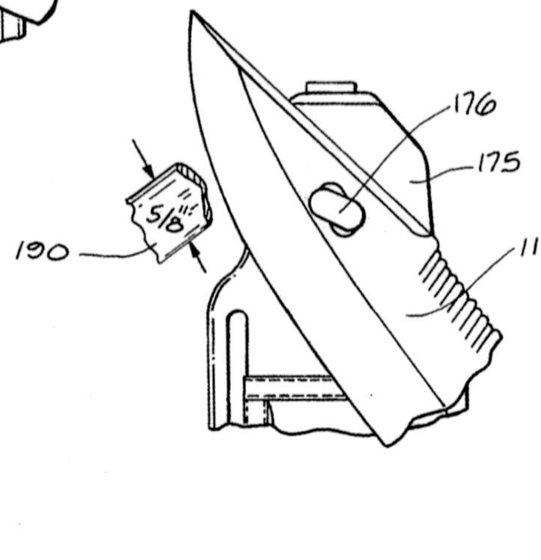

1

MILITARY BAYONET AND SCABBARD

BACKGROUND OF THE INVENTION

The bayonet has been an infantryman's additional weapon from earliest times and, in fact, is an outgrowth of the pike, the first infantryman's weapon. The bayonet has evolved, changed in length, changed in method of attachment and other details through the years without significant improvement. Bayonets have had a primary function in close hand to hand combat affixed to the barrel of the basic military rifle.

Recently the need has been recognized for a multipurpose bayonet which must serve the functions of a bayonet, a military field knife, a combat knife and also a sawing and wire cutting instrument. These requirements have been recognized in recent U.S. military specifications such as Mil-K 70606 Mar. 21, 1986.

Some of the requirements tend to be contradictory in the design parameters. For example, a bayonet with a sharp blade which maintains its sharpness tends to be brittle and subject to fracturing if used as a prying tool. A bayonet which is long for greater reach on a rifle becomes unwieldy when used as a knife. A bayonet with a suitable sharp edge for cutting barbed wire becomes dulled after repeated use and can not cut cables by mere sawing action alone.

It has been proposed to use a bayonet blade when pivotally interlocked with a rigid scabbard similar to that disclosed in my design patent application Ser. No. 766,101 filed Aug. 15, 1987 as a scissor type wire cutter.

Such an arrangement is shown in U.S. Pat. No. 3,842,458 of R. E. Bauer. The scabbard is releasably connected to a belt by a clip of the type disclosed in the U.S. patent of Bianchi U.S. Pat. No. 4,690,315 issued Sept. 1, 1987. The Bauer patent describes prior bayonets of that type which use a notched cutter plate on the scabbard and an unnotched blade as unreliable since the wire or cable to be cut may slip out of the scabbard plate notch. The Bauer patent proposes the use of a notched hardened steel blade cooperating with the notched scabbard plate as the solution to the wire slippage problem. The Bauer patent further discloses the blade as keyed to the scabbard during cutting operation.

BRIEF STATEMENT OF THE INVENTION

I recognized that the bayonet can be designed to meet these conflicting requirements and should, in addition to its use affixed to the barrel of a rifle, act effectively as a combat knife, a survival knife for the infantryman and additionally, act, if the occasion arises, as an effective wire and cable cutter and an effective prying tool, bottle or can opener and saw without danger of breakage or premature dulling of the blade.

If the bayonet is to be used as a prying tool, it must exhibit resiliency not found in hardened steel knife blade edges.

My invention involves a bayonet, having a blade length between 6 and 8 inches, having a cutting edge and a hollow ground rear edge which includes a cutter blade toward the tip and saw teeth similar to the survival knife disclosed in my U.S. Pat. No. 4,622,707 issued Nov. 18, 1986. The blade is manufactured of hardened steel. The blade, in the tip region, has an oval opening therethrough which cooperates with a pin on the exterior of its sheath to provide a pivot for a wire cutter. A U shaped recess in a hardened plate on the sheath provides the shearing surface for heavy wire or

2

cable cutting. An arm secured to the cutter plate overhangs the blade and holds it in cutting relationship with the cutter plate.

The knife blade includes a short tang which is secured to a tang rod which acts as a core for the handle. The rear of the handle is secured to the tang rod or extension by a threaded adapter which loads the tang rod in tension. The tang rod is manufactured of a stainless steel having a higher degree of resiliency than the bayonet blade whereby any deflective forces on the handle, if it exceeds the predetermined load on the blade, will cause the handle and tang rod to deflect rather than applying fracturing stress on the blade. At first glance, a bending handle would appear to be unacceptable, but in fact such a property insures that the bayonet may be used for prying without danger to the blade.

I have also provided two different wire and strap cutter arrangements using the bayonet scabbard as one handle mounting a cutter plate. I have determined that an effective solution to wire slippage in the wire cutter application of my new bayonet does not require blade notching. In my bayonet scabbard, the cutter plate employs a deep notch in the cutter plate and an overlying arm of length greater than the notch depth. The overlying ar and the cutter plate embrace the blade and securely lock the wire to be cut in the plate notch prior to cutting. This avoids the apparent problem of prior art cutters in which the cutting action tended to push the wire out of the notch. Furthermore, the wire cutting blade and cutter plate cutting surface each include a minor (10, for example) draft angle which serves to urge the blade and cutter plate together rather than apart during the cutting operation. This eliminates the need for keying the blade scabbard.

In another and referred embodiment, the blade is secured to the scabbard cutter plate by a T headed pivot, similar in certain respects to that shown in the Bauer patent and providing a changable cutting surface by means of an enlarged blade opening. It further provides for blade clearance adjustment for wear.

Altogether, my bayonet provides each of the required functions of a modern bayonet without compromising its basic function.

BRIEF DESCRIPTION OF THE DRAWING

This invention may be more clearly understood by reference to the following detailed description and the drawing in which:

FIG. **1** is a side elevational view of the bayonet of this invention;

FIG. **2** is an exploded view thereof;

FIG. **3** is a side elevational view of the scabbard for the bayonet of this invention;

FIG. **4** is an exploded view thereof;

FIG. **5** is a fragmentary view of a preferred form of belt hook for use in connection with this invention;

FIG. **5A** is a side elevational view of the belt attachment clip assembly of FIG. **5**;

FIG. **6** is a perspective view of this bayonet being used as a wire cutter;

FIG. **7** is a perspective view of this bayonet being used as a saw;

FIG. **8** is a top plan view of the bayonet of this invention shown under bending loading;

FIG. **8A** is a fragmentary sectional view of the handle portion of this invention shown in its normal unstressed condition;

4,821,356

3

FIG. **8B** is a view similar to FIG. **8A** under moderate bending loading as illustrated in FIG. **8**;

FIG. **8C** is a view similar to FIG. **8A** under further bending loading;

FIG. **9** is a top plan view showing the blade under torsional loading.

FIG. **9A** is a fragmentary sectional view of the handle portion of this invention under torsional loading.

FIG. **10** is a fragmentary side elevational view of the bayonet and scabbard of this invention ready for cutting a wire or cable;

FIG. **11** is a fragmentary side elevational view similar to FIG. **10** with barbed wire trapped just prior to cutting;

FIG. **12** is a fragmentary side elevational view similar to FIG. **11** with a different area of cutting surface in use;

FIG. **13** is a fragmentary bottom end view of the bayonet and scabbard of this invention in cable cutting arrangement;

FIG. **14** is a fragmentary elevational view of the bottom end of an alternate embodiment of the scabbard of this invention;

FIG. **14A** is a horizontal sectional view of the scabbard of FIG. **14** taken along lines **14A—14A** of FIG. **14**;

FIG. **15** is a side elevational view of one form of cutter plate of FIG. **3**;

FIG. **16** is a side elevational view of an alternate and preferred form of cutter plate of FIG. **3**;

FIG. **17** is a rear elevational view of the cutter plate of FIG. **3**;

FIG. **18** is an exploded view of the cutter plate and overlying arm of FIG. **3**;

FIG. **19** is a perspective view of the alternate of FIG. **16**;

FIGS. **20–22** are fragmentary sequence diagrams showing the cutting of $\frac{5}{8}$" stapping employing the alternate embodiment of this invention.

DETAILED DESCRIPTION OF THE INVENTION

The Bayonet Generally

Now referring to FIGS. **1** and **2** of the drawing, a bayonet **10** is shown including a blade **11**, a finger guard **12**, a handle **13** and a latching mechanism **14**, the latter of which is designed to engage the bayonet mounting lug of an M 16 rifle or other military type weapon.

The blade **11** includes a primary cutting edge **15** which is hollow ground, a single beveled shearing blade **16**, a set of recessed teeth **20** forming a saw and an elongated opening **21** used in connection with the scabbard for shearing or cutting of cables or heavy wire. The blade is fabricated of type **425** stainless steel produced by the Allegany Ludlum Steel Co. and preferably has a shot peened or other finish providing a low reflective surface and good abrasion and corrosion resistance.

The blade **11** is given a heat treatment to provide each of the cutting surfaces a Rockwell C hardness of **58** to **59** with the main body of the blade having a hardness of **54** to **55** Rockwell C. The rear of the blade **11** includes a short rectangular tang **22**, unshown in FIG. **1** but appearing in FIG. **2**, which extends through the fingerguard **12** and into the handle **13** The tang **22** which has a hardness in the order of **38-40** Rockwell C terminates in a threaded end **23** into which a tang rod or extension **24** may be threaded.

The tang rod or extension **24** includes a union portion **25** internally threaded to match the tang end **23** and

4

joins the main body **26** of the tang extension **24**. main body **26** of the tang extension **24** is likewise i nally threaded at opposite ends to receive the hand and attachment mechanism **14** and securing screv The tang extension **24** extends through an opening the handle **13**. The screw **30** extends into a matin cess **32** in the attachment mechanism **14** and ap compressive stress on the attachment mechanism **14** handle **13**, the latter of which bears against the rear of finger guard **12** while tensioning the tang exter **24**.

The screw **30** provides a primary function main ing the entire knife **10** assembled and allows for its d sembly into the form shown in FIG. **2** by its rem using a hex wrench or screw driver. The relationsh the parts interior to the handle **13** is best illustrat FIGS. **8A–C** and is described below, in connection those figures.

The finger guard **12** is best seen in FIG. **2** as inclu an integral ring **17** for encircling the barrel of weapon, a lanyard ring **18** and a pair of prying slo on opposite sides of the blade, particularly usef opening capped containers.

The attachment mechanism **14** includes a bod defining a slot **28** into which a pair of spring lo pawls **29** extend. The pawls are retracted out of sl by compressing their handle portion **32** and **33** toge against the resistance of an internal compression sp (unshown). This attachment mechanism **14** allow bayonet **10** to be slipped over the end of the barrel onto a conventional bayonet mounting lug foun American military rifles and other weapons. Th tachment mechanism **14** is secured from rotation respect to handle **13** by a pair of split pins **34** w extend through the attachment mechanism **14** into ing recesses (unshown) in the end of handle **13**.

The tang extension **24** as described above is n tained in tension by the screw **30** when the bayon assembled. The tang extension **24** is fabricated of series (**303** and **304** types recommended) stainless having a yield strength of the order of 35,000 psi a the preferred embodiment, has a diameter of, for e ple, 0.375+0.002 in., and overall length of app mately 4 inches and a length of the rod portion **26** inches. The union portion **25** has a diameter in the c of $\frac{5}{8}$ inch and a pair of flats **37** one of which appea FIG. **2** used to allow a wrench to tighten the tang e sion **24** onto the tang **23** of the blade **11** to a torq the order of 200 in lbs.

The tang rod **24** extends through a clearance ope **38** in the handle **13** of, for example, 0.390 inch dian surrounding the rod section **26** and having a $\frac{1}{2}$ de taper outward from the rear of the handle to the f

The tang extension **24** is not heat treated to chan normal resiliency and hardness.

The handle **13** is preferably fabricated from Du "Zytel" ST8018 glass filled Nylon and a yield stre in the order of 10,000 psi at normal ambient condit It has a total of 5 knurled sections separated by gro The cooperation of the handle **13** with the tang r extension **24** cooperating further with the finger g **12** and blade **11** and the attachment **14** by sec screw **30** is responsible for the blade saving capabi of this invention. This feature is described in conne with FIGS. **8–9**.

The Bayonet as a Prying Tool

As indicated above the soldier's bayonet is often needed for prying as well as twisting purpose despite the fact that ideally designed blade can be fractured by either of those motions. However, illustrated in FIG. 8 A–C, bending loading placed upon the blade **11** of this invention allows the handle **13** and tang rod **24** to bend as the blade approaches excessive loading. This signals to the user to avoid greater loading which might result in blade fracture although unlikely since the handle **13** and tang rod **24** will absorb additional loading by further deformation.

FIG. **8** shows a typical prying situation with the tip of blade **11** inserted in a vise-like device. Prying is accomplished by applying force to the handle in either of the directions of the arrow in FIG. **8**. As shown in FIG. **8**A, tapered clearance exists between the tang extension **24** and the wall of the aperture.

In FIG. **8**, the handle **13** has deflected until it engages the tang extension **24**. The apparent stiffness to the user of the handle to the user then increases as further deflection results in the tang extension **24** bending. The material, dimensions and heat treatment of the tang extension **24** are selected so that its resiliency is greater than that of the blade **11** resulting in handle **13** bending prior to any danger of blade fracturing. Thus the soldier is warned by the apparent stiffening of handle **13** of any approach to blade endangering loading.

Extensive testing of the bayonet has been performed in which one and one half inches of the pointed end of the blade was held between rigid supports and the handle **13** on the bayonet repeatedly deflected to a minimum arc of one and a quarter inches to the left and to the right and held without blade fracturing.

Similarly the bayonet has been tested by twisting as illustrated in FIG. **9** with one and half inches of the end of the blade measured from the finger guard or quillon end held. Twenty-five foot pounds, (thirty-five Newtons-Meter) torque was applied to the handle **13**, both clockwise and counter- clockwise direction without encountering fracturing of the blade. These test procedures serve to demonstrate the fact that significant twisting and bending forces can be applied to the blade without fracturing even though the blade has been hardened to the required hardness to maintain the cutting edge, the shearing edge, and the saw edge. In use, as a knife, by the military man any tendency to over stress the blade will be felt in his hand by the deflection of the handle prior to the fracture inducing loading of the blade **13**.

THE SCABBARD

Another feature of this invention is best illustrated by reference to FIG. **3** in conjunction with FIG. **6** in which the bayonet is used as a cable cutter. The bayonet **10** is normally housed in a scabbard or sheath **40** shown in FIGS. **3** and **4**. The sheath is similar to the sheaths shown in my design patent application Ser. No. 766,101 filed Aug. 15, 1985. It constitutes, in its preferred form, a molded plastic body **40** including an upper flared end **41** and a lower extension **42** carrying a cutter mechanism **43** which is secured to the body **40** by a pair of machine screws **44**. The body **40** includes a pair of side flanges **45** and **46** towards the upper end and a second pair of flanges **50** and **51** towards the lower end of the bayonet. The side flanges **45**, **46**, **50**, & **51** each include openings therethrough **45**o, **46**o, **50**o, and **51**o through which straps may extend for securing the bayonet sheath to baggage or other implements. The scabbard **40** is preferrably fabricated from plastic material such as, ST801, a glass filled Nylon resin produced by the Dupont de Nemours company of Wilmington, Del. The scabbard **40** includes an internal spring unshown in FIG. **2** which applies a mechanical bias against the side of the bayonet blade as it is inserted into the sheath **40** to secure the bayonet **10** within the sheath **40** under all norma circumstances.

The scabbard **40**, as is best shown in FIG. **4**, is supported by a fabric strap **60** including at its lower end a tie down loop **61** and at its upper end, one half of a plastic clip **62**, the other half of which is illustrated in FIG. **5**. The strap **60** includes a bayonet retainer strap **63** which is sewn at an angle with respect to the length of strap **60** and includes at its end region as shown in FIG. **3** a snap fastener **64** which has its mating part on the front face of the scabbard body and unshown in the drawing. The clip **62** is secured to the strap **60** by an sewn end loop portion **65** of strap **60**.

The strap **60** is held to the scabbard body **40** by two machine screws passing through grommets **66** and **70** in the strap. The machine screws engage recessed threaded inserts **71** in the body **40**. The lower fastener **72** in actuality is a male half of the snap fastener and the grommet **70** the female half so that the lower end of strap **60** is removably secure to the scabbard **40**.

The removable securement of the strap **60** is desirable since the scabbard body **40** in the lower region includes a sharpening stone **73** on the rear face and indicated in FIG. **4** by dashed lines. The sharpening stone **73** is normally covered by the strap **60** but may be uncovered to be used in sharpening the bayonet **10**. The sharpening stone **73** lies in a recess in the surface of the scabbard **40** with its surface slightly above the scabbard whereby the bayonet blade may be sharpened by being drawn across the surface of the sharpening stone **73** while the scabbard **40** is held by its upper end.

The lower end **42** of the scabbard **40** includes a pair of holes **74** designed to receive the a cutter plate **75** which is held in place by machine screws which are unshown in the drawing. The cutter plate **75** in one embodiment includes an up standing round circular pin **76** approximately ⅜ of an inch height and threaded into plate 75. An angular cutting surface **80** and a circular recess **81** as well as a rounded cutter region **82** are dimensioned to receive the largest size wire or cable to be cut by the combination of bayonet and scabbard. An overlying finger **83** of stainless steel is secured to the cutter plate **75** by a base portion **84** and a pair of mounting screws unshown in the drawing but extending through matching holes **85** in the finger piece **83** and **86** in the cutter plate. The rear face of cutter plate **75** includes an alignment bar **77** which rests in a meeting recess **77** R of the scabbard as shown in FIG. **4**. The alignment bar **77** transfers loading from the cutters plate **75** to the scabbard body **40** during wire cutting.

The finger **83** and the round cutter employing this embodiment portion **82** of the cutter plate **75** embrace the bayonet blade **11** when it is in place for cutting. The cutter plate **75** includes a screw driver blade **89** at its lower end to be used with the scabbard body so acting as a handle.

The operation of the bayonet as a cutter is best seen in FIG. **6** and FIGS. **10–13**. The embracing relationship of the finger **83** and the cutter plate **75** is best illustrated in FIG. **13**. The presence of the overlying finger **83** insures that a wire or cable does not slip out of cutting engagement without the necessity of a notched blade as in the prior art discussed above.

The Attachable Clip Assembly

The quick detachment arrangement of this invention from the wearers belt is illustrated in FIG. **5** and **5A** to which reference is now made. The mating half **62A** of the clip **62** of FIG. **4** appears at the bottom of FIG. **5** secured to a strap **100** which, in turn, is secured by rivets, unshown in FIG. **5A** of the drawing, to backing plate **101** which constitutes the body of the quick release clip. This clip is of the type disclosed in the U.S. patent to John E. Bianchi, cited above. The body **101** defines a pair of inwardly opening hooks **102** and **103** and at integral hinge tube **104** at the opposite of top end thereof. A spring member **105** including a pair of legs **106** and **107** have inwardly extended ankle portions **110** and **111**, respectively, ending in rounded feet portions **112** and **113** which maybe easily grasp by the fingers of the soldier even when wearing heavy mittens. The plate **101** and the spring **105** define a generally rectangular belt opening as illustrated in FIG. **5A**. The quick release assembly of this invention is completed by a transverse strap **112** including mating snap fastener parts **113** shown from the rear and **114** from the engaging female side.

In applying this assembly the entire scabbard **40** and its strap **60** may be instantly removed from the belt merely by depressing inwardly the two flexable fingers **68** and **69** of the clip portion **62A**.

When the entire assembly is to be removed from the belt. the feet **112** and **113** are compressed inwardly towards each other to release the spring member **105** from its retaining plate **102** and then the entire scabbard, bayonet and quick release assembly maybe removed by lifting the entire assembly upward. The clip assembly maybe used to attach the bayonet and scabbard to various straps in addition to the wearer's belt.

The Bayonet and Scabbard as a Wire or Cable Cutter

The normal use of the bayonet **10** and scabbard **40** is cutting in shown in FIG. **6** in which a double strand of barbed wire **90** is engaged in the cutter and the user is in the act of drawing the scabbard **40** and bayonet **10** together to effect cutting o the barbed wire **90**.

Rapid cutting of wire and cable is facilitated in accordance with this invention as illustrated in FIG. **10** in which the blade **11** particularly the cutter edge **16** acts as a guide for the barbed wire **90** to enter the cutting recess **81** of the cutter under the finger **83**. By sliding the bayonet blade along the wire to be cut until it reaches the recess **81**, then commencing rotational movement of the bayonet **10** and its scabbard **40** serves to first lock the wire or cable **90** in jaws and next complete the cut.

Where the user may be required to cut many strands of wire or use the cutter for a long period of time without being able to sharpen the cutting blade **16** another feature of this invention is incorporated and illustrated in FIGS. **11** and **12**. In those figures note that pin **76** does is not include any key hole shape which would limit the longitudinal position of the blade. Instead the opening **21** is elongated so that the blade has nearly a half an inch of longitudinal movement while still presenting an effective cutting edge **16**. This prevents undue wear on any localized area of the cutting edge **16**. The user need only make a number of the cuts with the blade drawn as far out as the elongated opening **21** will allow

and then move the blade forward as illustrated in FIG. **12** for additional cuts on a different portion of the cutting edge **16**.

Further facilitating the use of the bayonet **10** and scabbard **40** as a cutter is the fact that the base **84** or the finger **83** defines an OPEN stop **87** in use in FIG. **10** and a CLOSED stop **88** just after completion of cutting. Therefore the finger member **83–84** provides three additional important functions in this invention.

Alternate and Preferred Form of Cutter

Another and preferred form of cutter plate is illustrated in FIGS. **16** and **19**. It comprises a cutter plate **175** similar to cutter plate **75** of FIG. **15** with its alignment bar **177** and screw driver blade **189** similar to their counterparts in FIG. **15**, upstanding pin **176** includes a head portion, oval in shape corresponding to the oval opening **21** of blade **11**. The head of pin **176** holds the blade **11** from separating from the cutter plate **175** during cutting and substitutes for the overlying arm **83** of FIG. **18**.

Elimination of the upper arm **83** allows the bayonet and scabbard to cut material such as strapping which is actually wider than the cutter plate opening **181**. This is illustrated in FIGS. **20–22** in which a strap **190** is wider than opening **181**. Strap **190**, typically is a steel strap ⅜" in width and used to secure military ammunition boxes as well as palled loaded material.

Employing this invention, the bayonet **10** is engaged with the scabbard **40** as showing in FIG. **20** and the blade **11** slipped under the strap **190**. Rotating the blade **11** causes the rounded cutting surface **182** to grasp the wide strap **190** at about its midpoint. This is illustrated in FIG. **21**. The concentrated load at this midpoint allows the strap **190** to be pierced at its center region. This action appears in FIG. **21**. Completion of the cut appears in FIG. **22**.

Where cutting of wide straps as is illustrated in FIGS. **20–22** is required, the embodiment of cutting plate **175** is required. Since it cuts smaller stock as well, it is the preferred embodiment.

BLADE TIGHTENING FEATURE

Also, employing either embodiment of cutter plate, I have incorporated a manual blade tightening feature to insure effective wire and strap cutting. This feature is shown in FIGS. **14**, **18** and **19**.

FIG. **14** shows the bottom end of the scabbard **40** as having two holes **74 A** and **74 B** therethrough. They are of different diameter. Hole **74 A** provides full clearance for screw **92** and **192** and an upper integral plastic collar **193** which approximately the diameter of the head of screw **92** and **192**. The screws **92** and **192** are of sufficient length to extend to the cutting face of the cutter plate **75** and **175** when new. Screws **92** and **192** are located below the blade **11** during wire or strap cutting operation.

If the blade becomes loose after repeated cutting, driving the screw **92** or **192** inward, locally crushes the plastic collar **193** of FIG. **14** and allows the head of the screw **92** or **192** to bear against the cutter plate side of the blade. This holds the blade **11** tight against the finger **83** of FIG. **18** or the head **177** of FIG. **19**.

The Bayonet Used as a Saw

Now referring to FIG. **7** the use of this invention as a saw in clearly illustrated therein. The bayonet **10** is used inverted. Approximately three inches of saw teeth **20** are raked forward at an angle of approximately 10 and recessed even with the upper surface of the blade 11. The saw teeth 20 are tapered from the full blade width at their base to approximately 1/16 inch in thickness at the front edge. This allows rapid cutting through sheet metal and wood while maintaining the full strength of the blade in the central section of nearly one quarter inch thickness.

SUMMARY

All together I have developed an improved bayonet which secures to the end of the military weapon with a conventional bayonet clip to provide a fully functional traditional bayonet. Additionally the bayonet is effective as a saw, a prying tool, a cable or wire cutter when used with its scabbard and as a container opener.

When used as a prying tool the danger of breakage of the blade is greatly reduced not only because of the blade thickness and lack of any notches in the tip region but by reason of the fact that the handle **13** and tang extension **24** cooperate with the blade to provide energy absorption on twisting and deflection at two levels prior to the blade endangering flexing. Altogether, the bayonet and scabbard of my invention provides an effective life saving weapon and tool.

What is claimed is:

1. A bayonet comprising:

a blade;

a tang having an inner end secured to said blade; said tang having a modulus of elasticity lesser than the modulus of elasticity of said blade whereby said tang exhibits greater deformation under loading than said blade;

a handle securable to said blade and means securing said handle to said blade and to the outer end of said tang with clearance between said handle and said tang; and

means for attaching said bayonet to the muzzle region of a firearm barrel.

2. The combination in accordance with claim **1** wherein said tang is a rod secured to said blade as an separable extension.

3. The combination in accordance with claim **1** wherein said tang is threadably secured to said blade.

4. The combination in accordance with claim **1** wherein said means securing said handle and tang comprises a threaded member co-acting with the attachment of said tang to said blade for maintaining said tang in tension.

5. A bayonet in accordance with claim **2** wherein said tang and handle have a clearance therebetween at least at one end region of said handle whereby said handle may deform under lateral force as in the case of bending loading of the blade without initial distortion of the tang and indicating a first stress limit condition.

6. A bayonet in accordance with claim **5** wherein the clearance between said tang and said handle is sufficient whereby after a predetermined degree of deformation of said tang, bending deformation of said handle occurs signalling to the user a second stress limit condition prior to blade failure.

7. A bayonet comprising:

a blade including a blade portion and a tang portion

a handle including an elongated opening therein dimensioned to receive the tang portion of said blade;

means tensioning said tang portion within said handle;

said handle having a yield strength less than the yield strength of said blade portion whereby on deformation loading applied to said bayonet, said handle deforms prior to deformation of said blade.

8. A bayonet in accordance with claim **7** wherein said tang portion of said blade has a yield strength greater than said handle and less than said blade portion of said blade.

9. A bayonet in accordance with claim **7** wherein the opening in said handle exhibits clearance with said tang whereby said handle may deform under loading prior to engagement with said tang portion.

10. A bayonet in accordance with claim **7** wherein said tang portion of said blade is separable therefrom.

11. A bayonet in accordance with claim **10** wherein said separable tang portion is in threaded engagement with the blade portion of said blade.

12. A bayonet in accordance with claim **7** wherein said tang portion extends through said handle; and said bayonet includes means engaging said handle and said blade tensioning said tang portion.

13. A bayonet in accordance with claim **12** including spacer means between said tang portion and said blade portion of said blade and wherein said tang portion is tensioned between said spacer means and said handle engaging means.

14. A bayonet in accordance with claim **13** wherein said spacer means extends transverse to the length of said blade and constitutes a finger guard.

15. A bayonet in accordance with claim **9** wherein said clearance toward the blade portion end of said handle to greater toward the outer end of said handle.

16. A bayonet-scabbard wire cutter comprising

a bayonet including a blade and handle

said bayonet blade including a wire or cable cutting blade surface and a opening therein in the region of the tip of said blade;

a rigid scabbard including a cutter plate secured thereto in the region of one end of said scabbard;

an upstanding pin secured to said cutting plate;

an edge opening recess in said cutter plate dimensioned to receive a wire or cable to be cut and including an edge of said edge opening recess as a cutting surface for such wire or cable;

said upstanding pin located on said cutter plate with respect to the cutting surface of said edge opening recess whereby the wire cutting blade surface of said blade engages said cutting surface of said cutter plate when said elongated opening encloses said upstanding pin; and

an arm secured to said cutter plate overlying said blade when in engagement with said cutting surface whereby said arm engages the blade on the opposite side from said cutter plate and insures close contact between said blade and cutter plate during wire cable cutting.

17. The bayonet-scabbard wire cutter in accordance with claim **16** wherein said arm extends beyond the end of said edge opening recess whereby said arm blade and cutter plate capture a wire or cable therebetween before cutting operation begins.

18. The bayonet-scabbard wire cutter in accordance with claim **16** wherein said arm is supported above the level of said cutter plate by an integral base secured to said cutter plate.

19. The bayonet-scabbard wire cutter in accordance with claim **18** wherein said base defines at least one stop for rotational movement of said blade.

4,821,356

11

20. The bayonet-scabbard wire cutter in accordance with claim **19** wherein said base includes a pair of surfaces defining both beginning and ending travel stops for said blade during wire or cable cutting.

21. The bayonet-scabbard wire cutter in accordance with claim **16** wherein said upstanding pin of said cutter plate is circular and said opening in said blade is elongated and round ended whereby said blade may be movable longitudinally on said pin to present different cutting surfaces thereon.

22. A bayonet-scabbard wire cutter comprising
- a bayonet including a blade and handle;
- said bayonet blade including a wire or cable cutting blade surface and a opening therein in the region of the tip of said blade;
- a rigid scabbard including a cutting plate having a surface thereon located in the region of one end of said scabbard;
- an upstanding pin secured to said cutting plate;
- an edge opening recess in said cutter surface including a protruding portion and a recess portion, said recessed portion dimensioned to receive a wire or cable to be cut and wherein the edge of said edge opening recess including said protruding portion constitutes a cutting surface for such wire or cable;
- said upstanding pin located on said cutter plate with respect to the cutting surface of said edge opening recess whereby the wire cutting blade surface of said blade engages said protruding portion of said edge opening recess surface of said cutter surface when said elongated opening of said blade encloses said upstanding pin.

23. The bayonet-scabbard wire cutter in accordance with claim **22**, wherein said protruding portion of said cutter surface comprises a curved cutting edge which serves to capture a wire or cable before cutting operation begins.

24. The bayonet-scabbard wire cutter in accordance with claim **22** wherein said cutter surface is on a separate cutter plate secured to the lower end of said scabbard.

25. The bayonet-scabbard wire cutter in accordance with claim **22** wherein the cutting edge of said blade is straight in the region of said cutter surface of said scabbard whereby the blade cutter portion and said protruding portion of said cutter surface of said scabbard can capture an object to be cut thereby which is wider than the recess of said scabbard.

26. The bayonet-scabbard wire cutter in accordance with claim **22** wherein said scabbard includes adjustable means extending through said cutting surface to bear upon one side of said blade and maintain said blade in adjustable engagement with said scabbard during cutting use.

12

27. The bayonet-scabbard wire cutter in accordance with claim **26** wherein said adjustable means comprises a mounting screw for said cutting surface.

28. The bayonet-scabbard wire cutter in accordance with claim **24** wherein said cutter plate is secured to said scabbard by at least one mounting screw and said mounting screw is extendable through said cutter plate to engage the blade of said bayonet and to adjust its engagement with said scabbard.

29. A bayonet-scabbard wire cutter in accordance with claim **28** wherein said scabbard is fabricated of a material which is at least partially crushable by said mounting screw when adjusted.

30. In a bayonet-scabbard wire cutter, comprising a bayonet blade having a cutting edge adjacent one edge and a handle at the opposite end, a scabbard having a cutting plate portion adjacent one end thereof, means for pivotally joining said bayonet and scabbard adjacent said one ends thereof for scissor-like movement with respect to each other during which said cutting edge moves across the surface of said cutting plate portion, the improvement comprising a wire-receiving recess extending inwardly from a constricted opening in one edge of said cutting plate portion in the path of the scissor-like movement of said cutting edge;
- additionally including a tang having an inner end secured to said blade, a handle securable to said blade and means securing said handle to said blade and to the outer end of said tang with clearance between said handle and said tang;
- said tang having a modulus of elasticity lesser than the modulus of the elasticity of said blade whereby said tang exhibited greater deformation under loading than said blade.

31. In a quick detachable bayonet and scabbard assembly including a scabbard and a bayonet removably received therein with a handle projecting from one end thereof, the improvement comprising an attachable clip assembly having means thereon for detachably securing said clip assembly to the projecting handle of the said bayonet and means thereon for detachably securing said clip assembly to said scabbard in which said last mentioned means comprises a fastener including a socket member having oppositely disposed lateral openings, and a clip member receivable within said socket member and having oppositely disposed resilient fingers engageable with said lateral openings and releasable by compressing said resilient fingers of the said oppositely disposed resilient fingers.

* * * * *

Notes

1. *Of Men and Bayonets*; Major James M. Gibson, Infantry School Quarterly, Volume 43, Nr. 1, Page 105, July 1953.

2. *Of Men and Bayonets*; Major James M. Gibson, Infantry School Quarterly, Volume 43, Nr. 1, Page 106, July 1953.

3. Operation tempo or the rate of operations

4. *The Bayonet - Spirit Weapon*, MAJ Schiller F. Shore, The Infantry School Quarterly, Volume 37, Nr. 2, page 6, dated 02 October 1950

5. Institutional memory is a collective of facts, concepts, experiences, and expertise held by a group of people. As it transcends the individual, it requires the ongoing transmission of these memories between members of this group.

6. "A sword is defensive or offensive depending on which end is pointed at you." Aristide Briand, 1930

7. General George S. Patton, *The Patton Papers Vol II*. C1 Fig 20.

8. *Stick with the Bayonet*, CPT Carlton G. Barber, Infantry Journal, page 52, U.S. Army, dated April 1959.

9. "all Marines, regardless of age, sex, rank or job will do this training." Gerry J. Gilmore, May 16, 2001.

10. *Department of the Army Historical Summary*: FY 1974

11. Reagan's March 8, 1983, speech to the National Association of Evangelicals in Orlando, Florida, is his first recorded use of the phrase *evil empire.*

12. AN/PSN-11, Precision Lightweight GPS Receiver (PLGR)

13. *Department of the Army Historical Summary*: FY 1987

14. *Research, Development and Acquisition-Army Acquisition Procedures*, DA PAM 70-3

15. A sutler, or victualer, is a civilian who sells provisions to an army in the field, in camp or in quarters – Wikipedia

16. *War's Greatest Workshop*, Arsenal Publishing Co., of the Tri-Cities, Not Inc, page 108, 1922

17. "Rock Island National Cemetery was established within the confines of the U.S. Arsenal located on Rock Island in the Mississippi River near the cities of Davenport, Iowa, and Moline, Ill. In 1863 an area was set aside to bury Union soldiers who died while serving as guards at the large Confederate prison camp established on Rock Island by the U.S. government.

In 1868, the inspector of national cemeteries reported that the Rock Island cemetery contained 136 remains, including seven unknowns and six women and children. He described it as rectangle of 216 feet by 96 feet, enclosed with a 'paling fence.' At the time, the arsenal's commanding officer, General Thomas Rodman, indicated that the location of the burial area would ultimately conflict with his plans for extending arsenal-complex buildings. He recommended the remains of individuals currently interred at Rock Island be moved to the upper end of the island; the inspector of national cemeteries further suggested that Civil War decedents interred in Oakdale Cemetery in Davenport, Iowa, be removed to the new site on Rock Island, as well. Subsequent property transfers from the Rock Island Arsenal Reservation in 1926, 1936 and 1950 brought the national cemetery to its present 31.5 acres.

Today, Rock Island is the final resting place of soldiers who served in the Civil War, as well as the Mexican War, Indian Wars, Spanish-American War, World Wars I and II, Korea, Vietnam, Persian Gulf and Iraq.

Rock Island Confederate Cemetery: Between 1863 and 1865, the federal government established a second cemetery of a little more than two acres for the burial of Confederate prisoners of war. Approximately 1,950 soldiers died at the Rock Island Confederate Prison, founded there in 1863. The first POWs, captured during the battles of Lookout Mountain and Missionary Ridge in Tennessee in November 1863, arrived in December. Throughout the war, Confederates were brought to Rock Island from battle areas throughout the South; eventually, more than 12,000 POWs were confined there. Prisoners died from a variety of causes, including exposure to the cold, harsh winters, malnutrition and diseases such as smallpox." -http://www.cem.va.gov/CEMs/nchp/rockisland.asp

18. Each *Fiscal Year* begins on 1 October, and funds are dispersed at the beginning of each Quarter, such as on 01 October, 01 January, and so forth.

19. *Political Aerodynamics: Technical Decisions in a Political World, Why the Acquisition System Cannot be Reformed*, MAJ Gary E. Slyman, USMC, CSC, Strategic Issues Thesis, Conference, Group 10, 12 April 1995.

20. The official nomenclature of the P38 is Opener, Can, Hand, Folding, Type I, and its National Stock Number is: 7330-00-242-3506.

21. Bakelite is a synthetic produced by reacting phenol and formaldehyde under heat and pressure.

22. See patent drawings and descriptions in Appendix H for multifunctional features.

23. *Miscellaneous Documents Referencing Pocket Knives*, United States Marine Corps Equipment Board, Marine Barracks, Quantico, Virginia, January-March 1944.

24. *Report of Project Nr. 2811, Service Test of Fighting Knife, DA Project Nr. 502-08-006*, United States Army Infantry Board, 17 June 1959.

25. *Final Engineering Design Report for Knife Cutter-Bayonet*, Benhof, Inc, Land Warfare Laboratory, Aberdeen Proving Grounds, 10 May 1974.

26. *TRADOC (Training and Doctrine Command) Letter of Execution for Knife-Bayonet, Product Improved*, ATCD-TM, TRADOC Project No 1-C9-7-CEP058-08, and dated 21 January 1977.

27. *TRADOC Letter ATCD-ML*, dated 17 December 1985,

28. U.S. Patent Number 3842458, dated 22 October 1974, issued to Russell E. Bauer.

29. *Multipurpose Bayonet System*, Infantry Magazine, page 10, U.S. Army, dated November 1986

30. Phrobis III: The Winning Edge, The Blade Magazine, March/ April 1987, page 38.

31. *TECOM, Independent Evaluation Report of the Multipurpose Bayonet System (MPBS)*, CPT Keith G. Frost, Jr., January 1987.

32. *Army Competition Advocacy Program*, Army Regulation 715–31, 9 June 1989 (Effective 10 July 1989).

33. *Phrobis & The M9 Bayonet: Part 4*, Homer M. Brett, The Society of American Bayonet Collectors, Volume 21, Fall 1997.

34. *Military Standard, Army Nomenclature System*, MIL-STD-1464A, Picatinny Arsenal, New Jersey, 15 May 1987.

35. *Ordnance Committee Meeting minutes*, Numbers 22 and 28, Nomenclature System, 1925.

36. LOI, or Letter of Instruction.

37. The agency responsible: Ordnance for weapons, JAG for legal, etc.

38. History of Ordnance Drawing Numbers and Ordnance Part Numbers, Rock Island Arsenal, 08 October 1945.

39. Piecemarks are marks placed on an individual piece of an assembly, designating its location in the assembly as indicated in shop drawings.

40. A major end item is a final combination of end products which is ready to use.

41. Contract number DAAA21-87-C-0001, dated 06 October 1986.

42. *Phrobis III: The Winning Edge*, The Blade Magazine, March/April 1987, page 38.

43. The original patent called for steel produced by Allegany Ludlum Steel Company.

44. Buck Knives website.

45. *Phrobis and the M9 Bayonet – Part Two, The Chevron Bayonet*, Homer M. Brett, The Society of American Bayonet Collectors, Newsletter No. 14, Fall 1993.

46. *Buck Interoffice Memo*, dated 20 January 1987, signed by Theodore E. Tarlston, Quality Assurance Manager.

47. U.S. Patent Office, Patent Number 4,821,356, 18 April 1989.

48. See Appendix F for details.

49. Phrobis: $15,641,000.00/325,000 = $48.13. Lan-Cay $1,427,400.00/30500 = $46.80. These were the prices of the initial contracts, not considering any addons.

50. *The Military Knife and Bayonet*, Page 386, Homer M. Brett, World Photo Press, Tokyo, Japan, 2001

51. *The Military Knife and Bayonet*, Page 386, Homer M. Brett, World Photo Press, Tokyo, Japan, 2001

52. See contract data in Appendix E for details.

53. IAW- In Accordance With

54. *Chicom green*, or Chinese Communist green, is a yellowish green commonly used to paint equipment of the Chinese army.

55. An MWO is a Modification Work Order, or an authorization to change a piece of equipment by adding to or removing from it some new part or component.

56. Espirit de Corps simply means Spirit of the Corp, that is, unit or organization pride.

57. Long range is generally considered to be distances beyond 300 meters.

58. A *rack weapon* is a standard issue rifle capable of placing three rounds within a four inch grid at 100 meters. It is has not been accurized.

59. To *bring scunion* is to inflict great distress, injury, or destruction, in this case as a result of incredible accuracy.

60. *Barrel lash* is a phenomena peculiar to rifles wherein when fired the front portion of the barrel actually bends upward, then returns to its original axis. It is similar to *cracking the whip*.

61. Muzzle velocity of the M16A2 is 3050 feet per second, down from 3200 fps for the M16A1.

62. *K-D targets*, or Known Distance targets.

63. *The Military Knife and Bayonet*, Page 375, Homer M. Brett, World Photo Press, Tokyo, Japan, 2001

64. *DX'ed* or *Direct Exchange,* the exchanging of one piece of equipment for another.

65. Defense Reutilization Management Office, or DRMO, is the activity responsible of disposing of unwanted property. Every installation has a DRMO which runs local sales or auctions, or processes the equipment and sends it to regional DRMO activities who dispose of it.

66. MARCORSYSCOM (Marine Systems Command) is the activity responsible for all Marine Corps research and development.

67. *Buck Barrel Nut M9 Bayonet*, Bill Porter, The Journal of The Society of American Bayonet Collectors, page 13, Volume 40, , Summer 2002

Bibliography

A History of Ordnance Department Drawing and Part Numbers, Edward Scott Meadows, The Gun Report, November 2005.

*American Military Bayonets of the 20*th *Century: A Guide for Collectors, Including Notes on Makers, Markings, finishes, Variations, Scabbards, and Production Data*. Gary M. Cunningham, Scott A. Duff Publications, Inc., Export, Pennsylvania, 1996.

Bayonet Wire Cutter, Report Nr. 239, United States Marine Corps Equipment Board, Marine Barracks, Quantico, Virginia, 28 June 1944.

Commercial Item Description, Knife, Pocket, General Purpose, A-A-59100, U.S. Army Natick Research, Development and Evaluation Center, Natick, Massachusetts, 10 April 1997.

Federal Specification, Knife, Pocket (Heavy Duty), GGG-K-00484D, Federal Supply Service, General Services Administration, Washington, D.C., 14 September 1966.

Final Engineering Design Report for Knife Cutter-Bayonet, Benhof, Inc, Land Warfare Laboratory, Aberdeen Proving Grounds, 10 May 1974.

Force Development Testing and Experimentation Operational feasibility Test of Product Improved (PI) Knife-Bayonet, United States Army Infantry Board, February 1977.

History of Ordnance Drawing Numbers and Ordnance Part Numbers, Rock Island Arsenal, 08 October 1945.

Knives Pocket, General Purpose, Report of Infantry Board, Nr. 1877, Ft. Benning, Georgia, 28 September 1945.

Knives Pocket, Report of Infantry Board, Nr. 1741, Ft. Benning, Georgia, 21 December 1944.

Letter Requirement for the Multipurpose Bayonet, USMC, MCO - 3900.4C, 01 July 1989.

Military Specification for Knife, Pocket, General Purpose, MIL-K-818A, 12 August 1955.

Military Specification for Knife, Pocket, General Purpose, MIL-K-818C, 08 June 1964.

Military Specifications, Bayonet-Knives, MIL-B-1309E, Rock Island Arsenal, Illinois, 08 May 1975.

Military Specifications, Notice of Validation, Bayonet-Knives, MIL-B-1309E, Rock Island Arsenal, Illinois, 28 May 1987.

Military Specifications, Bayonet-Knives, MIL-B-1309E, Amendment 1, Rock Island Arsenal, Illinois, 22 June 1992.

Military Standard, Army Nomenclature System, MIL-STD-1464A, Picatinny Arsenal, New Jersey, 15 May 1987.

Military Specifications, Knife, Bayonet, Multipurpose with Scabbard, MIL-K-70606 (2), 15 September 1988.

Military Specifications, Knife, Bayonet, Multipurpose with Scabbard, MIL-K-70606, Amendment 2, 1993.

Military Specifications, Knife, Bayonet, Multipurpose with Scabbard, MIL-K-70606, Amendment 3, August 2000.

Miscellaneous Documents Referencing Pocket Knives, United States Marine Corps Equipment Board, Marine Barracks, Quantico, Virginia, January-March 1944.

Multipurpose Bayonet System, Infantry Magazine, page 10, U.S. Army, dated November 1986.

Of Men and Bayonets, MAJ James M. Gibson, The Infantry School Quarterly, Volume 43, Nr. 1, July 1953.

Ordnance Committee Meeting minutes, Numbers 22 and 28, Nomenclature System, 1925

Partial Report Nr. 3 on Investigation Nr. 40 on Flaming Bayonet, Lt H.W. Asire, 01 May 1918.

Phrobis and the M9 Bayonet – Part 1, The Chevron Bayonet, Homer M. Brett, The Society of American Bayonet Collectors, Summer 1992.

Phrobis and the M9 Bayonet – Part 2, The Chevron Bayonet, Homer M. Brett, The Society of American Bayonet Collectors, Fall 1993.

Phrobis and the M9 Bayonet – Part 3, The Chevron Bayonet, Homer M. Brett, The Society of American Bayonet Collectors, Newsletter No. 14, Fall 1993.

Phrobis & The M9 Bayonet: Part 4, Homer M. Brett, The Society of American Bayonet Collectors, Volume 21, Fall 1997.

Political Aerodynamics: Technical Decisions in a Political World, Why the Acquisition System Cannot be Reformed, MAJ.

Gary E. Slyman, USMC, CSC, Strategic Issues Thesis, Conference, Group 10, 12 April 1995.

Project No. 3533, Operational Feasibility Test of Product Improved (P.I.) Knife-Bayonet, Final Report, February 1977.

Proposed Military Specification for Knife, Pocket, General Purpose, MIL-K-818B, 22 May 1959.

Report of Project Nr. 2811, Service Test of Fighting Knife, DA Project Nr. 502-08-006, United States Army Infantry Board, 17 June 1959.

Revision of U.S. Army Specification Nr. 17-170, Knife, Engineer, Four Blade with Clevis, The Engineer Board, Ft. Belvoir, Virginia, July 1944.

Solicitation 10; Bayonet 2000, Solicitation Number M67854-01-R-3080, PSA #2959, Commerce Business Daily, 18 October 2001.

Stick with the Bayonet, CPT Carlton G. Barber, Infantry Journal, U.S. Army, April 1959.

TECOM, Independent Evaluation Report of the Multipurpose Bayonet System (MPBS), CPT Keith G. Frost, Jr., January 1987.

Test Report Nr. 22470-87M (Rev 1), Final Test of Fungus Resistance, A. Eickhorn, GmbH, Solingen, Germany, 29 August 1986.

The Bayonet, CPT A.L. Thompson, British Army, CGSC Military Review, Volume II, Nr. 05, May 1988.

The Bayonet, Common Sense Lessons, Major Roland J. Tiso, Jr., Infantry Journal, U.S. Army, August 1990.

The Bayonet, Simple But Dependable, Robert J. Behrens, Infantry Journal, U.S. Army, May 1988.

The Bayonet, Spirit Weapon, MAJ Schiller F. Shore, The Infantry School Quarterly, Volume 37, Nr. 2, 2 October 1950.

The Corps Gets Ready to Fix Bayonets, Harold Kennedy, National Defense Magazine, Issue of May 2002.

The Military Knife and Bayonet, Homer M. Brett, World Photo Press, Tokyo, Japan, 2001.

User Manual for XM9 Multipurpose Bayonet, A. Eickhorn, GmbH, Solingen, Germany, 07 May 1986.

War's Greatest Workshop, Arsenal Publishing Co., of the Tri-Cities, Not Inc, 1922.

Index